HARD AT WORK

WORK

Life in Singapore

T0345356

HARD AT WORK
Life in Singapore

Edited by **Gerard Sasges and Ng Shi Wen**
Photographs by **Ng Shi Wen**
Foreword by **Teo You Yenn**

RIDGE BOOKS
SINGAPORE

© Gerard Sasges and Ng Shi Wen

Published under the Ridge Books imprint by:

NUS Press
National University of Singapore
AS3-01-02, 3 Arts Link
Singapore 117569

Fax: (65) 6774-0652
E-mail: nusbooks@nus.edu.sg
Website: http://nuspress.nus.edu.sg

ISBN 978-981-325-050-5 (paper)

First edition 2019
Reprint 2020

National Library Board, Singapore Cataloguing in Publication Data

Name(s): Sasges, Gerard. | Ng, Shi Wen, author.
Title: Hard at work : life in Singapore / Gerard Sasges & Ng Shi Wen.
Description: Singapore : Ridge Books, [2019]
Identifier(s): OCN 1090190815 | ISBN 978-981-325-050-5 (paperback)
Subject(s): LCSH: Labor--Singapore. | Work--Social aspects--Singapore. |
Working class--Singapore. | Singapore--Social conditions--21st century.
Classification: DDC 306.36095957--dc23

Printed by: Markono Print Media Pte Ltd

CONTENTS

FOREWORD

Cities hum. For people who live in them, the humming is a kind of complex ugly beauty. It is magnetic – it draws one in, and becomes a kind of life force that keeps one there. Descriptions of cities often focus on their status as financial hubs, shiny skylines, and the various consumption choices they offer. Living within, city-dwellers are tethered to something else – less glamorous, cast in shades and shadows, harder to describe, too messy to put one's finger on.

I remember being mesmerised as a kid by Richard Scarry's books – the ones where buildings are bisected so that you get to see their cross-sections and be privy to everyone doing busy work in them; where every inch of road is filled with busy creatures, busy-ing away at various occupations. There is so much doing in a city – so many specialties and trades, so much busy-ness in the air, at once utterly chaotic and somehow magically harmonious. Connectedness and isolation, noise and quiet, conflict and conviviality, and it all comes together to produce something that is the city, humming along, more than the sum of its parts.

The interviews and accompanying photographs in *Hard at Work*, when I explored them as a collection, remind me of the childhood pleasure of scrutinising those busy pictures. The book is a rarity for presenting relatively raw data. The interview transcripts are lightly edited; analysis is eschewed and in its place the interviews are subtly organised to leave space for meandering, discovery, with rewards at multiple turns. Venture a few steps and face direct revelations about the nature of jobs that every city-dweller takes for granted – cleaner, bus captain, doctor, postal worker. Take a few more steps and be surprised – a teacher turns out to have an unexpected story; you encounter a pet crematorium worker, a monk, a bet collector, a law student with a part-time job his classmates cannot begin to imagine. We find too, as we meander, evocative photographs that are hard to look away from, so rare it is to see so much backstage. The images remind us of the corporeal realities that make up our days and hours, as well as the significance of ordinary spaces and everyday acts in bringing into being that which we share in a city.

Reading the stories, we see dreams – some broken, others being chased; we witness craft, expertise, and the corresponding beauty of people taking pride in their labour. Against the backdrop of relentless national discourses in Singapore that privilege straight and narrow pathways, we meet people who reject (or are rejected from) straight paths who turn out to be true path-seekers and path-finders. Seemingly without being prompted, interviewees speak relentlessly of human connections – with family, friends, co-workers, but importantly also with strangers. These human encounters are both persistent and fleeting, sometimes affirming and other times frustrating, and here lie the threads of complex and messy human connections that make a city. Where words end, pixels carry the book forward, sustaining the feeling that this thing we're staring at is lit up from many different directions.

Together, the stories reveal the generic engine of any big city, but also the specific engines underlying this particular one. The city of Singapore: a cacophony of languages colliding; we refer to it simply as Singlish but it is not easy to describe to people not of here. *Hard at Work*, though ostensibly in English, somehow manages to convey, and legitimise, the many sounds and rhythms that make up local language(s). The city of Singapore – a city but also a nation state and therefore with particular kinds of borders and boundaries, specific articulations of belonging and otherness. Academics, attuned as we are to certain norms of political correctness, sometimes struggle with describing these, but ordinary people have no such qualms. In *Hard at Work*, they cut to the chase with persistent references to ethnic, religious, national difference – one wants to sum it up as "diversity", but the word does not do justice to the picture that emerges as the collection of interviews unfold. Most big cities are diverse places, but these are heightened tensions and contradictions of a city that also feels compelled to guard its borders in order to simultaneously be a nation. The city of Singapore: a city governed with a strong hand. No one appears to ask about the government, but it pops up everywhere. City-dwellers who hum but watch their back; city-dwellers who buzz, unheard; city-dwellers who search for gaps, spaces, because sometimes that is all one can do. Together, the stories bring comfort, a sigh of relief, because here is a city I finally recognise, not a city one is supposed to conjure in one's imagination – Global City passion made possible – but a city, and country, real in its complex ugly beauty.

There are two jobs hidden from view in *Hard at Work*: Professor and Ethnographer. In both cases, the authors embody craft and expertise, commitment and pride. Like the many people interviewed, they take their work seriously, and have made something solid and durable in the process. I see only the final product, so this is me reverse engineering: The Professor gave his students tools of the trade – these are the questions to ask when we think about what work is, here is how you approach strangers, this is how you should ask questions, this is the way to listen, these are the ethics of conducting yourself as an interviewer, as a human being. The Professor looked at his students' work and recognised value, their potential contribution to knowledge-production. He went beyond grading assignments to what must have been deep labour of conceptualisation, selection, editing, organisation. A product that ends up looking elegant and effortless usually entails intense labour – like making a garment so that its stitches do not show.

The Ethnographer, in this highly unusual case, is a composite of many students and a photographer. They brought their openness and curiosity to the field, suspending judgement to cede space for their interviewees. They asked and they observed and they listened – simple tools of the trade, too often unused and which turn out to be what anyone needs to learn more about the world. They used their selves and their tools skillfully: we see this in the sustained candour and occasional meanderings of interviewees' stories; in the documentation of quiet, unremarkable, habitual moments embedded in work; and in the aunties and uncles turning the ethnographic gaze around to ask the students questions about their lives.

One or two interviews do not constitute an ethnography and individually each person is not necessarily an ethnographer, but by bringing together their work, they have created something that embodies how ethnography deepens our understanding of the world: everyday, nitty-gritty labour, the sensibilities and wisdoms of ordinary people, and the ways in which individual acts interact with social forces beyond the person – these matter for how we experience our society and should matter for how we imagine our collective selves.

The students and the photographer – The Ethnographer – together with The Professor, have created something unusual for amplifying the unseen, surfacing the under-acknowledged, elevating the mundane. And like the magic of a city, it is more than the sum of its parts.

A city hums, and it draws us in. If you let it, this book will too.

Teo You Yenn, June 2019

INTRODUCTION

Aiyah, all jobs hard one lah.

Work is hard. Despite exhortations to follow our dreams, find our passion, and never give up, these few words from a tea seller in one of Singapore's hawker centres probably come closer to the reality of employment for most of us. It's particularly the case for Singapore, where people work some of the longest hours in the world. Statistics compiled by the Ministry of Manpower show that despite a long-term decline, as of 2017 Singapore residents still work more than residents of any other OECD country. Meanwhile, media stories with titles like "Age of golden workers" (*Straits Times*, 30 April 2017) extoll the benefits of working into one's 80s or even 90s. If we take these reports at their word, many Singaporeans will be working hard from the moment they enter the workforce until the day they leave this earthly existence.

All this hard work has produced extraordinary results. Singapore's spectacular skyline, garden-like setting, superb airport and transportation system, world-leading schools and universities, and public housing scheme are all held up as models to the world. Much of the nation's success can be attributed to the vision and pragmatism of its leaders. At the same time, though, it's important to remember that the extraordinary Singapore we know today would never have been built nor would it continue to function without the labour of millions of ordinary people.

What follows are 60 interviews with the people who make Singapore possible. These interviews are the outcome of a collaborative project at the National University of Singapore between 2014 and 2017 that saw almost 100 students interview nearly 300 people. From the resulting interviews, we selected a number that we felt came together to form a wide-ranging story of Singapore. These include not just more visible occupations such as doctor, police officer and hawker, but also less obvious ones such as pet crematorium worker, wedding groomer and drag performer. Some of the people we interviewed even flirt with illegality, like a singer in a Thai disco working without the correct visa or a bet collector. Yet licit or illicit, respected or reviled, all of them form part of Singapore's working world.

When transcribing and editing the interviews for publication, we tried as much as possible to let people tell their stories in their own words and on their own terms. Thus, even if these interviews were originally conducted as part of a university class, they leave out commentary, analysis, or references to scholars with difficult-to-pronounce names. Instead, as much as possible what follows is simply the words of the people we interviewed, in the first-person style that they used with us, edited as if they were talking directly to the reader. They were kind enough to share with us their thoughts and experiences, hopes and disappointments, and now we share them with you as simply and directly as we can. What you make of them is up to you.

This commitment to share the stories of the people we interviewed includes the language they used. Singapore is a place where language, dialect and class converge, combine, diverge and recombine, sometimes in the course of a single conversation. One famous result is "Singapore Colloquial English", more commonly called Singlish, itself a broad category that encompasses multiple variants and registers. Many of the interviews were conducted in whole or in part in some form of Singlish, and we've attempted to preserve the original vocabulary, syntax, grammar and rhythms, with as little editorial explanation as possible. This was a conscious decision. Despite state-sponsored campaigns like the "Speak Good English Movement", we felt it was important to acknowledge and to validate the unique codes, expressions and ways of speaking used by millions. Nevertheless, we know some of the interviews may be hard for non-Singaporeans to read. If that includes you, it may help to read the passages out loud.

While many of the interviews were conducted in Singlish, others had to be translated from Malay, others from Mandarin Chinese, a few from Hokkien, Cantonese or other Chinese "dialects", and a few more from other languages depending on the skills of the interviewers. Choosing the register for the translations was also complicated. One reason for the linguistic diversity is Singapore's complex ethnic mix. Another is the prevalence of foreign workers in the workforce. In addition to a domestic population of 4.5 million citizens and permanent residents, Singapore is also the temporary home of almost 1.4 million foreign workers. This means that at any given moment, over 50 per cent of the people in waged employment in Singapore are from elsewhere. This includes about 400,000 professional or skilled workers, and close to 1 million labourers or service workers from places like Malaysia, India, Bangladesh, China and the Philippines. The interviews that follow acknowledge this fact by including the voices not just of Singapore residents but also the foreign workers who make such an important contribution to the nation.

The explicit topic of the interviews is work: the mundane reality of what people do to make a living. Yet because our jobs are so intimately entwined with our lives more generally, these stories of work are also about much more. In a sense, personal work histories chart how ordinary people live national and global history. For an ice cream seller, for example, long-term processes of economic restructuring may be experienced in terms of job loss and the struggle to find gainful employment. For a camera retailer, technological change since the 1990s is lived in terms of a cycle of boom and bust and the hope to keep his shop open until he can retire. For the tea seller whose words opened this introduction, contemporary urban redevelopment is felt in terms of rising rents and the imminent prospect of relocation. Taken together, these interviews contribute to a kind of people's history of Singapore.

These stories are also about people's place in society and the systems and structures that shape their lives. A young man fresh out of National Service might leverage the connections of his well-off parents to turn a passion for food into a successful career as a restaurateur. A tennis coach might dream of coaching Singapore's next tennis star but spend his day playing matches with bored housewives and wealthy expats. A cleaner in a hawker centre might find herself unable to take rest breaks for fear of being photographed by customers and reported to her supervisors. All of the people we interviewed are active subjects who seek to provide for themselves and their families while leading lives of dignity and self-respect. At the same time, however, their capacity to do so is both enabled and constrained by complex global processes and by factors of class, ethnicity, gender, age and others beyond their control.

Stories of work are about the objective conditions that determine our place in society. Yet they are also about where – and who – we would like to be. They shed light on our hopes, aspirations and values, with all the complexities and contradictions they entail. The interviews that follow include a presenter from the Singapore Zoo who idolises Jane Goodall and hopes to devote her life to working with animals. They feature a police officer determined to give back to the society that has given him so much, even while upholding laws that he disagrees with personally. They reveal a grocery stocker who hopes simply for stable, long-term employment and a little less work to do. And the story of an unlicenced tissue seller reminds us that personal dignity and fierce independence can be found in places and people we might not expect.

I feel privileged to have been part of this project. No matter how many times I read these interviews, I discover new things and I find myself moved. Some of the interviews are funny, some of them sad. Some frustrate me while others inspire me. All of them help me think about what Singapore is and what it might be. Mainly, though, I find myself humbled by the stories of ordinary working people who struggle, adapt and survive in the face of challenges large and small. This book is dedicated to them and to all people who work to make Singapore possible.

Gerard Sasges

THE HARD AT WORK PROJECT

The interviews in this collection were conducted as part of a class I taught at the National University of Singapore between 2014 and 2017. The class used the topic of work as a way to explore how people in Southeast Asia generally and Singapore in particular were experiencing processes of economic, social, cultural and political change that we often lump under the term "development". As part of the class, students interviewed people working in Singapore about their jobs. And while the explicit topic of the interview may have been work, implicitly we hoped to use it as a way into the issues that shape Singapore today.

Students were free to choose the people they interviewed. Sometimes they mobilised networks of friends or family. Other times, they interviewed complete strangers. Our project also benefited over the years from the participation of exchange students. Their critical approaches challenged those of us who assumed we knew Singapore, and their improvised networks allowed us to interview people we might not otherwise have met. Unfortunately, the realities of publishing a book meant that we weren't able to include interviews from all students. Even if their interviews aren't included, the perspectives, questions and comments of everyone who participated were an important part of our success.

Our project was guided by three commitments. One is to what professional scholars call "informed consent". Before we began an interview, we told potential participants about the nature of the project, let them know the name and contact information of both myself and the student interviewer, and made it clear that their interviews might be published. Everyone was given the choice to participate in the project or not, and if they chose to participate, signed a consent form. The consent forms have only been seen by three people – the interviewer, the interviewee and myself – and are kept in a secure place. With a few exceptions, when the person is obviously identifiable and where they gave us explicit permission to proceed on that basis, all interviews are anonymous, and details that might make people identifiable have been changed or removed. None of the people we interviewed appear in the images that accompany the interviews.

The second commitment was to interview people attentively, responsibly and empathetically. Over the course of each semester, the students and I developed our interviewing skills in a range of ways. We began by thinking about our own position and about the power dynamics involved in interviewing. We paid attention to issues of class, race, age and gender and how they might shape the interview process. We learned to follow up and to encourage people to elaborate and expand on things that might otherwise go unspoken. We practiced how to listen to people, paying attention to silences, pauses, intonation, and movement as much as the words that were being spoken. Most generally, we tried to treat each interview as a conversation between equals, shaped by our questions and our methods but ultimately determined by the stories people wanted to tell and the ways they wanted to tell them.

Our third commitment was to respect the stories we were told and the people who told them. One part of this involved translation. Most of the interviews were conducted in some form of Singapore English, but some were conducted in part or in whole in other languages. When this was the case, the task of translating was left to the interviewer. Not only were they the ones with the necessary linguistic competences, but also they had the first-hand experience of the interview itself. This combination, we felt, gave the best chance of success at a process that is as much about context, idiom and even emotion as about the words themselves. If the speaker was Singaporean or a long-term resident, then we translated into Singlish; if they weren't, then the translation is in Singapore Standard English. To take one example, an interview of a Singaporean cleaner, conducted in Chinese, would be rendered in Singlish while an interview of a Chinese national doing the same job would be in Standard English. No translation is perfect. Yet it still has to be done. As the translator and critic George Steiner put it, "Without translation, we would be living in provinces bordering on silence."

The other part of this commitment involved editing. Few of us would want to read an unedited transcript of a conversation. Even the most coherent, composed person will backtrack, digress, repeat themselves and punctuate their conversation with innumerable "ums" and "ers". So as much as we wanted to provide an authentic account of every conversation we had, we also had to take account of the need to make interviews engaging for readers. The first stage of editing was carried out by the interviewer themselves. The most obvious change was to turn a conversation into a first-person monologue. Taking out the interviewer's questions and contributions, we felt, was the best way to foreground the speaker and their story. Interviewers might also remove parts they felt were repetitive or unhelpful, or in some cases reorder passages within the interview. The second stage was carried out by the two editors. For the most part this involved editing the interviews for length, which was made necessary when our desire to include as many stories as possible met the publisher's need to keep the end result to a workable length. In a few cases, we made further changes to the ordering of passages within an interview in order to create a more coherent flow from beginning to end. If major changes seemed warranted, we made them in consultation with the interviewer. At all stages of translation and editing, we were guided by the desire to respect the interviewee and their story, both in their words and their intent.

Gerard Sasges

PROJECT PARTICIPANTS

Alan Ang Wee Chuan

Ang Wen Min

Irene Arieputri

Alexandra Chamberlin

Chan Sun Hei

Yuen Ling Chan

Felicia Chia Qi Min

Rachel Chia Su Erhn

Charlene Choe Tze Yi

Choo Ruizhi

Chng Shao Kai

Nathene Chua Qi Qi

Perlita Contridas

Quentin Dampierre

Melissa De Boer

Samuel Devaraj

Dong Chenchen

Carmen Ferri

Jona Frasch

Irene Fung

Levonne Goh Yan Xin

Rachel Nadia Goh Yuling

Mia Gonzalez

Harith Redzuan Bin Mustaffa Qamal

Abigail Rose Ho Jia-Yin

Robert Hoehner

Kang Li Ting

Cheryl Ko Hui Ling

Sara Lau Jin Ee

Liz Lee Hui Xin

Lee Liu Yi

Vivien Lee

Nicole Lee Mei Ting

Candy Lee Shu Hua

Corliss Ler Jia Yi

Eunice Lim Chian Hwee

Lim Kai Hui

Bernard Loh Meng Chin

Lok Weng Seng

Elza Loo Hwe Ning

Bhavika Mahtani

Tiffane Mak

Muhammad Fathul Ariffin Bin Ayub
Muhammad Syakir Bin Hashim
Nadira Binte Mohamed Aslam
Nasuha Binte Nizam Thaha
Cristina Nearing
Nicholas Neo Yan Hwee
Mathias Nielsen
Violet Ng Hui Zhi
Ng Li Ying
Joanna Ng Sue Ann
Nur Atiqah Binte Rosli
Nur Nadzirah Binte Abdul Halim K
Nur Qistina Binte Ahmad
Angie Ong
Ong Lin Yee
Ooi Yong Ann
Alina Pahor
Charmaine Pang
Yoga Prasetyo
Signe Rasmussen
Grace Rigby
Ros Amirah Binte Rosli
Justin Rotman
Said Effendy
Saw Su Hui
Pearly Seah Hui En
Seri Ariyani Binte Zulfakili

Shabirah Binte Mohammed Sidek
Siti Nurfatin Binte Raja Ali
Olivia Sng Mun Yi
Evelyn Tan
Jeanette Tan Li Ying
Tan Sing Yee
Charmaine Tan Wen Qi
Tan Xin Hui
Trini Zerlina Tan Zhao Ling
Tan Zhuorui
Teo Boon Hwee
Althea Toh Wern-Rae
Sarah Tong Ren Xuan
Try Sutrisno Foo
Tseng Yi Ying
Sarun Udomkichdecha
Vern Varin Urairat
Rina Wang Miao Qin
Wee Min Er
Jennifer Williams
Xie Ziqi
Joycelyn Yeo Lin
Yeo Tze Yang
Leonard Yeo Zong You
Audrey Yong Hui Ling
Ting Zhang

DRINKING

CHAPTER ONE

DRINKING

Barista

My name is Amy. I'm turning 21 this year and I'm currently working as a shift supervisor cum barista at Starbucks. The location explains why my store is always packed with customers. It gets really bad in the morning at around 7 a.m. onwards but the crowd will die off after 10 and that's usually when I get to have my work break. I take turns with my partners to go for our breaks because there's a limit to the number of partners allowed to go for breaks at a time. We call the baristas working in a store "partners". I think that's how the company wants us to see each other, but we're definitely more than just partners. More like my family, really. Having been working here for almost a year, seeing the same faces five times a day for like nine hours if I'm working single shift, and twelve if I'm working double shift, I've gotten really emotionally attached to each and every one of them.

When I first started working as a barista at Starbucks, I thought that the benefits were really attractive and I especially loved getting to bring home the marked-out foods. And don't get me wrong, I still do, but not as much. I don't find the benefits as enticing as I found them a few months ago. It gets really boring bringing home the same food every week and consuming the same things every day. A partner is entitled to two beverages and a food for every shift you've worked in a day. So if you work double shift, that you'll get to have four beverages and two pastries. That's the reason why you see some partners secretly giving drinks to their friends for free.

On some days, I'll bring home the granola bars that are not marked-out yet. Meaning, I'll bring home the food that are not allowed to be brought home because they haven't expired. It wouldn't really make any difference to the sales anyway and the granola bars are really, really good! I bet the other partners do the same too. I'm only working here for the money, although they don't really pay me much. Ironic, isn't it? And also because I love coffee a lot, of course. I could've chosen to work for Coffee Bean but Starbucks has a higher reputation for their drinks so I chose Starbucks. The pay rate for Starbucks in Singapore is about $6 per hour for part-timers. For full-timers like me, it varies depending on your position in the store and the number of hours you've worked. I bring home about $1,350 a month inclusive of CPF (Central Provident Fund). That's very little, considering the fact that I have a diploma. I mean, I didn't work my ass off in polytechnic to have a job paying me lower than $1.5K per month, right?

The thought of me quitting this job never leaves my mind. I'm always thinking about it because this job gives me no life. Every day, I wake up at 5 a.m. Shower. Walk to Choa Chu Kang MRT station, board the train and queue up with a lot of elderly at 5:45. Reach my store before 6:30 a.m. Clock in. Do the opening. Set up the pastry case or bar. Perform. Clock out at 4. Take the train home. Wash up, have dinner and go to sleep. Repeat. It's so mundane – so, so mundane that I'm always looking for things to spice up my life. Just today during my break, I tried a new brand of cigarettes for the fun of it. So I had like four sticks of Winston Red today. I might change to a new brand next week.

There was actually a point where I almost quit because of the overwhelming stress I had to face when I was training to be a supervisor. Honestly, I could get a job with a better pay but it makes me sad leaving my partners behind. Since I've gotten this far to get the position of a supervisor of my store, why not wait a little more before I quit ... right?

I'm saving up for the next phase of my life, which is university. I've gotten a place in LaSalle but I took a gap year after graduating from polytechnic because I felt that I would need some time to replenish my savings after spending on my graduation trip to Korea. [laughs] I'm the eldest so I'm quite independent financially. I don't want to increase the burden of my parents who still have to pay for my brother's school expenditure.

If I have free time, or during my off days, I'll play the guitar, draw, go shopping or meet up with friends. Ever since I worked at Starbucks, I barely have the time to have proper conversations with my friends because the strenuous work makes me too exhausted to even hold long conversations. Some of my friends who don't understand think I'm antisocial. Some say I'm being difficult with making plans but I have no control of my working hours. You see, when people get their off days for public holidays, that's when we have to work for extra hours.

My biggest struggle would probably be finding time for my family. It's really frustrating sometimes. I go to work even before they're awake. When I get home, sometimes I'm so tired I'll sleep right away after my dinner. And also because I had to spend all day with customers, I'd rather have me time when I'm at home. Basically I just spend my time at home stoning from exhaustion. It's like we're so close yet so far, you know?

My customers are mainly students, tourists and office ladies and businessmen. We're encouraged to make small talk with our customers so they won't feel bored in the queue. It's part of Starbucks' strategy to retain customer loyalty. It's quite easy for me because I've been doing it for a while. We just have to tune in to their age group and try to ask random questions like "Where are you from?" "Do you have class today?" "Are you studying at SMU (Singapore Management University)?" or just give them a smile. But you know … there are some days where you're not really in the mood or having sibeh (Hokkien: extremely) negative emotions but you still have to face the customers with a smile. As baristas of a company that's known for service, we're trained to put the commitment to our work above our emotions.

People usually think that us baristas are uneducated and have no future, so we tend to be ordered around and looked down upon. I have never felt so disrespected before I get a job at Starbucks. Everyone looked up to me in school. Eh, not because I'm tall, but my grades were. I used to be the top student in class for most of my modules and I got a lot of respect from my friends. So it's a big change for me here. Maybe it's just my luck to get arrogant customers. The line between giving good customer service and letting someone get away with anything is so blurred that we have to put up with their shit. But on the bright side, we get to pick up good conversation skills here. I used to be a little shy but after a year of talking to my customers every day, I feel like I could make great conversation with anyone. Even with my pet cat.

For now, I'll just take a day at a time. I'll make a mountain from the little pay I get every month and when I'm satisfied with my mountain of savings, that's when I'll quit my job to continue my studies at LaSalle. Or maybe I'll just quit when my motivation runs dry. Which is probably soon.

Nur Atiqah Binte Rosli

Thai Disco Singer

Sawadeeka! I am Oil. I am from Bangkok, Thailand. I am 20 this year. I can speak English but not good. I am work in Club V3 Thai Disco now as singer. I come here to Singapore 30 days only because I come as tourist. A lot of girls here same-same. All tourist. I like Singapore. Very clean, very safe and everything very nice. But very expensive. That one I no like. I stay condo here with other girls also from Thailand. But I no tell my family I come here. They no like. I tell them I come Singapore holiday with my friends. I first time come here. Five days liao (Hokkien: already). I never take aeroplane before. Also my first time. I very lucky can come here work. Can holiday and work together very good. Because I work in V3, got free aeroplane and free home for us in Singapore. No need money, everything free and no boyfriend. Because before I come here I break up him, he call me every day. I very angry at him so I break up him. After we break up he follow me home and always wait for me downstairs when I in Thailand. Now no more because I in Singapore. I won't see him anymore. He no good. Very "chao chu" (Thai: flirtatious). You know what's that? Thai men like "butterfly" (having several girlfriends at once). My boyfriend too. But Singapore men good. No "chao chu". They bring me go eat after I work finish here. At Geylang or somewhere. I meet them in V3. They my customers. Very nice.

I work night time because V3 open 9 p.m. Close at 4 a.m. but if no people, can close early. Last time I work morning in Thailand in office. So I feel tired very easily now but work here very fun and easy. A lot of people come on Friday see us. Today (Sunday) not so many people. We need go V3 early prepare, and clean the place after work finish if no customers bring us go out eat. But I very lucky. I always go out eat after work so no need to clean up V3. My good friend ask me come here work V3 because I can sing. She say can come Singapore, free holiday and can earn a lot money, go back. I don't know how much I will earn but she say very easy money and a lot so I want. She ask me send her photo and she show her agent then he ask me come work here. She not in Singapore now. Go home to Thailand. We same agent, Peter his name. I can sing a lot of songs. English, Chinese, Thai songs. Chinese song I learn for this job. Yesterday I learnt 她说 (Chinese song). Very difficult to remember but I love to sing. I cannot speak Chinese but I want to learn Chinese song. I hear other girl sing 海阔天空 (Cantonese song), first day I come here work. Peter say that song, a lot customers like. It's very nice, I want to learn too. Last time I working office in Thailand, only speak Thai. I come here can learn Chinese songs and speak English. Singapore speak English.

Before I come here to work I need buy clothes for working here. I buy at Pratunam. You got go Pratunam? Shopping very cheap. So a lot people go. Singapore people also go. I go there buy. I spent around 5,000 baht (approx. $215) buy clothes and high shoe. A lot of money but I need to buy because I don't have working clothes for work here. I won't wear them when I go back Bangkok because I want work back in office. But lucky I buy, need change new clothes after I sing a song. I sing a lot so one night I can change three or four clothing. Sometimes V3 people give us clothes but I always bring mine.

My job very easy. Every day just sing, dance and play games with customers. But I need to drink a lot. Need go around and ask customers buy tequila from me. I need learn four games. The games can help me get customers buy drink from me. Now I only know two games – "5, 10" and "1, 2, 3". I play with customers. They very nice, will buy drinks when I say I thirsty. But I no like small boy. They come here no money buy tequila. My friend also say young boys buy very little. I don't find guys buy tequila from me when they bring girlfriends. Girls don't like us talk to their boyfriends. We all know that. A lot of guys and girls then I go ask them buy. One tequila $15. [laughs] Three hundred baht, one tequila! But guys will still buy. Peter says I need sell 15 tequila every day. If not I can also get flower.

When I sing got customers give me flower. Peter say the flower can change for money. Different flower, different price. Some $50 some $10,000. That's a lot. I got some flowers from customers. After we take flowers from customers we need go and say thank you to them and talk-talk with them. Talking is good. They will buy tequila from me. But I don't know how much I earn already. Peter say can earn a lot money, go back. But I don't know is how much. Must see how many tequila I sell and how many flower money customers give me. I like flower because I don't need to drink and can earn more. Don't need sell so many tequila. I want to know how much I earn already but Peter say count next time. Ask me sell a lot tequila. Sometimes easy. Sometimes difficult. I still learning how to sell. A lot girls here customers can buy from.

Anyway I don't like drink a lot. When customer buy a lot I need drink many-many with them. Wake up head pain. Lazy to work. But still must come, like yesterday, if not Peter not happy. I want them buy flower. Yesterday I saw one customer give $500 flower money to a girl but I only got $50. I want to get more flower money … but a lot girls in V3 very pretty. I don't feel pretty here. The breast big one, guys like to buy tequila and flower for them. That day got one girl she go out with customer, never go home. We all know where she go. [laughs] But I never because I don't like. I go home every time after eat with customers.

I don't go a lot place in Singapore. No time. I want go walk-walk around here. Go see the Merlion and Orchard Road but I no time. Only can work and sleep. After work I eat with customers and friends then go home sleep till 3 or 4 p.m. Then we wake up and eat "mama" (Maggi noodles) and prepare go work. Peter fetch us once. But I

always take cab go work with the other girls in our house. I don't know them before I come. But we all friend now. We talk, laugh-laugh then now good friend. We stay together also. Downstairs condo got swimming pool but we haven't use yet. No time.

I want come back Singapore work again. Very easy money. But I miss my family. I call them and talk to them when I reach Singapore. I got Facebook and Instagram. But I don't like put pictures up there when I come Singapore. They will know. A lot of girls do this in Thailand. But I don't want my parents sad. But this job very good. I can run away from my ex-boyfriend and holiday here free. Who don't want? A lot of girls here also like me. They don't need money because they okay. But they still come here sing and play then go back Thailand and come again. If can I also want come here work again.

Olivia Sng Mun Yi

Tea seller

My name Mary. I'm boss of this bubble tea shop. I work in hawker centre, but I not hawker hor. I am boss, an en-tri-pu-nur (entrepreneur)! Not many people brave like me to try adventure of opening my own business. So I proud of myself lah.

This my first business and venture. Two years ago my husband learn to make bubble tea from his friend who train in Taiwan. At first the shop was joint venture between me, my husband and my husband's friend, but my husband's friend don't want continue the business because some conflicts. Aiyah, work with people very difficult one lah. They cannot agree on rotation of shifts, so my husband's friend don't want continue the business with us. So I take over loh. My husband still has a full-time job, he cannot become boss. I learn how to make bubble tea from my husband and run this shop by myself. I become the boss.

Why I choose to sell bubble tea ah? Bubble tea quite popular in Singapore mah. See lah, now got many bubble tea shops everywhere. So many the Gong Cha and Koi in shopping centres. But I not selling bubble tea in shopping area. I sell in hawker centre so my price very cheap, very reasonable. You know right, each cup only around $1.50 to $2. My bubble tea shop also the only one in this hawker centre, so people want drink bubble tea, they come to me. Business here quite good lah. I have many regular customers. Mondays to Fridays, from 11 a.m. to 6 p.m., office people come and buy bubble tea from me, especially during lunch time. Saturdays, I open from 11 a.m. to 9 p.m. and my customers usually the church people. I don't open my shop on Sundays because Sunday is family time. Actually business quite slow recently lah. Some offices have moved out, so less office customers now. But I still make some money ah, not bad. I also deliver bubble tea to schools when they have event. Last month, I cater to Hwa Chong students and they love my bubble tea! Next month I going deliver to Nanyang Polytechnic. See, my tea very popular ah because is cheaper than Koi and Gong Cha, also healthier and nicer.

The tea I use very high quality one leh! The Koi and Gong Cha only use assam tea to make bubble tea, which is cheap and low quality. I use more expensive earl grey tea. For women better avoid drinking assam tea, ah, because very cooling, no good for your body leh! Even though I spend more on high-quality tea, is okay lah. When quality good, this what attracts customers and makes my bubble tea different lor. Every morning, I brew the tea myself and make the juices. I don't hire other people help because I need train them and make sure the standard there. Very mafan (Mandarin: troublesome). Also must pay them, not worth for small shop like mine. I do everything myself better. Sometimes is tiring lah, especially when got a lot of orders, I work overnight just to brew tea. Then must bring the tea to the schools. But all worth lah, when I see my customers really enjoy my tea. Customers are like my family lor, when they happy with my tea, I also happy.

For the past two years work here I never met bad customer. Only one time when customer come and scold me badly because he thought I put chemical in his tea and he said I want him to die. Siao (Hokkien: crazy) one leh! I told him that I am selling here is juice, not syrup. My tea no chemical one. If you want chemical go to Koi and Gong Cha, that one is confirm have. I know they use syrup and cheap tea there, so I don't drink from them. I don't allow my kids to drink also. Really not healthy hor. So I make tea that is good and not harm to my customers and also my kids.

Yah, I have three kids. The eldest 17 years old, second one 13 and youngest is 11. My second one always help me at my shop doing cashier on Saturdays. He like to work here. The customers also like him, because he cute. Every time they see him they always smile. Maybe next time my second son can take over this shop in the future. This brand is a lifetime trademark mah, so can give it anytime to my second son lor. But my eldest one don't like ah. He never come to our shop one. Maybe he shy or feel uncomfortable, I don't know. He never tell me. But anyway he also busy studying. He want go to polytechnic, study some video thing, so I let him lor. I don't pressure my kids much lah. Their life, so they must choose their own path and try their best. I cannot choose the path for them mah.

Like me lor, this the path I choose, so I must try my best. You know, work in office actually much better than work here leh. Work in office you get benefits like CPF and fix salary, here don't have anything. I worked as secretary all my life after O Levels, I thought I will stay that forever. But in the end, see where I end up! Life is adventure lah, so this adventure come, I take it up lor! Actually I quite proud of myself. Work as boss for the past two years already, I quite happy. I meet many friends, and make tea also fun. But I also upset lah. The rental here is very high. Is $1,800 and this not including the table cleaning fee and electricity bills. So total every month I pay around $2,500 to $3,000 leh. I only earn $1,000, or $1,000 plus on good months. Quite little but I still can survive lah. My family live very simple one, so that good. But to me the government should do something leh. They say the rental already very cheap but not true lor! They don't understand what is like to work here and how much bubble tea I must sell to pay rent. My bubble tea cost around $2, I have to sell around … 2,000 cups every month to make profit leh. Hard for me, you know. Need take care of my three kids and also my parents. [sighs] I actually also want expand my business and get another shop in Hougang but minimum rental bid there is $2,500 leh! I where got that kind of money? If I take that shop hor, my bubble tea price confirm have to increase, then not cheap anymore. Aiyah, government should step in and lower the minimum bidding price mah. Help us do our business better. Don't know what they thinking sometimes.

But I think in the future hor, hawker centres like this will be no more already. The rental so high, some more all the young people don't want this hawker life. The government also demolish hawker centres leh. You know, this place in the end December this year going to demolish already. I very sad. This place like my family. The aunties and uncles here all very nice, we all help one another. The customers who come here also like my family already. See, I remember all of you and your regular orders. I very sad must move out lah. I still finding a place to move to, don't know where also because the rent everywhere so high. Just hope that can continue this business and pass it to my second son next time lor. If not, I have to go back my office job.

Now got the 99 per cent SME (small and medium enterprises) campaign thing, you heard before or not? My friends ask me join that so I can earn some advertisement money then can help my business. I still thinking if I should join lah. But actually hor, I also don't think I can win … my shop so small, even if get all my regular customers vote, not enough lah! [laughs] But, now got the Facebook hor, really help a lot. Recently I make Facebook page for my bubble tea, got few people like my page. Some of my regular customers all very young mah, so must connect them lor. Sometimes they also help me post good reviews on my Facebook and share their friends.

My regular customers help me spread my bubble tea to their friends, I thank them. But of course that's not enough ah, I also try my best to engage the new customers and talk to them when they buy my bubble tea. I try make sure I remember their orders so when next time they come, I know what bubble tea they want and there is personal touch, you know. Like how I remember your order when you come visit me every Saturday! Yah, I treat all my customers specially. Sometimes I will also ask them about their day and if they have kids, about their kids. So we always chit-chat lor. Nice lah, I like to talk to my customers. Makes my job not boring also.

Aiyah, all jobs hard one lah. My customers very nice but what I worry most in this job is money lor. Whether I can pay my rent, whether got money for family, whether can pay supplier, whether got money to expand. But even if hard hor, I want do my best to sustain this business and not give up halfway. Anyway my dream just for my life to go smooth and retire with enough money. So even if don't earn a lot, still okay lah. I very simple one. But I think for young people like you, want aim high and get promoted, work as a boss in hawker centre really not good ah. Confirm cannot survive one. Need hard work and never-say-die attitude. Singaporeans very funny hor, always complain about a lot of foreigners here in Singapore. But what to do, no one want to do all these low pay jobs mah. Of course have to ask foreigners lah. Singaporeans now where got want do this.

So I special lor. Actually I am only 40 years old. I still got a long, long road ahead of me leh. Just hope I can continue doing this until retire and pass on the shop to my second son if he want take over. In life, must always try adventure no matter whether it work out or not. This is path I choose mah, so even when it gets difficult ah, I also don't want to give up. Next time you go work, must remember not give up halfway even when tiring, okay?

Ang Wen Min

Craft Brewer

I'm a craft beer brewer and I sell my beer at my own stall in the Chinatown Complex. I did not do this for my whole life though. After high school I served as a regular in the Singaporean army for 21 years. I quit after some policy changes were made and because I didn't see my future there. I wanted to do my own thing and be my own boss. Together with my friend, I opened a factory that produced adhesive tape. This didn't last long though. After one year, the Singapore government established new environmental regulations. Implementing these new regulations would have cost a bomb for us. We didn't have a choice, so we decided to move our business to Shenyang in China. The government incentives were very good and helped us a lot in the first years of doing business. I was there for about four years, then we opened another factory in Shanghai, because the winter isn't that cold and long in Shanghai, so we didn't have to spend so much on the heating. Additionally, Shanghai is more central and commercialised, so it was easier to do business there. After 10 years, things started to not go well for us. The Chinese government decided to take away subsidies and tax reductions we had gotten before, because they weren't very interested in the foreign low-tech industry anymore. They tried to encourage local citizens to start their own venture for these kinds of businesses. Of course that wasn't very helpful for us and our product wasn't competitive anymore. I decided to pull out and sell my share of the business.

When I got back, I started to live the life of a retired man. I travelled a lot and was especially interested in the West, because I'd only been in Asia my whole life. I did a tour through Europe and saw lots of nice places there. And I had my first taste of craft beer in Munich. After I got back home, I bought some small-scale brewery equipment for about $200 and started to try remaking the beer I tasted in Munich at home. I was a retired man, so I had the spare time to try something new, haha! In one batch I made between 10 and 20 litres of beer, but it was very bad in the beginning. I taught myself how to do it with internet research and books. My brewing skills got better and after a while, my friends talked me into opening my own microbrewery and making a profession out of my hobby. In order to do that, I had to become more professional. Especially in terms of the beer brewing equipment. Suppliers always try to rip you off, that's a lesson I learned during my time in China. In order to avoid that, I had to know what I was talking about before I would start to buy professional equipment and supplies.

I also went back to Germany for half a year. I lived in Munich and did a half-year programme about brewing at a local university. The time there was very educational for me. I learned a lot and I saw that Germans really have a great acceptance of other people, mindsets and cultures. The other students in my class were a whole lot younger than me and very energetic. Besides me, the oldest student was in his early 30s. On the weekends I travelled a bit, but mainly I went to the various pubs and tried and tried and tried. I especially liked the smaller pubs, because the brewers there were very talkative. In half a year you can pick up a lot. They really want to exchange ideas with you and don't hold back. Asians are more protective with their knowledge, which is a cultural thing. They don't want to pass on their full knowledge, because they are scared that the student might get better than the master. A shame!

After I came back from Munich, I started setting up my micro-brewery. I bought parts of my equipment in China and in Germany and set it up in an industrial park. It's a Singaporean law that you can only brew less than 30 litres at home and only for your own consumption. If you want to sell your beer, then you need a licence to brew and a licence to sell. It's mainly about hygiene and the tax. It's very hard to set up a business like that in Singapore and you need to follow lots of regulations. For example, the brewery and your storage have to be monitored at all times and you have to take a course on how to estimate the alcohol amount that will be produced with a certain amount of raw material, which is important for the taxes you have to pay. I also needed to get the approval of the NEA, of the HDB (Housing & Development Board) and of the town council. Setting up the business took me about a year and I opened up about 14 months ago. I'm running the business together with my brother. He's an accountant, so he helps me with the financial part of the business. If there's a lot of work, then he sometimes helps me with the delivery as well.

I was never really keen to go high end, like opening a bar at Clarke Quay for example. This would cost a bomb because of the rent, furniture and manpower. You also can't simply sell craft beer there. You have to offer other drinks and some food as well, which I never wanted to do. I want my beer to be taken seriously and I only want customers who really appreciate it and who know the difference between craft and commercial beer. In order to get that kind of customer I need the exposure to middle and lower-middle income people. And where is the best place to do that? The hawker centre! I have a large variety of customers and I have to pay special attention on the nationalities. Americans, for example, like to have foam on their beer, but English people don't like that. If I don't recognise that correctly, my customers might be unhappy. Lots of experts and foreigners come to my stall, all of different ages. I have Singaporean customers too, but they are usually younger. Older Singaporeans stick to Tiger Beer, because they are used to that. They don't want to change after so many years and the friends they take their beer with feel the same way. So there's kind of a peer pressure. Even if some older people like my craft beer better, they still stick to Tiger because their friends like it and they don't want to drink alone at my stall.

I sell about 200 litres of beer per day and brew four times a week. One batch of beer takes about nine days to brew. Bigger breweries like Tiger and Carlsberg can do it in just two and a half days because they use less grain and they add sugar in order to speed up the process, but you can definitely taste a difference. I offer several different kinds of beer and I like to experiment with new recipes. In fact I'm working on a red ale right now. It will have a full body and a lasting aftertaste. Very nice, but not quite done yet.

Except for experimenting with new recipes, I enjoy selling my beer more than producing it. I really like being at my stall and selling beer every day. I get to talk to young people like you, which makes me very happy, because I don't feel that old. [laughs] Not everyone wants to have a conversation, but a lot of my customers do. Even the Japanese! Their English is not very good, but they usually still want to have a conversation. I think I am quite good at talking and making friends, whether they are old or young. I know two Englishmen who are about my age and are still working. Whenever they go back to England they bring me English beers and some sausages from their hometown. And then I have an Italian friend. I call him Tomato. [laughs] I know that this isn't his actual name, but it sounds like it. I think his real name is Tomaso, but I am not quite sure, Tomato is better. Whenever his mother sends him goodies from Italy he will come to my stall and share them with me. Last year he broke up with his girlfriend. I didn't know about it. Whenever he came to my stall before, he would sit on the other side of the table. But that night he came alone and sat here, right in front of my stall, so I knew that something must have happened. I asked him if he wanted to talk about what was bothering him and he told me the story. I said, "If you still love her, then don't be angry with her. Go up to her and then think of the first time you saw her." And now they are back together. I've been married to my wife for over 30 years now and this has always worked for me.

Yesterday an American came to my stall who'd been at home for three months and just returned to Singapore. So I said, "Hey, welcome to the haze!" He asked me if the haze would affect my business. I answered that about 40 per cent less people came to my store in the last week. Do you know what he did? He started making calls to his friends and after a while, six more people came to my stall. And do you want to know the best part of the story? He told the six of them, "Don't order a jug for the first round and refuse to take the change!" So they only ordered the smaller, relatively more expensive glasses of beer. Everyone gave me $10 bills and refused to take the change. I didn't notice that they have been told to do so until the same order of the third person in a row. [smiles] I do get tips sometimes, but not that much and not in this way. I was very touched that my friend tried to help me in this difficult situation.

Four months ago I hired a brewer to help me with the production. The demand is getting higher and I can't do it alone anymore. I want to further expand my business in two ways. My first concept is that I help people setting up their own bar or stall and then sell them my beer. That's better than a franchise system, because I have less work and my partners can focus on selling as much of my beer as they can, without worrying about a franchise fee. We're all happy this way. My second approach in expanding my business is that I set up stalls and run them myself until they're successful. Then I hand them over to someone else and collect a deposit for my equipment. I stay the owner of the equipment, another person pays the rent for the stall and I sell him or her my beer. So I don't have to worry about paying wages for more employees and I can be sure that they really put their heart and soul into the business. The income in this business depends highly on how you run it and how you interact with your customers. In fact, I think that this is why I'm so successful. You just have to love what you are doing.

Robert Hoehner

Coffee Wholesaler

My name is Uncle Heng and I own a shop selling coffee since 1984. In the past, my grandfather's shop was in Bugis. Now it's a big office block. We were chased out when they wanted to build the MRT station. So they relocated us and gave us a special rate under the resettlement rent in 1984. Every time I pass by the office block, I think about the past. It was better then, before all the old folks moved away. Mine is a family business, started in in 1939, but there's nobody to take over the business after me. I don't have a next generation because I'm not married.

I started helping my father in secondary school. When I didn't have homework, I would go to the shop or follow the other workers in the delivery van. I started learning there. Before taking over this business, I was a technician with the air force for 12 years. Even during that period, I helped my father. Then, continue lor. Working in the air force and selling coffee are different. I can't compare them. The experiences are different. I can't say which I like better.

In the past, I used to work the deliveries for my father. Now I do more shop work. Normally I start at 9 a.m. and end at 6 p.m. During my second quarter at 12 to 3 p.m., I'll close the shop and deliver beans to hawker centres and coffee stalls. I don't have that many to go to anymore. Many have given up their businesses as most are run by old people who have no more energy to work. I don't have many walk-in customers. Only people who know me will come, and they know what time I'm open. At 6 p.m., I wash my hands and go home! You need to learn how to rest and switch off. It's productivity when you work longer but there's no life. I need to break off and disconnect completely, force myself to shut down so that I will not burn out.

If you calculate my real working hours, it's probably longer than seven or eight hours, because behind the shop, I still have to prepare my coffee beans. These are the extra hours not included in retail hours. I get my beans raw from the bean wholesaler before sending them to the roasting factory. After roasting, I need to do some preparation before grinding. Selling, grinding ... that's the simplest part of the job. Do you see these gunny sacks? Before I can sell them, I have to do shifting and sort and clean the beans. It's not difficult, but it is menial and tiring. I use a sieve to remove the small particles in the mix. Husks fall out when you roast coffee beans and sometimes these husks are not cleared properly. Or margarine and sugar break down into fine particles. These account for the sour and bitter taste. It's like a ... clean-up process. Not everyone does it, but the majority does. The difference is how thorough they are. For me? [laughs] In some urgent situations, no choice, I have to let go. But if I have time, I do it.

The hardest work is the shifting because I am old. I'm already 52 years old! It is manual and I run a one-man show. I feel exhausted from my job, but not every day. If I'm tired, I just don't work! If I've prepared enough for the next two days, I'll relax a bit. I need to rest leh. In 1980s, we piah (Hokkien: go all out with little concern for rest or safety) and we opened every day from Monday to Sunday. There were no off days aside from half a day on Sunday. This was in my father's time when we were still in Bugis. We worked from 7 a.m. to 6 p.m. After we moved here, we cut the hours. Now the shop is in my hands … the hours are even shorter. [chuckles]

Here I sell two grades of Arabica beans and two other grades of Robusta beans but I have three different roasting methods. Each shop will sell a different type of coffee even if we buy our beans from the same plantation. That's because we have to tell our roasting factories exactly how we want them roasted. I decide the length of time and the temperature of the roasting of my beans. Sometimes I go and watch my beans get roasted. I do my homework you know. I read articles on the internet, go to coffee exhibitions to learn and to look at machines. I saw a documentary once and I was interested in getting a roasting machine, but it costs half a million. But that was about 10 years back. Anyway, even if I buy it, I have to ask HDB, NEA (National Environment Agency) and the fire brigade. I'll need a lot of permits. If I could afford it, I would do it, but it'll be a different niche of customers that I'll be catering to. Besides, for this business, roasting is the most difficult part. The fumes are really pungent. Once you finish roasting and open the oven, wah, cannot tahan (Malay: endure). Everyone thinks, whoa, the aroma is so nice! But they don't know about the smelly part. My shop lies closer to the end part of the coffee production chain so I'm lucky I don't do the roasting.

In the past, business ran on a chain of wholesalers, middleman, second middleman then retailers. The second middleman is now gone because of competition. The seller goes directly to the wholesaler. Like me! I go straight to the wholesaler as a seller. So I am not the middleman. That is if I'm at the end of the chain. For coffee shops, I'm the middleman, but if they have the ability to go straight to the wholesaler, then I'm done for. If the fellow can go straight to him and save 20 per cent, then I'm gone. So if you look around, the middleman business is not slowly, but clearly [with emphasis] gone. But by the time I get cut off, I think I won't have to worry anymore. [laughs] Maybe in 10 years. But for now, the coffee drinking niche is still there, I still have that group of people. No doubt it's smaller, but it's still there, maybe there'll be some younger ones, but not many lah. Their lives are too hectic. They have no time to brew their own coffee, so they go for instant coffee, or go to cafés where someone will do it for them. I give the trade 50 years to die.

Sad? Well … it's life. The cycle will go on. Eventually, this method will die out. Like everything else, the cycle goes around, after a while it goes down, and new changes will come up. In the past, there were a lot of shops like mine. In the 1980s, you would have been able to find one everywhere. In the '90s and early 2000s, they started to shrink. I don't see many anymore. I am the only one here. You can find some in the markets, as little corners in provision shops. You have to know exactly where we are, or you wouldn't be able to find us. A lot of the older generation who used to sell coffee gave up when their kids didn't want to take over. The kids are more educated so they don't go for this sort of work. It's not because it's not profitable, but more of a lifestyle change. This is hard work, you know.

I did think about expanding, but I need to piah all the way. I can spend money, get it into an upmarket look, but it doesn't suit the way this coffee business is. See the display rack? It came from my grandfather's shop. I thought about it, though. I know this man who did it but he collapsed, and then where is the business? He became the business. My life is worth more than this.

I'm happiest when my customers say my coffee is nice and they're happy to buy it again. It's like an achievement and my effort is not wasted. My old regulars make me happy. Some are so old that we talk and joke like friends and buddies. Most live here, but not all. Some stay in Bedok. They'll come because they're regulars. They just need to come and say hello, and I'll know what they want. My weirdest customer wanted "all mixed". She said she went everywhere to look for coffee but she couldn't get what her father wanted. She came here to try three types and two mixes. Finally, she came back and asked if she could mix everything. I said sure. So she did. She went back and he liked it. So she came back and we worked out the proportions and ratio.

Sentimental? Cannot be lah. I think about the past sometimes but I am like, "Eh? Last time was like that" [points his finger upwards with a jerk] ... but not those who "Ohhhhh. Last time was like that ...". [drags his tone and looks sad] No, not me. I keep these posters and my signboard because of their value. The signboard is from 1939, so it's almost 80 years. Some collectors came and told me that I should sell them my signboard. As long as my shop is still around, how can I sell it? Our brand is already 55 years old!

Happy? Okay lah. If I weren't happy, I wouldn't have continued after my father left seven years ago. Even if I run for the next 20 years, the business will continue winding down for the next 20 years. It's not really a plan. It'll run until the day I physically cannot do it anymore. That's the full stop. Life is taking one step at a time. Who knows what will happen tomorrow?

Rachel Nadia Goh Yuling

EATING

CHAPTER TWO

EATING

Hawker

Actually I'm a third-gen hawker. My grandpa was a hawker and my dad took over. It's funny, my dad always says his least favourite job is to be a hawker but somehow he ended up being one because he was helping out since young and felt it was natural to take over. For me it's also very natural, like we are doing pretty well in Kovan so I want to help expand the business because they've already spent 30 years perfecting their craft, and they've always wanted to open more stalls but it's very hard for them. Because in Kovan, they're very famous, a lot of customers buy because of them, sometimes if my mum isn't there you can really see a reduction in queue numbers. I think it's partly because of the relationships, you know, some people buy also just to chit-chat with you for a few minutes. And some people see other uncles cooking and my dad is not there they will think, "Oh, I don't think his noodles are as good as the original one." Then they end up not buying also. And it's very competitive there because there are three fishball noodles stalls and all three are doing very well. So they cannot go out even if they want to expand another shop. So since I'm done with school, I just decided to help out lor.

Actually last time I didn't really spend much time in the hawker centre leh, like I was always in school. I always wanted to go uni. Personally to me there's no conflict between going to uni and being a hawker, and I can always become a hawker after going uni. Although I must say that going to uni instead of choosing to work as a hawker directly means I might have lost out on some connections I could have made. But I have no regrets on going to uni lah. NUS (National University of Singapore) was a period of my life that I really enjoyed.

Growing up, I didn't get to spend much time with my parents because they were always working long shifts, and only in recent years they got extra help so I could see them more often. Plus I don't stay with them lah, since they work from morning to night I stayed with my grandparents and aunt. I'm definitely closer to my aunt lah, as compared to my parents. But now my dad comes over every night to help clear up and stuff, so in recent years I've grown closer to my parents. So I guess I didn't spend much time with them in my growing years but it's better now lah.

That's my aunt, [points to woman working in stall] she often comes in the afternoon after the other auntie has left. The other auntie, she actually lives a few blocks away and she came here looking for a job. So she was like surveying this area and asking around and that's how we got her lor. We are actually quite okay with people with no experience if people are just taking orders and collecting money, serving people, that's quite easy so not much need for experience. But for the cook we prefer to have someone who has experience, so at least he will know whether the noodles are cooked or not. [laughs]

So last year my friends tagged me on Facebook and said that Tiger Beer is giving out this Hawker Fund for aspiring hawkers. So I applied for it and I heard that there's quite a number of people who applied, but I was one of the 20 or 25 lucky chosen ones lah. It's like $10K but it's not a lot lah, the stove itself is already over $10K, but it definitely helped a bit. But this just made me realise that opening up a stall, right, you need to have a quite a bit of capital, I would say around $30K. All the renovation, the stainless steel, actually cost quite a bit and my parents helped to chip in. We didn't get all these second-hand unlike most other stalls. So we paid extra for new stuff lor. And then we have to pay three months of deposit as well as a security, so there's a lot of money involved. And because we have only started for about a month and a half, we haven't really been making money as well. And the location ... we didn't expect it to be so poor as well. Last time I just heard from people that, oh there's a lot of stalls available in Yishun, and that it's very good because it's in the middle of a residential area. I also heard that there's only about 43 stalls here and 700 applicants, so I thought it would be pretty good if so many people applied here. But then when I applied and got it, it was like ugh ... not that good. But the good thing is my dad drives. So he will send me here in the morning then help with the set-up of the stall, like cook all the soup, laksa gravy, or prepare all the minced meat, veggies and other ingredients.

I think the main problem I'm facing now is that there is no crowd in the hawker centre. It's definitely not the food that I'm selling, because if that was the problem you would see long queues at other stalls and not mine. But now everyone's stalls are always very empty! Very sad lah. This hawker is not the traditional kind of hawker. The new hawkers now like this one are managed by private companies. Last time they used to be managed by NEA, but nowadays a lot are managed by Kopitiam, Koufu, NTUC (National Trades Union Congress) ... for us it's Timbre. And I think that's because in this market they impose this 50 cents tray return system, so we have to collect extra 50 cents from the customers along with the cash they pay for our food. The idea is to encourage customers to start returning their trays, so basically they pay this extra 50 cents right, but when they return the tray they get 50 cents back. So a lot of elderly who are very unhappy with the system refuse to come back anymore, they go like, "Wah! So troublesome, I don't want to come here already. First and last time here." Then they really do what they say and never appear again leh. Sian (Hokkien: frustrated and weary). But for me depends lah, if customers sitting nearby and no need the tray I'll just bring the food to their tables lor.

You see they sending us trays right, actually we have to pay for the trays one, so it's sort of like a closed cycle. We collect the 50 cents from the customers, then end up since the tray return people will pay them 50 cents back, that's how they get the 50 cents back from us. I'm not making money from it, and customers don't lose money from it as well. But it's just very troublesome lah. Some people will really complain, like, "Wah, I come eat your noodles, you still ask me to self return the tray." Especially the older people. But some younger people like those parents with kids don't mind doing this because they see it as a lesson for their children. But most of our customers here are old people, right, so quite bad.

There are also hawkers who are not so nice lah. Like for this hawker centre there's a WhatsApp group chat with all the tenants mah, then you remember the tray system right? Actually we have to impose and make it compulsory one. But a lot of elderly don't want the tray especially if they're sitting nearby or if they're holding a walking stick also, then if they have difficulty walking doesn't make sense to ask them to carry the tray back also mah. So some hawkers will see one, then if the customers don't want to take then just give them the choice not to take lor. But then hor, some tenants, right, they'll actually tell the management, "Eh, I see which stall never give tray to customers." Like they'll complain to management eh. You would think that as tenants in the same hawker we will have each others' back, but no leh.

Daily, I get maybe 80 to 100 customers? That's considered not very good. My dad says this is one of the worst hawker centres. In comparison to my dad's stall, I don't know how many bowls exactly he sells daily but they really have much more customers lah. That's why I say location is very important. In Kovan right, there's the MRT station, there's a shopping mall and wet market. So it's like always crowded. And over here there's a lot of kopitiams across the street, so a lot of competition also. Still have to take a bus from Yishun MRT station. Aiyah, very sad already.

Competition is good lah, that's how it made my father's business so successful mah, because it drove him to work harder. But personally for me, I guess I'm not so driven? If I see the other fishball noodle stall doing much better I will think of ideas to improve also lah, it's natural. But as of now nobody in this hawker is doing very well. [sighs] But quite funny lah, since we got so much time we always will walk around and check out the competition one. Like sometimes when I walk back from the toilet I'll go peep at the other fishball noodle stall, see got business or not, like see how many customers they have. [laughs] But okay lah, from what I see we got more customers, I think because for theirs they only got fishball and fishcake and is a bit cheaper at $3, but ours got more variety of ingredients like mushroom, meatball, fishball, fishcake, vegetable ball, you know? Plus we have more variety since we have laksa gravy also. Okay lah, before I moved into this stall I actually heard of them coming to Yishun also, so I went to the Geylang outlet and tried theirs. Average only leh, so when I tried it already I also feel a bit more comforted.

The rent per month? If business is bad it's $2.3K minimum but if business is good they actually take about 15 per cent of your gross profit. But they cap it at $3K lah. They are quite smart actually, they track our sales from this system that we have to rent from them every month. We actually have to key in every transaction so that they can track it from the system. People can't even cheat this system lah, with the current crowd I don't think most people will earn a lot also. To be honest I would rather have to pay more rent if the location is good leh.

I guess as long as we can still make a profit we won't increase the price of the noodles. But I must say that the ingredients have been getting more and more expensive. But we won't increase unless we really are not earning profits anymore. As of now we're not really getting much profit lah, if you count in all the labour costs. Plus for our stall we have more ingredients offered, like fishball, vegetable ball, mushrooms, meatballs. Other places only have like fishball, fishcake, maybe some minced meat. All these slowly increased, like over the years we added in more stuff.

It is very tough to be hawker, I guess maybe that's why not many people choose to be a hawker. I don't think I would have considered this line if I didn't come from a family of hawkers, like for you, you also never considered this, right? If no one you know is in this line it probably won't be a consideration because it's just not the first thing in your head. There's another guy here who's doing like Korean BBQ food, and the reason why he got into this business is because his parents also own hawker stalls. His parents are pretty experienced in the line, his father owns maybe 20 stalls? And they're the supplier for seafood for several other hawkers. So, yeah, that's how he got into this. Then another guy who does Western food he studied in culinary school then worked in a restaurant for some time before coming to do this. Then the other two who got money, I'm not sure but I think they're just trying out lah, anyway since they getting most of the stuff for free. But for me it's because I know someone doing this and I think I would like the work lor.

If not for my parents, setting up would be super tough. It's really much tougher than I originally thought leh. Like, for example, first

you have to pick a stainless steel guy and tell him what goes where because you have to make everything work for you. Because they're not in the stall working, right, so you have to decide where the basin goes, or where to put the noodles so it's easy for you to work around things. Then you have to find a guy to do signage, take pictures for your food and all. And if you don't have any experience or haven't had any help, you won't know who to look for because there are so many choices in the market and you need to know who's the best. And there's also the plumbing work, like maybe must plan the wires to be arranged in a certain way also; like this tube must put strategically so that it will link to the sink…. Aiyah, I also don't know what they are talking about lah. Then lighting also must decide where to put it so that it's bright enough, use what light or don't know what, also must decide leh! So confusing sia. But lucky I had my dad to help me out for this lah. I'm glad my parents are hawkers too. I guess I've never felt embarrassed by them. But I can't say for sure that if their stall wasn't so popular I wouldn't be embarrassed by them. But now I'm always like, "Eh, my parents are hawkers, come down and try our food leh," and try to get customers.

I work every day except for Mondays. It definitely impacts my social life. Because I'm here from 6 a.m. to 10 p.m. and on weekends as well. We definitely cannot take weekends off because those are our best business days. I got friends, I got boyfriend, aiyah very sian, but got to sacrifice lah. But they're understanding. And sometimes they come over to my stall and visit. Honestly, right, hawkering is really a tough job. For example when I wake up, my friends are still asleep and when I end I'm too tired to go out because the next day I have work and I have to wake up at 5 plus again, so there's practically almost no social life lah.

When I go out to eat with my friends, I die-die also don't want to eat fishball noodles. [laughs] I eat until sian already leh. But for my dad, right, he everywhere also will go eat. I think it's because he really likes fishball noodles lah. And also because he wants to scope out the competition, you know? Okay lah, but I think depends on how each person was brought up. I was brought up eating my parents' fishball noodles, and I think that their recipe has been so refined already, like no need improvement mah, so I don't see any point in comparing with others and trying to improve the current recipe also.

I guess what determines a good fishball noodle bowl to me is the chilli and the lard. The ingredients definitely have to be fresh also. Like the chilli has to be fragrant, and this differs in every stall because every stall has different recipes. Like for our chilli we have big onions, small onions, lemongrass, garlic, normal chilli paste, chilli … a lot of ingredients lah, then must do all the portioning and all. My aunt will help us peel the onions and garlic before coming for her afternoon shift. Then just chop with the machine and fry it lor. Then once we mix it together we bring it to Kovan and fry it again since raw chilli doesn't taste as good. Then my dad will bring the chilli here to Yishun in the morning for me lor. I mean ultimately, right, to me fishball noodles taste the same, it just depends on the freshness of the ingredients, and the types of ingredients they use. Some stalls also put more chilli mah, then it gives the bowl a whole new different taste also. Some places also like to put a lot of vinegar in the noodles, and personally I think too much vinegar just spoils the taste lah.

Alright are you finished with the interview? [joking tone] Five plus already, I need to start finding customers. How to find ah? Just make eye contact with those that walk past and smile, smile, normally can attract someone. Thanks for coming to entertain me ah. Really nice to meet you eh, come again next time okay!

Ong Lin Yee

Restaurateur

I'm pretty sure I'm a supertaster. The sensation of eating is very, very intense for me. So I'm always trying to recreate these experiences for other people. My parents gave me the benefit of education through travel. We travelled a lot, ate all around the world. So even as a kid I was exposed to lots of different food, all over Asia, the Americas, Europe. Even today, when we go to a restaurant I will order the most obscure item on the menu just so I can taste it. I feel like I keep a record in my head of all the flavours I've ever experienced. My motivation to cook for other people I think comes from my sensory relationship with food.

I would classify myself as a business owner and an F&B consultant. I own two F&B businesses. I also spent the last 24 months as a full-time consultant working on emerging markets mostly in Asia. I've been to various cities around Asia helping to tighten up processes in hotels and restaurants, redesigning kitchens, reconceptualising menus, doing a lot of branding work for food identity.

I come from a middle-class Chinese Protestant family. My parents are both professionals, an engineer and a lawyer. By the time I was 17 or 18, it was already clear that their ideas of what was a proper career and how to measure success were very different from mine. So even broaching the topic with them was difficult. Food and the service industry in general is seen as "can't make it anywhere else then you go into F&B". But I enjoy working with people, interacting. And I chose food, simply because food is the best way to connect with people.

I started cooking in NS (National Service), just as a way to feed people who came over. At that point I had already met two friends in the army who were also interested in food. We were doing BBQs for army guys. At that point, aiyah army, you don't have much money.

So we figured it was cheaper to just buy the meat wholesale and cook for them. It evolved from that into our university days when we started to have third-party orders – friends of friends. Just cook and then leave. Make $300 a day. Then other people started to contact us and said: "Hey! I heard that you do this, can you come and cook for us?" Then because now we didn't know our clients directly, we actually had to get our shit together: reply proper emails and stuff. Can't fuck up, right? So we were doing this private dining thing the entire time we were in university. Chefs for hire.

Of course we started out with family connections, which is why I will never say that I am displeased with my lot in life or where I started. As much as my parents felt like F&B was a strange thing, they also said ok lah, eh, this friend wants to ask if you do private dinners. So eventually we were getting twice monthly dinners of maybe $180 to $200 a head, 20, 30 people. And these are at people's houses where they host. If you can host 30 people at that price, you're wealthy. And they would be very generous, they'd give us angbaos (red packets) and stuff. Cos we were very young guys, we charm the aunties and all, right? We were making more than what most fresh grads earn. But of course, with money comes trouble lah, we had different ideas about the business so eventually we decided to part ways.

My first job right out of school was in a cooking events company that also ran an amateur cooking school. I wasn't hired because I was a very skilled cook, but because I could talk and I had a degree. I found later on in the food industry that this was a huge advantage, because in the industry there are so many fuckers out there who can cook very well, but very few who could explain what they were doing in a clear and cogent manner. If this audience needed to be very highbrow, I could do that. If this audience needed it to be very dumbed down – really, like pidgin English – I could do that too. And I had a lot of fun doing it. It's a bit of an act lah, like theatre.

That was the second thing that drew me in – the performance of the kitchen. It's all about the performance.

I'd say I only really learnt how to cook when I graduated and was working in the events company. That's when I was forced to know what I was doing because I had to teach people how to do it. Before that? Bullshit! Junk! I was getting by memorising two or three recipes and doing those very well. I would use those recipes for all those dinners I made. It was amazing because people would pay me for that. Of course a lot of that was also upsell lah. We wouldn't just make the food, we'd go out and talk about it. So we don't just serve the food, I'd also tell them how I got the idea. I'd say something like: "Oh I heard that you like this ingredient, so we incorporated it into this and that …". So when I go back into the kitchen all my guys were like, "Oh my god, you are such a slut."

These are very upper-class people. Many of them have a massive kitchen that has never been used. There was this one time we went to a home to check out the kitchen before the event, and this tai tai (Singlish: a wealthy woman who does not work) came tottering down. I asked to check the kitchen to make sure everything works, and she goes "Um, Wati, help me turn on the oven! Can you help me turn this on, turn that on …". Wah, you mean you don't even know how to turn on the oven? Ok, never mind. We turn on the oven just so I can check it. Then we go do something else. When we come back into the kitchen, there was this horrible smell of burning plastic. The manual, which is still sealed in plastic in the oven, has completely melted and fucked up the tray.

Generally speaking, I have two types of days. Operational days, and non-operational days. An operational day starts relatively early. By 9 a.m. I'm going to places like Pasir Panjang, speaking to my wholesalers to make sure that my orders for the day are coming in fine. Going to bakeries to check on the bread for the day. I don't go into the office straight away, but I will be fielding phone calls from the beginning. Requests for interviews, events, off-site events, recipe development, and occasionally now I get enquiries about takeover: people who want to buy up my restaurant. So just being on the phone takes up an hour and a half already. By the time I'm in the restaurant it's usually about lunch time. I'm in, I don't talk to anyone first, I just step in, put on the apron and start helping out with the grill, cutting stuff. Sometimes I'm a hindrance because they've already started doing stuff.

By lunch time, there will be at least 20, 30 people in the queue. As much as I feel dirty saying this, I'll have to go out to chat with people and a lot of that is just showmanship. The team will sometimes look at me and wonder: what is the owner doing? The managers understand that I have to keep doing these things, so that we create some kind of brotherly thing, and this feels like their neighbourhood sandwich joint, right? But the young staff don't see that. They only see us having a beer or a cigarette. But doing this is when I get to ask: "Hey, how's your office doing, you guys need office orders? Oh! You have an event next week? Let us give you a discount rate" or whatever. So this carries on from lunch until 2 or 3 p.m., at which point I'll be like, "Okay, I need to step out for a moment now." It could be to develop a seasonal menu, it could be working on the design for a new poster, figuring out where to get a contractor to build a frontage for an event, or going to look for a piece of equipment that we need. By 6 or 7 p.m. my day is usually over. But that's when I try and find a new place to eat or meet people for dinner and just talk about stuff lah. So that's my day as a business owner. Very soon that's going to change because I'm going to be back in the kitchen for a new restaurant.

When I have to work in the kitchen, the day starts about the same, I wake up at 9 a.m., by the time I head to the restaurant it's about 11.

I'll be there to see the first group of customers come in for lunch. And then our supplies usually come in just after noon lah, about 1. That's when I will check it, accept or reject things, and start thinking about what to order next. Fresh produce has a five- to seven-day lead time, so I need to plan in advance. Because the order takes two days to get to Europe, three days to confirm, and then three days to ship it over. The ordering process takes about an hour, because you always have a back and forth between the suppliers and the kitchen about what they have and what we can make. It's never straightforward, because the menu is always different. I try to have a weekly specials board that changes every few days. That helps with regular customers lah.

Okay, then the fun stuff starts to happen. After I make the orders, I have a pocket of time at about 4 p.m. This is when I do prep by myself. How it usually works is I will R&D a dish on my own, then we get the team to try it. I am more interested in the taste of the dish, but when I hand it over to the head chef they can then figure out the best way to make it. So it's a very creative process. At 5, we start to see a bit more activity. The front of house team, which has been closed from 2 to 5 p.m. is out polishing glasses, setting up the tables. The music comes on. We put on some heavy prep music: usually some very energetic music, something everyone knows and can sing to. You need everyone in a good mood putting the finishing touches and stuff. When the kitchen crew comes in at 5, we take everything out of the fridges, all the ingredients that they need for their dishes for each station. Your oils and seasonings, your cloths and towels and board etc. Make sure you have every damn thing. When it gets busy and you're picking up information from everyone, from the front of house staff and the customers and chef calling you, you can't stop and look for something. Everything has to be ready. It should be like muscle memory.

My favourite ritual is actually wiping the specials board clean at

5 p.m. and writing the stuff for the day on the specials board. I like making that commitment to my clients. Closer to 6, the kitchen is ready to go. The ovens and grills are back on, the heat is coming out from the kitchen. At 6 we do an opening brief. Everyone gathers, front of house, bars, kitchen. Usually I lead the meeting lah, it will be a simple how many guests are coming today, any notable guests, anyone that we pissed off before, we need to track that because we failed them the last time and we cannot fuck up again. Any links to owners, friends and family, any links to staff. Those are VIPs that we take special care of.

When we have staff's family come over for special occasions we will break out all the stuff for them. I will make you eat until you die then you can go home very happy. If you can make them proud of the space where their sons and daughters are working then you have a very motivated worker, right? The next day you can see that your staff come in and there's a spring in their step and they are motivated to do well. There is no better validation than having your friends and family come and say, "Hey, I had a wonderful time, thank you so much." I think that's very important. I have a team of 12 Singaporeans, not a single foreigner. My team has put their trust in me and I really need to make sure I don't let them down.

So from 6 to 7 p.m. you have early diners, families, your regulars. Seven-thirty you have your general rush crowd. Eight o'clock you're in the thick of it: the kitchen is a full crush. The timing is crucial, if not you get something ready before it's time to serve it, or things get overcooked or cold because they're just sitting there. You need to know exactly how long things take to cook and what's going on. At 9 things start to slow down and it is at this moment when the juicy stuff starts to happen.

A lot of the people who come here are regulars. I've seen you with your boss, the same boss you are bitching about today. I've seen you here with your wife, and now you're here with another woman, and your hands are all over her. And I have to pretend that I've not seen you before. The staff give me a look, and we all know we have to give a generic greeting: "Hi guys, how are you?" Not, "Hi Mike and Cheryl, how are you?" Because that's not Cheryl!

As soon as they have a bit of alcohol and the music is pumping, this is when the conversations really start. There are counter seats, which are so close to us, and there are also booths. People inside feel like they are in their own little bubble, their private cocoon. We've also seen people fighting. We have ... what we called break-up seats. Just jinxed seats lah. Back in my last restaurant, seats 7 and 8 have seen three couples breaking up. Wah, very fucked up. There was this one guy, a New Yorker who works here. The girlfriend, some kind of atas (Malay: upper class) Singaporean who spoke with a slight American accent. When she came in, everyone was looking at her, because okay lah, she's good looking. So all of us were paying attention to her, and we could also see her body language. She looked a bit upset, so we tried to chat with them a bit, make sure it's not our problem. And then she was like giving him all these one-word answers while he was chatting enthusiastically away, so we know something wasn't right there. Then in the middle of dinner, I bring over their main courses. And just as I'm about to present it to them, the girl goes: "I'm so sorry. I really can't do this anymore. I need to go, I've met someone." And she just gets up, gets her bag, and exits. I'm like literally here, holding the food, and it's so awkward. I put the food down, the guy gives me a look, and I call my manager over to get him a double shot of a very expensive whisky. He finished all the food by himself slowly, leaves a massive tip, then goes, "Thanks, guys." Very classy. He never came back.

We've also had a lot of young men come in with their girlfriends trying to impress them. And trying to order things that they cannot

pronounce. Then they will just point and at the menu and say, "Uh
… I want this one." Then they order lamb chops or something, and
when the food comes they complain that the lamb chop tastes too
lamby. They're just trying to impress the girl lah, all guys go through
that but it's still very funny to see. We also see all sorts of creepy
stuff lah. Seventy-, 80-year-old guys come in with 20-plus-year-old
girls. And these girls are good looking and well spoken, and they are
obviously on some sort of transactional date.

But the people that piss me off are the experiences where we
are not treated like human beings lah. We don't expect you to greet
us constantly or be very effusive, but at least respond when we are
saying something lah, make some kind of eye contact. They know
that there are no consequences, right? Besides us spitting in your food
or something. Which, by the way, doesn't happen. It really doesn't.
We might overcook some meat if you insist on it being overcooked.
If you complain after we give you a well done we might cook the
damn thing until it's like a hockey puck, but we won't create an
unhygienic experience lah. Sometimes people demand things without
even addressing us, and I like to treat this as some sort of a game. I'll
ignore them until they realise they're being rude and ask, "Excuse
me…." Then I'll go, "Oh! Sorry! Were you speaking to me?" But if
you are disrespectful to my staff, I will ask you to leave.

There are few things I appreciate in life more than the first cigarette
at the end of a busy service. Last order is usually about 10 p.m. to
10:30, you're out of the restaurant by about 11:30 after cleaning up.
This is when I'm most awake. I mean nobody goes home right after
work and just goes to sleep right? Need time to decompress. I love
the night. It's quiet and cool, nobody is calling me or texting me. We
clean down from 10:30 to about 11:15. That's when I sit down with
my notebook and record every single thing that was ordered. I will
also plan for the next day, and before we leave we make sure all the

fridges are on, because there's nothing worse than having a fridge that is accidentally switched off because then the next day you come in there's like $20,000 worth of food that's gone bad.

I usually wait for the last person in the front of house to be done because they have to mop the floors, clean the toilets, set the tables and wipe the wine glasses, right? I try and be the last one out because I drive and I can drop people off, but I also feel like, as a leader, if I always leave early, it doesn't motivate the staff to work hard. I come home about midnight or 1 a.m., for the next two or three hours I'm reading blogs, or on Instagram looking at food, or watching videos of food, I'm still in a food mode, still full of adrenaline. I'm still thinking about food, what was good, what needs to be improved, there is no way I can go to bed straight away. I do a good amount of work from 1 to 4 a.m.

So when do I eat my dinner? I don't. Initially I did a really unhealthy thing – I'd eat supper after work. And then I realised I would wake up really bloated and uncomfortable. So I figured out a better way was to snack and eat small things along the way, so I'm constantly at a 70 per cent full. The one meal I will try and have is family meal for lunch. At my restaurant, every day someone will make lunch for everyone. The budget is relatively high, and it's meant to be the time when no one bugs you, no suppliers come, no calls are made, the restaurant is closed just so that the team can sit down and enjoy some moments over food. This is really important because you are insisting on them giving others a good dining experience. They need to experience that themselves and have a love for good food. If they understand how to enjoy good food and ambience and conversation over food, then they will strive to replicate that kind of experience for the customers. I can think of no better training. So everyone comes for family meal. I don't care if you are a cleaner, a bartender, a new part-timer at front of house. The kitchen will cook for you, and you will have 20 minutes of unbroken time where we just talk nonsense and eat. So I don't see my family, and I don't have dinner, but everyone makes up for that by having a staff meal together. Because that's your family.

There are three main cost pillars in F&B. You have rent, you have labour and you have food cost. These three things represent 90 per cent of the costs of an F&B establishment. Singapore is one of the few countries in the world where all three are expensive. All this means a very competitive environment for the F&B industry. Seven out of ten restaurants in Singapore will close within three years, and out of those three that survive, less than 5 per cent make it into the double-digit profit margins, by that I mean just like 15 per cent profit. Most hover between 7 and 9 per cent. It's pathetic.

If you look at Tharman's (then Deputy Prime Minister Tharman Shanmugaratnam) industry route map for 2016, one of the things he wanted to implement was automation. This means making grants available to SMEs to automate processes and make them more efficient. F&B employs something like 13 per cent of the labour pool but contributes like 4 per cent of revenue. So Spring Singapore (the Standards, Productivity and Innovation Board, now part of Enterprise Singapore) and other programmes are supposed to help F&B consolidate and scale up by centralising food processing and production. For example, instead of five restaurants each making their own sauce, they want to have one central facility making sauce. But what do you get? You get lower cost, but you get homogeneity. Compromising. Lower quality. But the market needs it, I suppose.

Monthly rent in the CBD ranges between $9 to $20 per square foot. The average place is between 600 to 1,500 square foot. Larger restaurants will be in the excess of 2,000 square feet, so that makes it … $30 to 40 grand a month just for rent. You need to be earning more than $200,000 a month in order to make rent a 20 per cent component of your total cost. Your labour component is about 30, 35 per cent, so that should be about $50,000 to $60,000. Your cost of goods sold should hover between 25 to 35 per cent of your revenue. That's another 60 grand. How much are you left with to pay for utilities and admin costs and disposables? Best case scenario, $20,000. But then you have to buy insurance, you need to pay the workers their CPF and bonuses, NS incentives, leave, hire part-timers. Eventually you're left with nothing lah.

Opening a restaurant isn't a way to make money. It really isn't. There are some outliers that manage to do that. Tze char restaurants. QSR (quick service retail) fast food joints make money. Hawkers also can make money if their rental structure was from an earlier time. Michelin star restaurants don't really make money. They make their money through events, recipe books, special appearances. Or I guess if you go into manufacturing and services where you stock supermarkets and stuff. That's very lucrative. But you need massive amounts of capital to get into it and a central facility and a factory, that kind of thing lah. Not what your regular F&B guy is able to do. So yeah, I don't want to say it's a very bleak picture, but it is ... I don't know why we do it. I guess for some people they wouldn't be happy doing anything else.

It's actually quite manageable to keep a relationship going in the midst of all this, even though it's tough to think about settling down. I'm not going to think about having kids for the foreseeable future, even though I really, really like kids. But I know my passion for the industry will clash with my desire to be a good dad. I have a very understanding girlfriend, so it's okay. But it's challenging lah. The hours are crazy. Not crazy long, just ungodly. And I'm constantly working on ideas and stuff. Sometimes we go on a date, and we just want to chill and talk and stuff. But I'll be eating something and suddenly find myself thinking: there is something wrong with this soup … what is it? And then I launch into analysis mode. And she'll be like, "Do you have to? Can't you just chill?"

But I wouldn't trade it for anything else in the world. I'd do it all over again. If there's one downside, I would say it's the lack of a chance to save money and get a place and stuff…. [sighs] When you start your own business, you don't see any of the money for many, many years. I threw all my savings in. Thankfully my parents don't mind me staying at home. I see my friends, they've moved out, started families, they have two properties of their own. And that gets me thinking, what if I had applied myself to a different industry? Maybe I'd also do well … but I think about that, and I go, "No, no, no!" Then I wouldn't be elbow deep in butter, making stuff, sharing my passion with other people. When I think about it like that, then I think okay, I'll still be a food guy.

Ng Shi Wen

Ice Cream Uncle

Yes, what you want? Want to ask questions ah? I was about to go to the toilet leh. I already stand so long, still haven't go. Later okay? My stall no need to watch one!

So, girl, you want to ask me questions? Come, you ask. Ah, I have been doing this for eight years already, since I was in my 50s. I lost my job at the factory and had to look for a new one. I was hired to do quality control and quality assurance at Yong Tai – you know Yong Tai? They make clothes. It used to be at Hougang. Before that, I was a mechanic. But they hired me because they said, "You are trained as a mechanic, you will know how to do QC. It is similar."

I was a mechanic for over 10 years. Slowly, I got into higher positions, and became a technician. I was working for a toy manufacturing company. [suddenly gets excited] The toys we made

were very interesting! For example, there was one that could climb up the wall. The company was from America, and they opened a factory here. But when the company went bankrupt, the factory closed and we had to leave. There were about a thousand people working in the factory, I think. There were five floors in the factory and two working shifts – morning and night shifts. My job over there was to check the toys ... whether the toys worked. Not everybody could do, you know. You need to open up the toy and look to see what wasn't working properly. Sometimes we had to fix the screws, and test to see if the toy worked.

So, selling ice cream? When I was 55, I took out half of my CPF. I worked at different places for about three years. One day, I saw an advertisement for selling ice cream in the newspaper. You only need to apply for a government licence. The licence was given by NEA. I went for the interview, but I didn't get a letter from them until one year later. I thought they didn't want me already! For that one year, I didn't work, because it was difficult to find a job. Because I am old. Got lah, if I want. Wash dishes and clear plates. But I think I'm not suitable for it. I thought selling ice cream would be quite simple and easy.

When I went for the interview, they asked me whether I wanted to use a bicycle or a motor (motorcycle), but I really didn't think much about it beforehand. I thought that using a bicycle would be too tiring, and my legs were already not that strong. But using a motor means must have a licence, and need money to buy the motor. At that time, I spent $3,500 on the motor. I didn't have a licence, so I went to get one too. You know, the three-wheel one (motorbike with attached cart) more dangerous. Easier to flip over, especially when the cart is empty. The whole thing will go off the ground you know, when I do turning on the road! When I told my friend that I was going to ride the three-wheel one, he said, "Har? Must be careful!"

One time, when I was riding along Orchard Road, my motor flew onto the pavement! Yah, really. I was trying to avoid a car. After that time, I got scared and now I ride more carefully.

No one will teach you how to cut and sell the ice cream. Have to ask other people how to do. Okay lah, they got someone to teach me how to do it. A young person. After watching and trying, I learnt how to do it. At first, I chopped very slowly, but later you will get faster. Sometimes, I would also cut my hand accidentally.

Fridays and Saturdays are the busiest. But that's not always the case. Sometimes got people, sometimes no one. Five or 6 in the evening is when most people come. Because there is a cinema here, many people come in the evening. I usually work from 2 p.m., sometimes start at 12 p.m., to 11 p.m. because of the night movie screenings. Depends on what time I pick up the ice cream from the supplier – if pick up earlier, then start earlier.

Actually, selling ice cream is not good money. I thought it was easy at first. But actually, it is very complicated and there are many things to do. Last time, I sold the ice cream at $1, can earn half back. Now, sell at $1.20, can only earn about 30 to 40 cents. Cannot sell too expensive, because too many people selling on Orchard Road. Nowadays, some people sell at $1.50 or even $2. But if I increase to $1.50, then I will have no business. Sell cheap, got more customers. Most of the people along Orchard Road sell at $1.20. Only outside schools they sell at $1. See this person? Regular customer, so I give $1. How much I earn in a day? Depends lah! Sometimes, as high as $90. Other days, only $40 to $50. Sometimes I don't earn anything, or even suffer a loss. You guess when there will be no business? Yah, when it's raining! No one will buy ice cream. Also, when I cannot sell the ice cream, must buy more dry ice. Two dollars fifty for 1 kg. Need 10 kg a day, so that's another $25! Of course I try to sell as much as possible, but confirm have leftover. That's why I sing the song "I ask

Heaven" – I ask why Heaven makes fun of me!

I don't work every day lah. Mostly Friday and Saturday. The other days, I rest at home, or go down and walk-walk, or hang out with friends. My wife is still working, but my son is not working. He couldn't find a job – now very hard to find a job. Some of my customers tell me even those university graduates can't find a job. I ask you, if you can't find a job, will you go and sell ice cream? Some university graduates don't want to, they would rather walk up and down the streets than do that kind of work.

Here got many students come and buy ice cream. Got university here. But also got other kinds of customers. Local and tourists. So I need to know basic English and Malay. These days, if you only know Mandarin, then very hard. Some Chinese people, they don't speak Mandarin anymore, they speak English instead. They think they are better than other people! Even though they can speak Mandarin, they don't want. Singapore has changed a lot.

What is there to like about this job? Hand tired, leg tired. Here, here, here also pain! [points to back, calf and knee] This job is tiring, not only because must stand the whole day, but because after selling, you still need to ride home. The problem is when you have customers who cannot decide. Say want, then don't want, or don't want, then want. Some customers are also very stingy, they don't want to part with their money – so arrogant! Sometimes, I will also meet weird customers. Some of them are drunk, then they come and talk nonsense to you … just ignore lah! They never really do anything.

But no choice, don't like, also need to work. No job, no money. Who is going to take care of me? Nowadays, even children don't take care of their parents. You got see on the news? Actually, I will stop selling ice cream at the end of next year, November 2018. That is when the motorbike's COE (Certificate of Entitlement) end. I will look for other jobs, maybe a less tiring job. In Singapore, it's work until you die! I don't earn much now. Enough for three meals, and for clothes to wear. But not much left over. Skills upgrade? That one cheat people one! My son's friend went, then in the end still need to pay! Thousand over dollars. Anyway, my CPF money will finish this December. Only Medisave left. So you say, need to work or not? Need! Unless you are a rich person. People say: you cannot fall sick, if not, go jump off a building and die! Because medical bills are so high here!

You got any more questions? My favourite ice cream flavour? Haha ... chocolate and yam lah. Last time I used to eat red bean also. Not anymore ... because people say, leg pain cannot eat beans. So I stopped eating lah.

I got nothing much to look forward to lah. Just waiting to die! Nothing much that I'm interested in. People are also changing. It's so different from kampung days. Nowadays, everyone stays in their own box, they don't know their neighbours. If they open the door, it's to talk about money. They say no money, no talk. It's a harsh world. I just take one day at a time.

Nathene Chua

Farmer

This is lettuce, this is mustard, that's Okinawa spinach, this is purple basil – touch it and smell it – this long one is called luffa. I grew them all from seeds. Thank god for this, I don't know what I did right, the first two batches were torture, they didn't turn out too nicely. But now the narcissus has begun to bloom. I've never planted mustard that grew so big, and even though I'm already good at growing lettuce, it's never grown so big either.

This whole place is set up by my husband, John, this hard work. I only do the easy things lah: weeding, planting, watering and harvesting. We have a nice time here, he plays his part and I play mine, then we cook all these veggies and share them with other farmers. Every Saturday is chaos because everybody gathers to eat here, there is about minimum 8, at most 20. They are all farmers like us, so we gather here like a community, sort of like bonding, sharing ideas, learning from one another. We are all not professional farmers, so we will ask questions like, "Eh, why is your veggie so nice, what did you put, did you cheat or not?" [laughs] We share a very good friendship, but of course we quarrel amongst ourselves. You know old people can be quite eccentric so we quarrel over petty things. But next week we eat together again, we poke fun at one another. If I don't have certain things, I just go over to their plot and they tell me, "Just cut." There's a kind of community happiness here.

There is also this very weird thing going on – we don't look down on one another. There are lots of rich people who live in landed property and drive expensive cars here but we will treat everybody the same. Go to hell lah, you and your big car, you know? We don't care! We don't care! If you think you are rich, okay, keep to yourself, don't join us. There were one or two who didn't want to join us, we left them alone. If you want, you come over and eat this poor man's meal, if you don't want, then done! Eventually they will come join us, they feel lonely too. We don't show off things like brands, all our things are like that – dirty.

These are reasons why some people give up their five-figure jobs to do farming. It's the peace. The happiness within that money cannot buy. You can be a CEO but fuck you. Big deal! We joke amongst ourselves, you can be rich but if we don't plant veggie you will die. But young people like you can never come to this level. You have to fight for your future. You have to acquire your wealth first, right? When you get your wealth and are not worried about your dollar and cents, only can you begin to revert – come down to nature, the peace.

The farmers here are mostly retirees. We have a little bit of extra cash that we can afford to waste in things like these. In a lot of people's eyes, we are crazy, we waste our money. Practically every farmer here loses money every month. You count lah: the adoption fee is running at $400 per month, as years go by, the fee escalates. Besides adoption fee, if I have electricity, I have to pay for electricity, which is one and a half times more than the rate in HDB flats or households, then you also have to buy fertiliser, seeds or seedlings. But your production leh? How much can you sell, how much can you produce? Only that fixed amount. Not to mention your time, your transport, your food. So it's a total loss here.

But I recalculated. [slams table] Instead of going to the gym, to massages, and detox sessions which cost $3,888, I think it's still cheaper here. This is my heaven, my paradise. Not only mine, but also my husband's. This is our paradise. The gain is freedom, the kind of exercise we have here, the sweat we purge out cleanses our bodies because you have to do the work without knowing it. Here you are really, we call it, "sweating like a horse", because inside the greenhouse it's like 40 to 42° Celsius. Everything gets soaked, your bra, your underwear, everything gets drenched in sweat, but we don't care. The sweat is literally like rain. Your toxins are purged out, and you're drinking a lot of water. When we plant our own veggie, we don't use chemicals, it's pesticide free, even the fertilisers, we use organic fertiliser. It tastes better, crunchier, safer. And then the air here, it's also fresher. Except my tobacco. [lights cigarette] Not all the farmers smoke, but we don't care lah.

I've been doing this for four years. Before this, when I was in my 20s, I worked very hard in the shipyard. It was hard work. After that, my health went down. I stopped work to go around travelling. Then I went to join a production firm, filming advertisements for some years, came out, started my own small production company, made some money. Looked after parents, looked after children. Eventually, children all grown up, parents gone. Then I found the vacuum, the loneliness. Die. So every day stone lah, nag lah. My mother's death was a big blow to me. I forgot where I wanted to go and would sit at the bus stop crying. For a period of time I went to work with John every day, I would sit in the car playing games while waiting for him to be done with his work. Then John brought me here one day. When I came here and saw what they were doing, I requested to have a bit of land to plant. Then that's how we started doing this. It was hard work in the first year. At that time I had pains all over. I had to hold one small shovel with two hands, and less than one foot into the ground, my shoulders and arms would began to hurt so much that afterwards John had to help me wash my hair. So slowly, I began to sweat it out. Now I can easily lift up 10 kg. This place gave me my health.

This piece of land was allocated for vegetable farming. All land in Singapore is owned by Singapore Land Authority. We bid for this land and got this land for 10 years. AVA (Agri-Food and Veterinary Authority) is our guardian. In land-scarce Singapore, 1 square foot of land also must be productive, 1 square foot must produce a certain amount of vegetables – they are going by the technical way. Three years ago, one lot had to produce 80 to 100 kg. This year it has doubled. So I tell AVA, "Can, no problem, I pluck the veggie, the root, the soil, I weigh them together, there will be 200 kg." They only want figures so I'll give them figures. I tell the other farmers to do the same. It is nonsense! Four years ago, 1 square foot of land has to produce 1 kg, but now you want me to produce 2 kg. Eh, the land is still the same, if I can plant 20 chye sim, it doesn't mean I can plant 30 the next year! It's not like stock market leh. The fella doesn't just grow like that. AVA wants everything to be productive. It's the black and white that comes from the top, the planners of Singapore. People who study and come up with a theory and then force it down upon us; in theory it might work lah, but physically it may not.

So when the AVA staff come and see our fan, our cooler, and me resting here, they ask me why are you not farming. To them, this shed is a waste of area, growing flowers is a waste of area, and they want it to be removed. In the past I used to get very frustrated, I used to quarrel like a bitch with them, swear and curse at them. But recently, I was thinking, aren't they also human beings who are making a living, aren't they also being pressurised by the boss, what if it was my son who's in that position, will I swear? So it came down to this hide-and-seek game. They come by the front door, I'd leave by the back. Or if not, I talk stupid to them. "Cannot plant flower lah auntie," they say. I tell them, "Okay, okay, sorry ah, sorry! I know, but auntie very old, I work very slowly." Then when they come three months later, I've shifted the flowers to the other side. They can see that there are some slight changes, they take photograph to show their boss as proof that they are doing their work. I hate them lah, but I pity them too. But what to do? We elect these people up there so who is to blame?

The other way is to choose to leave Singapore, but where would you go? I have been to many places but I still think Singapore is the best – safe, good education, good medical facilities. You live in a pigeonhole but at least you don't have to clean up so much. There's a little hiccup here and there, but being at this age, you're slowly getting half deaf and half blind, so it doesn't matter so much anymore. All these small naggings, it's peanuts. Sometimes we need them, if not life becomes very monotonous, there's no excitement. So I'm very thankful to whoever is up there, that we both have this little piece of playground to play in. This land contract ends at 2020, if I cannot find another place, I told John, "Okay, let's do it at home, the HDB corridor!" If not, I'll convert one of our bedrooms into an LED farm, grow some microgreens.

I call myself a tai tai farmer, because tai tais get to do things their way, tai tai will not succumb to working hours, I do it my way, my time – own time, own target. I have that freedom of not being controlled. I plant what I want to eat. If you are a real farmer, you'd have to wake up at 4 o'clock in the morning, work all day at the farm, day in day out, lunch time they sleep from 12 to 2 p.m. They can't work because it's very hot, and then they work till quite late. They are worried about production, they are chasing for time. I don't. The veggie decides to grow slower? Okay, I wait lah. The pests come and attack me? Okay lor, if I have to kill you, I'll kill you, but if you share your food with me, I won't kill you.

Nobody controls me; I do it by my own feel, my own timing. The end of last year, somebody offered me a job at Geylang East to look after their garden. So half a day, in the morning, I go there and play, there's no one there to control me. They just ask me to look after the garden nicely, no AVA coming, so there's no need to plant veggie, I plant a whole lot of flowers, fruit trees, plant some veggie, plant some herbs, some spices. I'm very happy there, boh zeng hu (Hokkien: no government). I'm there for half a day, and then I'll go on the train, enjoy the air con, sleep, talk all the way back here at 4 p.m. If it's hot, I rest for a while. If I want to sleep for two hours, I sleep for two hours, if I want to sleep for half an hour, I sleep for half an hour, then I will get up to meddle with something around the farm. So this is a privilege. That's why it's called tai tai farming. At 6 p.m., John will come here from his job and we'll smoke, admire something. 6:30 or 7, I'll tell him, "Eh, very hot lah, let's go home."

We eat the veggies we produce, sometimes we exchange with other farmers here, I bring it to my friends, majority of it, I send it to the old folks home where I work. Sometimes someone walks in and wants to buy our veggies. Everything is going at $10 per kg because

I do not know how to do calculations – so they can just take and put it on the scale; if it's 1.1 kg, 1.2 kg, aiyah, never mind lah, I'll just charge them $10. Sometimes they also want to buy some pandan leaves. I would just cut from the thick bush and give it to them for free. We give a lot of freebies.

I give to all this people I don't know. Then out of the blue, on Saturday, you have all these people coming with their food, a packet of kueh, chilli that they pound, but between John and I, we can't finish them all, so we'd gather everyone here. Then also, I'll end up with a whole big box of seeds, people who go overseas bring these seeds back for me, until today I've got this whole big box of seeds in my house. I take it because I know it's their appreciation. Mine is never a business model, never. If I'm doing it as a business, this will never happen because you'll always be thinking about cost, revenue. Then you can never give vegetables for free, you must be crazy to do that. So I learned sharing – if you share and give, it comes back tenfold. To me, this is the best thing that happens in farming. This is the joy.

Tan Sing Yee

MAKING AND REPAIRING

CHAPTER THREE

MAKING AND REPAIRING

Carpenter

My name Ismail. I from Bangladesh, Khulna. Singapore coming 2008. I carpenter: kitchen, room, wardrobe, all making. In Bangladesh, I do private job, selling phone. Manager monthly give 200 to 300 pieces, then I selling. But money little bit, little bit. I do three, four years, then my friend tell me Singapore very good, lot of money, so I come here. I selling house, paying agent 3 lakh (approximately $5,300). Wah, die already. I taking bus, six hour to Dhaka then sit in airplane, come Singapore. Here, I working six day. I stay Sungei Kadut now. One room, 20 people, 10 bed, stay upstairs-downstairs (bunk beds). Six o'clock must waking up because only four toilet, so taking turns for toilet. Eight o'clock lorry coming to take us and we coming here at 9 o'clock. Twelve o'clock lunch and then 4 o'clock coffee break. Lunch and coffee break, sometimes sleeping, sometimes talking, sometimes watching Bangla or Hindi movies. Then again, hard work. Seven o'clock lorry coming, I going, but sometimes, not here, factory working until 9, 10 o'clock. No rest. Go back, sometimes talking family, watching movie, sleep always not enough. Then wake up and coming back to work.

When I come Singapore, brother teach how to making, everything I learn. Now also, boss tell what to make, then I making. Singapore three company already. First time company, one year, second time company four year, this company coming three years. This one company very good, salary give every month, $1,000 plus. I send back $700; $300 I using here. One hundred and twenty dollars pay catering, rest I use enjoy: buy phone card, watch movie, eat outside on Sunday. Singapore food, outside very nice, especially chicken rice. But catering food no good. Inside cockroach. Chicken also like rubber. One day (once a month) they giving biryani, cow-making (beef), that one? Like. This side only two day coming, before Marina Bay. Here job have, working. No have, then working factory. I working, anything problem, telling foreman, this man talking, this man settle. But this company no problem. Last time, first time, company problem, two months, they no giving salary. No foreman also. Our brothers all telling no working because no salary, I scared but all brothers not working, so we all sitting down outside that time, then we get our salary. After that I company change, working four years, then company close.

Bangladesh family having. Sister have, brother have, father, mother have, wife have, baby have. Only one. We all talking every day. Marry only one year. I go Bangladesh, six months, see, see, see, choosing girl, baby-making and then coming back. Last time have girlfriend here, but she don't want me. I telling you, girlfriend have, money loss already. I see already. Makan (Malay: to eat), bus, taxi, phone card, and little bit give, money loss already. All women here only wanting money to buy thing. Bangladesh women, taking money, cooking, taking care of father, mother, baby. That time, when have girlfriend, I family no give much money. No good. Now I want giving them more money. I one man, everything settle, father, mother, sister, brother, wife, baby. I want my sister, brother and baby study, get good job in Bangladesh, so I must working every day for them only. Bangladesh student good, job have, no good student, no job have. I no have money study, so no good job.

You first Singaporean I talk to. Here not lonely, all brothers. But sometimes feel like only know the building Singapore, not people. I see here all people very busy, lot of money, and maybe don't like us. We dirty, smelly, but what to do, you tell me? My job like that. But we can friends. You, me, we doing different things, outside different but inside same. Same problem also: all need money. This permit finish, one month leave, no change company, I go Bangladesh sleep, then again coming. Always coming back, again and again. Hard work but money, very good. I telling you money have, everything have; money no have, everything no have. Bangladesh, Singapore everywhere same. I need money, this my job, so must do, must again coming.

Bhavika Mahtani

Motorcycle Mechanic

I have been doing this job for more than … roughly ah, I think about 15 years like that. Before this I was doing the same thing lor. But I was at another place, under one boss. I do all this myself, nobody help one. If you take someone ah, have to teach everything. Nowadays not like last time. Last time, when my time I learn, my teacher throw spanner at me if I do wrong ah. Spanner. Throw at me. [laughs] Nowadays how to do that? If you do, MOM (Ministry of Manpower), the police and the whole Singapore come and find you. Die liao. If you lucky, that guy will beat you up back. [laughs] If I employ a China worker, I need 13 Singaporean workers then I can get one China man. I need 14 people for what? I'm Snow White is it? [laughs] If Malaysia, need to have three Singaporean worker.

Singaporean? Worse ah. You come and ask your boyfriend to work for me. You think they want? I cannot pay them anyhow. Work so long, earn so little. I might as well do myself.

Every day I come to work at 9 o'clock, go back also 9 o'clock lor. Sometimes I end early but not so early lah, maybe 20 minutes early only. Sunday I half day. You see ah, once got family, you must think what to eat! Haha! Must be responsible. Survive lah. That's why ah, work, work, work every time, until Sunday also I still open shop. Until I go for holiday only one time a year. Where got leave, xiao mei (Mandarin: little girl)? I ownself work leh. Next month lor I go holiday! [grins] Um, for 10 days. Every year I go on a holiday for 10 days.

Sometimes this job is troublesome lah, like for example you do one bike – he already go to other people, do this do that, do until wah, then come to me. Piang, headache! Have to do, but cannot say you earn money because you spend a lot of time fixing. Then you cannot charge high prices also. If people understand, okay lah. But if they don't ah, "Wah, Ah Teck, so expensive?!" Then how? Actually, when they go to other place, they spend a lot of money one. No, I don't think I charge my customers a lot. I charge for labour, I never charge extra-extra profit from spare part or what. I charge for my labour because my labour ah, a little bit higher. Because I'm one person who is doing everything. Every day people come – accident lah, repair lah, piston jam lah. Sure got thing to do every day and not one bike, two bike – you see here lor how many bike? [points at line of bikes awaiting repairs] You ownself know how busy already lor.

I charge high for labour also because I really do properly one leh. I don't anyhow do. Some people fix already then, "Okay, you can go. Bye bye." Me, I fix, you go ride then see how, okay or not. If okay, come back and pay me. If not okay, come back I do for you but I never charge for that second time. That's why you see I spend a lot of time fixing one bike. I make sure I do properly not cin cai (Hokkien: haphazard) one hor. So if people come tell me, "Eh, Ah Teck, I need fast", I reject them then tell them you go other shop, then I recommend other place.

All my customers I tell them – I charge labour a bit high. Okay. Then the spare parts, you choose. You want original, or not original. If original, more expensive. But I don't take money for spare part. My customer all tell me, "Wah, got people say you charge expensive ah? I ever kena (Malay: to be on the receiving end of something unpleasant) before more expensive!" Got this one time, this two very young girls like you like that, ride Honda and come to my shop to repair bike. They wanted to change the signal light to the good one. I give them the price: $75 for the original one. They were shock. I thought, "Wah, jialat (Hokkien: to be in a dire situation)." That brand is expensive so of course it is $75 not like $30 plus. Sekali (Malay: once) one of the girl say, "Wah Ah Teck! So cheap! We go to that shop ah, kena $100!" That shop at the end there charge people crazy price. Every time customers come to my shop and ask me for the price, they get a shock. Very cheap, that shop very expensive. [laughs] I don't care one. Really, I don't. Sometimes some customer want to tell me about that shop – their new spare parts or the pricing. I tell them: "You don't tell me about that shop. I don't want to know." He is smart enough to profit from his customers, I'm just here to do my job until it's finish then okay already. But we never talk. They walk pass my shop, they look at the sky. Never bother saying hello or wave. So I do my job, and they should trust me that I am here to do my job.

You know those people go Malaysia do one? That one worse. Singaporeans think, "Wah, so cheap! How come you so expensive?" But they never think one. Really, all these people, mouth move but brain never work. Because the parts are actually different. Ah, you see? They don't know real or not, same or different. They only know:

price is cheap. Okay, let's go! But quality wise, lao ya (Mandarin: lousy) one! Okay lah, Malaysia also has good ones. But you think again, if they give the good one, they charge very expensive leh! More expensive than Singapore! You don't count the exchange rate now, you use the normal times two. You count, count then convert to dollars, Singapore cheaper! Like the mee rebus, Singapore about $2.50 like that. There how much? About 5 or 6 ringgit like that. See? Don't talk about exchange rate lah, where got cheap? Only Singaporean say cheap, haha! Everything in Malaysia also you all think cheap. Ringgit fall, you all buy everything in Malaysia. Never think good or not, or whether Singapore sell cheaper or not. Just buy, buy, buy. Kiasu (Hokkien: afraid of losing) mah! So if you want original part in Malaysia? Can, but confirm they charge higher.

That's why if you properly think, Johor motor shops are opened for 24 hours. Why? Not for their local people leh. All for Singaporeans one! You think Malaysian want to pay that kind of price ah? Crazy! Ever got this one Malaysian pizza rider accident in Singapore, come to my shop to repair his bike. I ask him, "Eh, why you come my shop? Go repair Malaysia lah, cheap what?" You know what he say? "Ah Teck lu gila (Malay: you're crazy). All JB (Johor Bahru) workshop open for Singaporean, because they know Singaporean very rich so they charge a lot! I'm a Malaysian and if I go there, I mati (Malay: die)! Expensive. Better come here do with you." Maybe same price as there but here labour and spare part got quality mah? Believe it or not, Malaysia guy come and told me this.

My hands ah, no price one. So cannot say that I earn a lot. But seriously, I don't earn a lot. I only charge labour. If I do like this, can survive lah, won't die. Better than working for somebody. You work for yourself, you work more, you get more money. Office or what, you work, work like crazy also, you get the same pay. This one – the more bike you do, the more money you get. Office? You look at papers until you blind, get more money meh? That's why sometimes Sunday I also work, then can cover lah.

But aiyah, Chinese say: you die, you cannot take your money with you. So okay lor, relax a bit when I go on holiday. Don't think about money. Lose also never mind, my mind and body must relax a bit. Tell you, if I really want, I can open 24 hours. Sure got people come. I open my handphone ah, people straight away call, "Ah Teck! My bike ah." But for what? No point. Work, work, work until I die then cannot be happy. How? That's why you want to ask me if I earn money or no earn money, I don't know. I just open the shop, charge them, they pay me today, tomorrow or next year. Sometimes I don't know how much I charge them, how much they owe me or who owes me. They pay, I take lor.

Record? No I don't write anything down, I don't do like all the big, big companies who do the finance or account thing. You ask me how much, I don't know. How to know? So much to think about! I don't want to know. I earn, then I earn lor. I lose, then I lose lor. Business mah? They want to pay they call me. I just work only, I don't know if I lose or earn or what. That's why my wife ask me, "Why your bank suddenly so much?" Then later, "Why your bank suddenly so little?" I tell her: "Eh, think so much for what? At least I pay bill, you all got makan, can support you all, okay mah?" Do until so big also for what, now I 50 already. Retire? I don't know. How to retire, cannot retire one! This is Singapore you know, you retire, you eat grass. Very hard lah.

If you work under someone, at least you can get an MC (medical certificate) if you are sick. I sick, I still have to work leh! You work for people it's different, "Towkay! (Hokkien: boss) I sick." Then okay bye bye. But not me. I have to be responsible. People want to collect their bikes as soon as possible. I cannot happy, happy delay. I also got utilities to pay for – the rental plus my stocks. Every month I fork out over $5,000. So, that's why Sunday I have to work. Haha. Last time only $2,000 or so. Unless your family rich then you get a good back-up from them. If not, mati.

But good thing lah because government don't disturb. They tell me: you cannot put your bikes here. Okay I follow. You cannot do this, I follow. Just follow lor, play safe. I can do my work peacefully, can already. But not all are nice. The old uncle types, they okay. Tell me to do, I follow. But the young ones ah, jialat. Never say, straightaway saman (Malay: to be issued a ticket or warrant) me. How I know if I cannot do it? Warn first lah, at least. This one straightaway kena. Like that, I no rice already. But even if I follow, sometimes I end up having to pay a lot! Got once MOM come, say I must do certificate. Safety one. I call people do everything already, sekali charged $800! One paper $800 hor? For nothing! Gold or what?

But I think the worst is those young guys who come to repair bike. Wah. Know a bit, act like they know a lot. "Eh, Ah Teck why do like this, why do like that? Why never do like that?" So pro meh? I do this how many years already, of course I know what I am doing. If I purposely do wrong to cheat your money ah, I can do a lot of things to cheat your money. Overcharge your spare parts, purposely do until like spoil then you come again then I charge you every time you come. Like that, you want or not? You know ah, sometimes people accident until very rabak (Malay: bad). But I don't tell them, "Oh, you must repair everything!" I only show okay this one need to repair, that one need to repair. I show all that is wrong with the bike lah, then they decide lor. I tell them how much, then see lor what they say.

There are even a few, after I repair for them already, then never pay. Got this one Malay guy, even put the IC (identity card) here, take bike then disappear. Don't know go where already. [chuckles] IC also don't want already. Aiyah, so troublesome report for what?

Don't want lah. Forget it. This kind of thing will happen. I think it was $500 to $600. I don't want to find him lah.

Ever I do one bike hor, was my customer's father. Then you all Malay ah, you believe when you pass away, must pay all your hutang (Malay: debt). If I say I don't accept then how ah? Because his father pass away, then one year later come find me. "Eh, Ah Teck. How much my father owe you?" He hutang me $100 plus only ah, the father never pay. Never come, then one year later, the son come and see me. One Malay guy already told me this one you know – that Malays when die, must pay back. If not, later he inside, ah, he suffer. Then how? I wanted to say, "Call your father come see me." Haha! If I don't accept, the father susah (Malay: difficult) already. I don't want to be so bad. So I say never mind lah, how much you want to give, you give. Serious, you know, the son come tell me the father pass away. I really stop for one minute and think: if I don't accept how ah? Haha! But I very happy, when my loyal customer come back and very close to me. I appreciate. Sometimes ah, I do extra for them, I never charge. If you go agent or big workshop company one, they will count part by part, count everything and charge you. Some of them very nice, like this Malay family who dabao (Mandarin: pack) food for me every Hari Raya! Very nice, I tell you.

That's why when you have your own business, it's good, but not say sure earn one, you know. Not guarantee. Sometimes you will lose also. That's why must give and take lor. Only Singapore government can earn 100 per cent ah! [laughs]

But you all should give it a try. Young, haven't marry, no children, no house, zero responsibilities – go out and try! You got nothing to lose what. But if my daughter wants to do this, I would tell her to think twice. Singaporeans need good income, stable income.

Ros Amirah Binte Rosli

Electronics Factory Worker

Lai zeh zeh, mai kei ki (Hokkien: come take a seat, don't be so formal). Just call me Auntie Siew Leng. This one interview for project ah? About work ah? Aiyah, I don't earn much eh … got ask my salary or not, later so paiseh (Hokkien: embarrassed). [awkward laughter] Work ah … got, I do a lot! Primary 6 study finish, come out and work already loh! That time only 13 years old cos I repeat one year. Friend recommend one … work at the firecracker company few months only … only make the casing and connect the string lah, cos that time underage … zeng hu come check must always run go and hide cos underage, always almost cannot make it on time you know. No good lah … one dozen few cents only, one day pay $2 only. Every day work from 8 to 5. Can bring home and do lah! Huh, no lah, no supervisor to check one, do more, earn more lor. Why want to do this job ah? You think I want ah? Boh gang zoh (Hokkien: no work to do) then friend recommend, go and work lah! Yah go and gain experience lor. My ah ma (Hokkien: paternal grandmother) lor! Keep ask me go and work, say what, I never study already then go and work, don't stay at home and waste time, waste food. [rolls eyes]

Then later zha si lang (Hokkien: explosion killed someone) ah! Got people die you know! [eyes wide open, nodding head slowly] Then close down, no job already. Then where I work ah? Mmmm. Ah! Yah! Then I work at garment factory. My father friend introduce one, that time still underage only 14. No check! Company don't check underage one, they need people what, but sewing too dangerous so can only do checking. Every day check lor for different department. Got sewing, got cutting. Then until 16 years old already, that time of age already so they let me do sewing lor. No lah! Nobody teach lah! You tan gu gu (Hokkien: literally "wait long long"). Ar boh then?! (Singlish: what else were you expecting?) People no time to teach you one! At first don't know lah, everything see people do then ownself learn lor, do already then know how to do already. Aiyah, very easy one lah. [waves dismissively]

Good? No good lah! I go in, old staff bully new staff give them do their work, then later new staff bully old staff. Aiyoh! I sew already, they not careful, tear it then tell me haven't sew yet. Wah, so fed up I show them the stitches lor! Don't come and play with me hor. Pay also low lah, one day $2, one month $500 plus only. Have to pay transport monthly, 50 cents. Every day also have to OT (overtime). [shakes head] Sew more, pay more lor, one dozen, I think 20 cents only lor. Different batch, different price; different design more difficult, more pay. Ah like that lor. But then this one I work very long, 14 years old work until 35 years old. Why stay so long? No choice what, family so big, need to eat one, need to bring back, feed family one, not good also must stay. But I also want to jump one (colloquial: change job) but then people always say electronic very busy lor, scared to jump lor! If I know so easy should just jump lor, now work, then know not difficult at all lor, those people anyhow say.

Then friend ask me to try other job cos work so long already. We go together ask factory if they need people or not. Last time no money, buy newspaper one waste money! Always friend recommend or ownself go factory ask. No cert (certification), no experience, company just employ one. So then got this company lah, ang moh (Hokkien: Western/foreign) electronic factory do assembly line, nearby Chai Chee only. You know the JTC (Jurong Town Council) Building? Ah, there I work five years. That time I was already 35 years old, have to test eyesight first. Assembly line always want young people, they scared people got lao hua (Mandarin: long-sighted), those they won't employ one. Luckily I pass and got in. That time I got no experience so starting do components only, arrange and sort out components. But then if assembly line got people never

come, have to go and take over. Wah, first time so scary leh! Cos don't know anything then the product keep coming. Always stuck! Have lah, people beside me got teach me, but then so many things to remember how to do well at once? People also busy with their own work, cannot always ask mah.

I work, then next time they let me join assembly line. Training? Got lah! Sure got training one! Every year also have, make sure you can remember mah! The person show me one time, wah haha! Totally blur hahaha! Show again still cannot remember. So many parts leh, this one join here, that one join there. [shakes head] Then she told me to see and memorise them little bit, little bit like spelling. Wah, she correct you know, really so easy. Line very busy cos got target to meet.

Ah! Got target to meet one! You think leh, where got so easy? But still can go toilet and take breaks. No lah, leader never do anything one! Assistant leader will take over, just don't always go and don't go too long. That time got this friend always go toilet so long ah, then her side keep on jam lor. No one know? Have hor! Leader walk here, walk there and see one. Do fast, do good, increase salary; don't do, keep on jam or go toilet? Cut pay lor. That time my leader strict but she same age as me, never dare to say much to me.

This company quite good lah, this job I got $600 starting pay then increment to $800 plus. Also got attendance pay. If only few times absent, got extra $30 or $40. I gian peng (Hokkien: greedy) one, every day sure go work. [laughs] Extra money why don't want? Also don't need to always do OT, good, good. But then later they shift to Malaysia so got retrench lor. But retrench pay good lah, one year one month leh!

Assembly line [in electronics firm] better lah, not so busy. Later, I do QC in plastic company. How long ah? Eight months I think. Pay ok lah, $800 but wah! Very stress you know! Every hour have to measure sample you know! Every hour leh! Ah, I measure sample then the machine operators can start up machine. Not only one machine, so many you know! Only me and another person. Yah lah, got shift lah, but still very busy you know. Machine start up already, still have to measure you know, think so easy ah? Why I want to work ah? No choice leh, I don't want one but forced to work eh, cos they say I got experience I do electronics factory before, two spaces only. This one or clean room. Wah! Clean room air so bad leh! All closed up, the plastic smell ah! [shudders and shakes head]

Everything also have to ownself learn, they (supervisors) teach you little bit, the rest have to see what they do, then ownself observe and follow already. Other people got their own work to do, not free one, no time to teach you everything. Ownself learn lor! Learn already, later know already, I boh tak chek (Hokkien: never went to school) also can do! A lot of things to do, run here, run there, check here, check there, everything also got to do. Supervisor still always nag. Har, why nag ah? Aiyah, keep saying we don't listen to him. Eh, we so busy, you tell me how to listen to him talk nonsense? Supervisor no good lah! Jin cha lah (Hokkien: so noisy)!

Then check already, still must reject and explain why reject, still must let operators know, but then those people always ignore and tear off the paper on the rejected item! Why ah? Cos don't want to redo mah! But then later head (team leader) come teoh suay siao (Hokkien: get into trouble). Orbi good lor (colloquial: serve them right). Yah, then got this woman, another shift one lah, wah! Ownself never measure always copy other people's measurements. Always write no reject leh, but then the thing come out always fail one. Sit there shake leg (colloquial: do nothing) think people don't know. Wah! One day head come, so angry face, so black, throw the papers in front of her. Scare me, first time saw him like that. Aiyah, you do this type of thing one day sure get caught one, just do your job properly lor, right? But then he good lah, never fire her, just give warning niah (Hokkien: merely).

But local company no good lah, move to Bintan, shrink company then retrench people. Chinese company jia lang ah (Hokkien: cheat people), retrench people already never pay, only one month lor! Yah can, they inform you in 24 hours, [shakes head] ang moh company better, that time got retrench still got one year and one month pay.

Then I work at electronics factory do assembly line one. Not local, ang moh. They do canister one, filter the air in printer yah. That one my sister recommend one. I think got work five years. That time salary only $650, then every year increment. Then now my company kena buy over ah, also ang moh one, they keep the same people, but now do another model (filter) already. You know those gold-gold thing stick on printer one? Ah ah! We do those. That time I do machine one, must operate machine. Wah, so noisy you know! Now I don't need machine but other people machine still very noisy! They got give us ear plug lah, but we always don't want wear cos want to talk mah! Wear already cannot hear. [laughs loudly]

Talk and gossip lor, very little guy – guy usually operate machine. Most auntie, all younger than me lah. Yah a lot Malaysian. Lazy lah, do assembly line one, still play game. Do work, put handphone in front and play game, product always fail lor. [shakes head] Supervisor never check lah, also play game. From same group got promoted to supervisor. Friend-friend, so close one eye lor, then department head come check then get into trouble lor! Promotion ah? Cannot anyhow promote one, must see cert then can promote one ah. That time got this guy work good but only primary school cert, cannot promote. Another one got study high school then got promotion. Yah factory also same one, no cert, no promotion, just increment. Same lah, everywhere same one! Paper (academic qualifications) very important you know! You study uni now hor? Yah, must study hard ah!

Here work close to 10 years already, pay not good lah, work so long already only $1,000 plus eh, no good lah! But this job I like lah, want to 60 years old already still can work. I'm the oldest you know! Factory all want younger people lah, need good eyesight. Also not so stress, still got tea break 15 minutes, if don't go tea break can take longer lunch, 1 hour not 45 minutes lor. Then medical also good lah, $800 go see doctor and dentist, food every day $4, then transport $60, leave at first start 14 days now 20 days already. Yah this one really not bad lah. You know last time, ah, still got team building go East Coast, go Sentosa play game, find treasure. Got annual dinner, Christmas got celebration, New Year also got buffet eat leh! But now business no good lah, now no more already, now economy so bad business shrink already. Next year worst ah.

Yah, this job good lah, benefit best one! Still can work, work lor, aiyah, who like working one? Don't like, also have to work, right? I don't like work lah, only like money hahaha! No dream lah, last time don't want work, just want to stay at home. Work just to earn money to survive lor. Last time I want to study night class one, my mother don't let lor, boh bian (Hokkien: no choice). Say she let me study also I never study properly, tell me don't waste money lah. All our salary have to give our mother to feed the family one, no choice lor. [looks dejected] But I got go and learn sewing, working already then go and learn one. Yah, I like sewing, very fun, can learn a lot of thing. Learn design? No lah haha! No standard lah, also can't speak English, cannot one lah. Got job okay already, people like us low education, as long as willing to work, got job, straightaway grab already, just work lor. Last time we only need experience, now paper also need. Aiyah, that's life lah, now you all better life already not so hard. You all can study next time tan duah lui (Hokkien: earn big bucks).

Rina Wang Miao Qin

Tailor

People here call me Kwok Seng, now I'm 76 years old. I work at City Plaza already a bit more than 35 years. The old people call this place not City Plaza, but just City. Yah, it's true, last time they have the watchdog here. At night time. After all the shop close. The dog black and very big. Because last time City very dirty one. You walking here, people can take your wallet. Sometimes people here fighting also. Last time and now different. Now weekend many Indonesian and maybe some Bangladesh and Indian people. Last time all kind. From everywhere have. Singaporean, Indonesian, Thailand, everywhere lah. Also, very busy every day. See now so empty. But okay lah, I still come here work every day.

So I every morning I wake up, I eat breakfast. Then eat lunch then I come out. I walk from Haig Road to here. About five minutes only. Few years ago I walk around for one hour first. I walk, walk, walk, until Katong there. Then I turn back. Now no energy already. But my stomach still flat. Because when I young I very active. Basketball, swimming, all I do. You want to become tailor very easy. Just need to learn how to use the sewing machine. You see this needle? Must be careful, when you sewing, do slowly. I until now never have accident. But now my eye not strong anymore. I do all these also follow feeling one. I don't go and see near-near. Just follow feeling.

I work tailor very long already loh. I stop Secondary 2, I only 14 years old. Last time I study at Chung Cheng school. The Chinese school. So when I stop school must find work, right? Last time Singapore 1960s very hard find work. Really. So I work construction for a while, but very tiring. Then I very lucky. Because I stay at the kampung near Joo Chiat there, right. Then around there got one tailor shop. And then the tailor looking for worker. So work there. I learn everything there. I also meet my wife there. After three years, I

keep money enough already, I open my own shop. At Galaxy building. The one near the Geylang Serai market. Got the movie theatre, that one. Wah, business very good. Many come find my shop, tailor this, tailor that. Until I must find my own worker also. My wife help me also lah.

That time the place still kampung area. The Joo Chiat–Geylang Serai area. I stay Joo Chiat, got many Chinese people from everywhere. Hokkien people, Teochew people, Hainan people, Nonya people. Then also got many Malay people and some Javanese Indonesian people. All stay together. That's why until now I know "Apa khabar?" (Malay: How are you?), "Sudah makan ke tidak?" (Malay: Have you eaten?), all these things. I'm Cantonese ah. Now more people like my children all grow up, only know English and Mandarin. My language they also don't know.

So when I got my children, my wife work less, help to take care they all two. Then also sometimes she take home some work. After a while my wife stop working with me at my shop and become cleaner. Now she not working already. After some years, other people buy the Galaxy building. Then slowly all the shop move out. So I move here lah, to City. At City that time so crowded. Business really good. Then my children slowly grow up, go university. Then now all working and got their own life. I also move out from Joo Chiat to Haig Road. Not too far, move far-far not nice.

Already eight years I never do make-to-measure things. Why? Because I don't have workers anymore. Last time I have five workers. Each one take one part home. I cut the fabric here. I give them the measurements. They take, go home and sew. Less and less people come here for make-to-measure. So slowly, I let go my workers. Because I cannot pay for so many people. I still need to pay the rent.

The rent go up a lot. From last time when I start $800 until now $2,600. Now must take care of the sewing machine some more. Want to ask people to repair, not cheap. Ask the repair person come down only, pay $50. Then when they repair, depend what they do maybe $80 or more. One sewing machine here around $1,000 plus. So two years ago I cannot tahan, I ask my boss (landlord) if I can rent half unit. So she say okay. Then now I pay $1,300 for half space. The other half last time, handphone shop. But two months ago they close shop. Cannot make business. I think they only tahan one year plus. Because here so little people. Some more, here so many handphone shop. I don't have handphone, only need this telephone here. Anything, my wife and two children can call me here.

The boss I pay rent money is very nice. She is Indonesian Chinese and always not stay in Singapore. So she give me one account number. Then I every month send the money to her. I pay every month. But if got anything, she always understand. So I think she is nice. Actually, here many shop the boss is Chinese Indonesian. Like my boss. They all come here when 1980s. From 1980s until 1990s got many Chinese Indonesia people come here. They all here because they scared in Indonesia. So they come here standby. They buy or rent the private house upstairs. So if anything happen in Indonesia, they can call their mother, father, sister, brother, all that come here. Very scary lah for them. They always tell last time people will hantam (Malay: hit) them, so feel more safe in Singapore. Yeah, so some stay here and make business. Some become like my boss, buy property and collect rent money until now. But after a few years not so bad already, some start to go back Indonesia.

Me? Oh, I never go anywhere one. My son always ask me to go holiday with him. He always say he can buy ticket go Taiwan, Korea, China, but I don't like. I only know how to work every day. I don't like to go holiday because waste money. I also don't know what to do outside. Who want to take care my shop when I go away? My son and daughter all understand. They from young don't do tailor work.

I work like this so they can study and do their own thing. Now my son old already, I ask him go stay himself. I stay with my daughter. I also don't know what she work. Same for my son. I also don't know what he work. I only know they all two got work, can already. My daughter last time study accounting. Then my son study computer engineer. So they all two got their own work now. But I don't know what they really do now. Want to ask, also I still don't understand. Of course, I got talk to them lah, but not important for me. I know they got their own money, can already.

I don't know why, they all two never marry. My daughter I know, change boyfriends three times, after that don't want anymore. I also don't want to force her. My son also, same. Until now no family for himself. I don't know why. But it's their life, what. How can I tell them? Now also I don't take money from them. I work myself so I can use my own money. Even I stay with my daughter, I also don't take her money. They all need to take care themselves. I still very lucky, got my wife. She got take care me. Every morning she cook, if not she dabao from the market food for me. When I go home I no lonely, can already.

But when I come work, actually sometimes very lonely. I share the unit with another shop, cramp a bit never mind. I still got space to sew, to cut. People still got space to use the dressing room. So that time when the handphone shop still have, I not bored. Always got people I can talk with. They all young man. So many things to talk. They always help me buy food if I ask. If not they help me get my kopi (Malay: coffee). When I go toilet, they help me jaga (Malay: keep watch). Sometime their customer also come to me for tailor their pants and shirt. Now they don't have already, I need to do all these myself. But I okay. Last time also got one auntie share shop with me do tailoring for women. She also after a while so few customer stop already. So now really nobody to talk with.

Now here I no friend. I cannot talk to my things. See so messy. The shop so many things people ask me to alter, but some a few years already still never take. But I don't care one lah. The auntie last time stop work, also leave her things here. Ask me to sell some the things she make. She last time make nightwear for women. There, the one I hang outside. She say if can, try to sell. Then if got money can pass to her some. Until now a few year already, nobody buy. Some days really nobody come. I can sit here do nothing. Nobody.

So I happy when have customer come. Give me something to do. If not, here really very quiet. Not like last time. Last time here so many shop sell clothes, all the people come here shopping. Buy something to wear. I always busy measuring people. Then cut the fabric. Then give my worker bring back to sew the different parts. Now I only do altering. Other shop here can alter simple-simple thing. But many things they don't know how to do. People know how to taper pants. But not all know how to make bigger. So yah, I do what I can do. Altering normally very easy. But the not so easy one I try to do also. If I can do, I do. When want to alter, must see the clothing. If people got idea, sure can make happen one. The other shop now all only know easy-easy thing because they not tailor like me. Some more, I charge cheap. If simple cutting, just $5, if a bit more $10. The more I must cut, the more I charge. The more troublesome also, the more I charge. Got one dress last time, I need to use so many fabric, I charge $80.

But now sometimes here quite quiet. Then yah, lonely lah. That's why I always on the TV. I also don't listen to the TV. Only maybe when have news I listen. But I on so here not so quiet. Got some sound. So when I do my work not just the machine sound. When the TV on, I feel less lonely lah.

Now I don't know how already. I must work every day. People like me every day work. Not take holiday kind, if they stop work …

aiyah. I don't want to think if that day can come. I really don't care about many thing now. I can wake up, have something to do, happy already. I have no hobby, my hobby is to don't care things. My friends, some no more already, some last time always come here chit-chat. But now old-old already, where got want to come here?

I really don't know how. Because they say City want to have renovation lah, en bloc lah, so many thing can happen, want to happen, but until now never happen. But I don't want to think so much. I can work, I happy already. See how lah. Wah, 10 o'clock already. Better go home, later my wife cook the thing become cold.

Try Sutrisno Foo

SELLING

CHAPTER FOUR

SELLING

Supermarket Stocker

My age is 22. I used to study at Simei ITE (Institute of Technical Education) learning about landscaping. Last time before that we learn plumbing also. First year was not very fun. This course ah, majority of them are boys. Very few girls will join this one. After graduation I went to find a job. My father suggested I work in a nursery at Choa Chu Kang. I was assisting the people there, taking care of the plants. Long time already, I was there last year I think … I was there for five months, after I graduate. I did my internship there. Because for the second year we have an internship. They have in-house and outside. If you do in-house, you won't get paid … I did it outside. My dad's friend recommended. So my father knew about it and then he asked me to go there. I think it is not a very safe place. It has all those kind of, you know, many creepy-crawlies – mosquitoes, insects lah. They will come and bother you.

Actually, it was that lady boss who told me that I don't need to go back already, cos I think she wants to hire new people, or maybe she think there's enough staff lah. So she let me go lah. After that, I rested for a while, then my father found a new job for me. I started this job in May. Yah, so now it's gonna be like five months already.

Time passes by quite fast. Yah. I like this job, even though it's very tiring. At least I got eight hours to work and then one hour to rest. So like from 12 to 3 p.m., I will be stacking up the products. Then from 3 to 5, if I'm free then I will pack coffee lah. Like those big packets you put it into small bags. Sell cheaper, like $4 or $5, like this lah. After 5, I will be eating my dinner until 6 o'clock. Then after that, 6 to 9 I will be at another place … CCK2 (Choa Chu Kang Hostel 2). There is CCK1 and CCK2 at the Sungei Tengah Lodge there. It's also at Choa Chu Kang. It's like a hostel for foreign workers.

There was no interview. Actually, my father's friend was the one who introduced this job to me. So my dad went to talk to the boss. And the boss was, like, okay with it. So the boss says that he wants me to learn slowly. I wanted to be a cashier, because I thought I was ready, but then my boss say not for the time being. Cos he is worried that I might count wrongly, then give customers the wrong amount. So I have to take it slow, learn slowly lah. But then I'm trying to, like, do my work faster, so I have more time to do extra. If not, from 3 to 5 I will be very sian, sit down at my desk doing nothing. I had three months training before I got the confirmation letter. So it's like all staff before they are confirmed, they will have to go through three months training. One of the girls that left, she was my partner, I was doing five sections with her. But after she left, I'm the only one doing it. So for the first weeks I couldn't cope lah, and I had to request for help, but these few days I'm trying to do things faster, and help others with their section. Very intense training but have to get used to it lah.

So it's like I'm at two places. At CCK2, I will go there and help lah. From 6 to 8 I will be packing flour, they need flour like 2 kg, 3 kg, so I'm doing all those kinds of stuff. Then 8 to 9, I will be helping my colleague at the counter lah, like packing things into bags.

My colleagues, they have to work 12 hours, I work only eight hours. They work from 9 a.m. to 9 p.m. Early in the morning there is not much people. So the boss say that I can come in the afternoon, from 12 to 9. But recently sometimes he will ask me whether I can do until 12 o'clock. Then I'm like, "12 o'clock can, but then I no bus already, only got company lorry." I don't stay at Choa Chu Kang. If I work until 12, then how am I supposed to go home to Seng Kang? I told him, "You want me to do 12 o'clock can, you come to my office at 12 o'clock and fetch me, you want or not? If not you give me taxi fare, I go back by myself." Then he said "Don't want, you just work until 9 o'clock, can already."

Mmm … I never buy anything to bring home before. I just keep in the office. Then if I want to eat, then I eat. If I want to drink, then I drink. Snacks and drinks lah. Those veggies and meat, I leave to my mummy to shop for it herself. Cos I don't know how to buy these things. I don't want to anyhow buy. Cos my colleagues, they know how to cook mah, I don't know how to cook, then I buy for what?

How many colleagues? Quite a lot. Boys' section quite a lot. Girls' section quite a few. So it's separate. The girls will be the ones stacking, then the guys will help us to take whatever items we need. I will ask the boys to use the ladder and then take for me. Cos I cannot reach, and sometimes it's very heavy, then I don't want to get injured. If I get injured my dad will be the one nagging at me. And I always get injured because the penknife always make me injured. It really hurts lah, when I see blood I get scared. Yah, sometimes it's here, [pointing to finger] sometimes somewhere else. My father ask me, "You can put on gloves to do it or not?" Then I said, "Stacking things only, need glove ah!" [laughs]

My colleagues are from Malaysia, Philippines, China. Yah, India also. To me it doesn't matter which country you are from. I treat you as my colleague and as a sister. Now I am quite close to one of my colleagues, because she is from China. Both of us talk in the same language, so we are close lah. Cos I talk to her quite a lot. Actually I did not expect so many of my colleagues were foreigners lah. But it turns out that I was the only Singaporean over there. My manager is from another country also. But then she can speak Chinese lah, but a little bit only.

What I don't like is that there are so many things to "top-up". I wish that there are less things to top-up, then I can do faster. Sometimes I don't even have time to do other stuff. Sometimes after I finish stacking, then new stock come, then I need to stack again. So it's like quite troublesome lah. And then the customers will keep on looking for me, asking me this one how much, that one how much … then sometimes I say I don't know, because I really don't know. And some customers they are very impatient, they like to cut queue also. Sometimes, the customers will get angry, especially when they are drunk. Got one time, my colleague was arguing with a customer. He shouted back at the customer, then the security had to step in leh.

Some customers, they will try to open the product, to see whether that one is the real one. Then they will open it to smell it, which the company doesn't like. So it's like my company has strict policy lah. So some customers they open it when you are not looking. When you are not looking, they try to be funny. I talk to my father about it also, then my father is like, "These customers they are like that one. They don't know what the products are like, so they like to touch and see and feel whether is it the real one." So, I have to think of ways and methods to stop people from opening lah. After you buy already you can go home and do whatever you want mah. You want to open also can, you want to give to people also can, but then don't open it at the shop itself, because there are CCTV cameras, they will know what is happening.

I don't find the job boring. Because I already thought about it, my father has introduced me to this job, and then I'm doing quite well at it. So I shouldn't, like, complain that much saying that it's

too tiring, "I don't want to do", and then "it's, like, boring", "every time do the same thing". So every day, even if I'm doing the same thing, I just tell myself maybe if I improve then maybe I get other things to do lah. Slowly adjust to the situation. I think it is my father's encouragement, and patience that motivates me. Because my father loves and dotes on me a lot. Sometimes when I'm tired, I tell him about it, and he says, "You must remember, even though it is tiring, you need to remind yourself that you need strength to do work." And my colleagues also motivate me lah, but in other ways. They will, like, say nice things to me, then they will treat me drinks. Sometimes they will also ask me to eat with them, share the food with them. I think it is the people surrounding me giving me the encouragement and the love lah.

My family, when they heard about the job, they were, like, quite happy also lah. Cause I earn money, I get salary then I can give to my brother also, my grandma also. So they are quite happy. My mum was the happiest I think. She's like, "Wah, you earned a lot of money already! You can go overseas already. Even Europe also can go!" Then she was like, "Then next year we go to Korea lor." And I was like, "Very good! Then I can go and see all the K-Pop groups I like!"

I will stay here for a very long time. Because I'm that kind who like to stay at the same place. I don't want to, like, straightaway change to another environment. Because it might take time for me to adjust. At first when my dad introduced me to this job I was, like, very scared that the colleagues will ignore me, treat me like a different person like that. Because I'm a Singaporean, so they are foreigners. But as I get to know them they are quite friendly also lah. So I hope to stay here for a very long time lah. I want to stay, I don't want to change. Forever. I would rather stay here.

Nathene Chua

Real Estate Agent

After NS, I didn't know what to do, I didn't have direction. Actually I wanted to be a chef. But it was too expensive. Then I wanted to be a technician. I went to Dover ITE to sign up for a course. They told me to come back in six months but when I did, the registration had already closed. Then while I was waiting I start work as a security guard. Last time the internet wasn't so popular, so you know security guard always got nothing to do, so I read newspaper and I always read the real estate section and think it's cool. I was a security guard at a condo and I always see property agents bringing their clients in. I like to talk to them. I asked, do you need to study or need a degree to do this and they said no. They said you just need to take the course to get the real estate licence.

So that's how I started my career in real estate in 2009. Yeah, the real estate market is moving in Singapore. I think I can say Singapore is a first world country in Southeast Asia. Every businessman, developer and private company from India, China, Indonesia, they all want to come to Singapore. Many old buildings they will tear down to build new things. Economy is doing better now. Actually, yeah, that's when we can tell there is buyer confidence.

Two years into my career is when I was at my peak, from 2011 to 2012. In 2011, I was doing very well for my age. That time I was only 22 or 23 and I'm not highly educated one lah. I just finished N Levels. When I closed my first deal, actually I feel very confused. I was happy lah, but as a security guard you earn max $2,000 per month, but when I closed my first deal I made $6,000 in commission. Actually it was supposed to be $12,000 but my manager helped me so she got a cut.

Is being mixed race an asset in real estate? Actually there's a lot us mixed race people in Singapore. I got a lot of Chindian friends.

Usually the mother is Chinese and the father is Indian. It's good to be bilingual but I would say Mandarin is more important now. But I also don't know why my parents choose Tamil as second language in school for me and my siblings.

Last time my aim was really chasing money one because, you know, I had the concept wrong. Because last time even though I do very well in real estate right, I wasn't really fulfilled. Though the money is good but I learned that money is not everything. Yeah … it's important but then there are other things that are even more important to have.

My parents are like, you know, the typical Singaporean family, so they don't really share, uh, tips on how to be happy in life and stuff. They're just typical, you know, old-fashioned parents so that's why a lot of things I learned came from outside, from people I respect. I like to learn from people a lot and try to take some risks.

So when I first join real estate, it was very tough also because I actually don't know how to communicate with people when I start. I actually never wanted to do sales one because I always thought that um … since when I was young I'm not good in talking. Very shy guy, low confidence. At the same time, I didn't know anything about real estate so it was quite difficult lah. So that's why I put all of my effort into making a successful career for myself, which I did but then there were other areas where I failed. I can say that I've changed now. I was forced to lah.

I want to have a family by 35. Actually since you ask, I can say I'm actually looking right now. I'm not really good with women one. [laughs] I've been subscribing to a lot of YouTube channels, email subscription. You know how Google knows what you search? I just saw the ad. I read up by myself online, you know. But it's one thing to learn these things and another to practice it. You must actually go out there and try for yourself. Dating apps don't work for me. I'm not good at taking photos. Girls get a lot of matches but guys do not. And, also, if you want to get matches, your life has to be interesting. My life is boring one.

So I'm attending a dating course, they call it a bootcamp. They teach you theory and how to talk to girls. You must go up to random strangers in shops and malls and start a conversation with them. The course is called Modern Man Academy. The guy who runs it is a real estate agent. I see him as a role model, he's a smart guy lah. They keep the class size small, only three people in one bootcamp. This is really part of trying to improve myself. Not being confident to talk to women is my weakness so I'm working on it.

Now, happiness, fulfillment, doing what I love are important to me. Being positive, having a good relationship with people, family, loved ones, you know … girlfriend, everybody, clients, make a difference in the world lah, try to impact as much as possible, inspire people, I think this is more who I want to be for long term maybe, till I die one day you know? It gives me more satisfaction.

Cristina Nearing

Electronics Store Owner

I'm John and I'm 55 years old this year. I started working since 16 years old. I worked with a dozen companies before becoming my own boss. I was a window cleaner, delivery boy, office boy, salesman. I didn't have it smooth at all.

I was educated only up to Secondary 3 because my family wasn't able to pay for my O Level exams. I had no choice but to start working at 16 years old. You know those that clean the outside hotel window one, now you see all the Bangla doing? They used to hire people like us. I think now they need some special licence to do it and their pay is higher since it is more dangerous. Last time they where got care all these? Dangerous? Of course it is, but I have no choice, I'm poorly educated, no special connection with anyone, I can only do this type of jobs. Now when I look back, I still cannot believe that I did such a job for $150 per month.

After NS I worked as a camera salesman at an electronic shop at Colombo Court. I earned about $200 per month. I worked there for about a year, then I quit and worked in another electronic shop at Lucky Plaza. At Lucky, my pay was $250. I quit after three months as I'd found another electronic shop at Paya Lebar airport where my pay increased to $450. Almost double! After a year or so, I quit and worked at Centrepoint, also selling cameras but this time my pay was about $1,000 including commission. Then I switch to Far East Plaza where my pay was $1,500 and finally the last place I worked for was an electronic shop at Paragon. I was about 25 years old when I was at Paragon and my average pay was about $4,000 per month. During better months I could even bring home about $6,000.

I was really happy at Paragon. My boss was very nice to me, he gave me special privileges like allowing me to come to work later because I was the top salesman. I really enjoyed it, I just need to work six days a week, serve the customers and wait for my pay cheque at the end of the month. I felt that finally life is fair as I get to enjoy, I got spare money to spend. Previously I had to scrimp and save. At Paragon, I was even able to go holiday in Hong Kong, bought my first car and even my first property. Not an HDB, but landed property. It was all good isn't it? But as I said, life is never smooth sailing. I enjoyed my eight years in that shop but then the management wanted to turn Paragon into a luxury shopping mall so they chased all the electronic shops out. All of a sudden I was jobless.

My old boss encouraged me to do my own business. He believed in my capabilities and he was one of the strongest pushes that make me into a boss. It was really a huge challenge but I accepted it as I thought that after working so many years for other people, I want to open my own shop some day. Therefore I started operating in 1996 at Far East Plaza. To start the business I needed about $100,000. But most importantly, it was my relations with my suppliers that was built over the years that provided me the financial support I needed initially. Electronic goods are very expensive and $100,000 alone is not enough to buy my stocks. But because of the trust I'd built up with my suppliers they were willing to supply me on credit. Business started picking up but then came 1997 Asian Financial Crisis. For a while I thought that I could no longer continue.

But I managed to hang on until 1999. That was a major turning point for me and my shop. With the help of a customer from the Philippines, I got into the phone business. He'd been my regular customer since I started the shop and he offered to supply me 300 pieces of Ericsson 788, then the smallest phone in the world. It was out of stock in many places and that 300 pieces all sold out very quickly. That's was when I started selling the other phone models with the profits I made from the 300 pieces and my business really started picking up.

Now with the internet many people would rather buy online. Business is a lot quieter now. We used to rely a lot on tourists but now they can buy their electronic goods online, so why do they need to come here to buy? I have tech-savvy employees working for me but I will never put my business online. Selling things online has no personal interactions with the customers: it's only the price that matters. There isn't any service or rapport like what I have built with my customers over the years. The service that we provide, it is irreplaceable. But people just want convenience. E-commerce is killing us retailers: they do not have any rental cost, so of course we lose out to them in terms of price. I know that the retail industry will die out some day, just like me as I'm getting old and my regular customers are also getting old. How long can we sustain?

As you can see many shops here have closed down. There used to be 10 electronic shops but now only three are left. These days, the shop has evolved into a meeting place where we talk about everything. Customers will just come to my shop for a box of rojak because they've already bought my latest gadgets and there is nothing new for them to buy. After 20 years, we've become friends: it's not so much about making money from them now. It's also not so much about them buying things from me as they can probably get their stuff cheaper online.

I'm still making enough to cover my rental and to pay my employees. I'm actually very scared the day will come when I can no longer make enough to sustain this shop as I wouldn't know what to do at my age. Thinking back, I ask myself would I be better off if I had worked for other people instead of becoming a boss? At least I would have one off day a week but now, my only off days are Chinese New Year. My kids always ask me why other people's parents have family day on Sunday, why they don't have.

Although it's really difficult to be a boss, this shop is an achievement for me. It's brought up my two kids, it provided stability for my family, helped me to pay off my house loans. Now that I'm old and business is slow, this shop is just a place for me to be. Where my friends can come find me and where I can feel that I'm still useful.

Kang Li Ting

Vitagen Auntie

Sit down, you need a table to write on, right? You are asking me about this job? Actually very early have already. I myself did it for 16 years already! I will tell you my story. At first, I worked at a factory in Jurong. I worked for … I think it was about … a few decades. That was my first job. I worked until our factory moved to China to expand. I did try to look for another job, but because of my age ... when I called employers they say, "Okay, just wait for the 'good news'." That means don't have already. At that time, my mother-in-law ordered Vitagen regularly. One day, the auntie came to deliver. She asked me, "Eh, you want a job?"

"What kind of work?"

"Deliver Vitagen lah."

"How much it pay then?"

"Sorry hor, no salary, only got some commission."

"And how much is that?"

"A few cents lor."

I replied, "This kind of job can do meh?" She told me I shouldn't think that way. If I think about a job at NTUC (a supermarket), it was $3.20 an hour. If I delivered Vitagen – totalling up the cost, the commission hor – it would be higher than the salary at NTUC. Yah, like that. I also didn't mind. Back then, the commission was 70 cents, and I thought, okay lor, just try and see. Anyway, staying at home was quite boring mah. Then I started lor! When I first started, I only did 26 packets a week! Twenty-six a week leh, I was thinking to myself, "Har, how to continue like that?" But later on, don't know how lah, but when I met other people, I just daringly asked them if they wanted to order. Then very quickly, it increased to 60 to 70 packets leh. Then the more I do, the more confident I get. Then do until now lor. Now ah? Once a week got about 150. It's also not a lot lah, the highest I got was 188 a week. Some customers moved away, so decreased lor.

When I first started, I had to go through a period of transition ... because ah, one day as I was pushing the trolley, I suddenly felt like I was going to fall. [chuckles as she recalls] I was really scared, so I quickly stopped. And I stood there and thought – my tears were about to fall – "Why do I want to do this job, when it's so tough? Have to push the heavy trolley." Then, I thought, "Aiyah, I'm relying on my own strength to earn money, there's nothing wrong in that." So I slowly grew accustomed to it lor.

Because in my earlier job, I was in charge of the store at the National Cap (capacitors) factory. Of course there was a huge change, it was totally different. When you go out, you need to face customers, and customers who reject you. Because not every customer will buy even when you go to them. This job is actually quite odd, because even though they call it home delivery hor, which means pre-ordered, the company also told us that the customer can still reject you, and you must still say thank you. So I find it very weird. But no choice lah hor, they say like that then we just accept lor.

For every area hor, there will be an "auntie" in charge. That means, you cannot go beyond your area. I don't know how the company demarcate, they told me that my area is between Block 631 to 643. You can't go to another area. But if you meet someone on the road, you can sell. Can. Because it can't be that someone wants to buy from you but you say, "Cannot sell." It's like buying in the market. But of course, for this kind of customers, we don't make a record lah.

We settle the bill once a month. Ah, so that means every month, before the 7th, we need to submit the accounts to the company. Last time, they would come to get the money, but later, it became better, can transfer from an account directly. You order first and sell, then they will send you a statement at the end of the month, telling you how much to pay. The company has their record, and I make my own record lor, that I bring out when I go on deliveries. Yah, so I can keep track. Because I have some customers, they don't want to pay the money every week, they say it's too troublesome, so they do it every month. I can't possibly remember so many, so I make my own record lor. [gestures to stacks of neatly stapled pieces of paper]

I split my deliveries into three days. On Monday, I deliver in the afternoon, on Tuesdays, in the morning, on Wednesdays, I deliver at night – that is when all the customers are at home lah. So the working hours are flexible lah, that's what I like about the job. If, for example, I was supposed to deliver on Wednesday, but I happen to have something on, I can let the customers know that I will change the timing or the date lor. How long do I take? Nowadays three hours or more. Wednesday slightly longer: if they are not around on Monday, then when I happen to go by on Wednesday, I will deliver the ones that I couldn't deliver on Monday. Because I see this as a service job mah, if the customer didn't say, then it's my responsibility to go over and check.

Have I taken any breaks? Got, got. In June, I went to stay in the hospital for a few days. Then for that week, I told my superior that I can't do it. But I was still the one who ordered the supplies, and the delivery was done by other aunties. Then end up my commission for that week no more lor. Yes, so I really don't go on a holiday anymore. I feel it's not very worth it leh, I have to order, then do paperwork, but other people earn the commission.

What do I like the most about this job? The flexibility in time. And also, my customers are now very familiar with me, very friendly. Ah. So on one hand, I feel that there is nothing much to do at home, and I can go out, walk a bit, and also chit-chat, and I can also earn a bit of pocket money. Pass some time lor. Exercise? Don't have lah, because the doctor say, this is not called yun dong (Mandarin: exercising), it's just lao dong (Mandarin: working). But it's hard lah. When one is old, there will be some leg pain lah. Will ache.

There wasn't much training leh. Just go to the factory for a tour. Then there was a superior who brought me for a trial – means they accompanied me on my first round. That's all. After that it's all up to you. The company only gives you a cooler bag, uniform, that's it.

Then for the other things: trolley you must buy your own, shorts, shoes, paper ... all your own lah. You also need to settle the electricity bill. They will lend you a fridge. Lend. If it's spoilt they will change, because their products are in my house mah. I have a lot of it, so I can't do without a fridge. My own fridge, cannot lah, hundred over packets leh, how to put?

Customers ah, honestly speaking, there are many kinds of people, with different personalities. Some of them treat you as a friend, they ask after you and care for you. "Auntie, have you eaten? Did you bring an umbrella since it's raining? Would you like to drink some water?" There are some that I can connect with better lor, they will really care for you. For example, if they are making cake, or some bread, or they happen to be eating something special that day, they will give me some to try. During the Malay New Year, I have two customers who are very kind, they will definitely give me some of their food: ketupat, lontong.

But then got other customers see you just as someone who delivers the goods: once they take it and have given the money, then that's it. So hor, if the customer is good, will exchange a few words, I will stay and talk for a bit lor. Ah, then for some that are yaya (Singlish: proud or arrogant), I just go lor. Just a greeting lor ... but all in all, basic courtesy is a must lah, because you want to earn their money mah ... to put it less nicely. Honestly, for this job, the main thing is that you need to have a smile, and also build relationship with people, must know how to build rapport. For example, I will try to accommodate the preference of the customers. For example, there are five to six colours (of Vitagen). I will ask which colour do you like. And I will try to give them what they like. For others who take more, I will record what they took the first round, so I can give them other colours next time.

Eh, actually, this industry quite a lot of people leh, I heard from my supervisor hor, just the home delivery people in Singapore, about 300 plus. Last time, when I first came in, I was … how old ah? I joined in 2000, [reaches for a calculator and starts tapping] year 2000, [hits enter with a flourish] I was 52 years old. At that time, the aunties were all about 40 plus, 50 years old. Er, apart from the aunties, also got one or two uncles lah. Nowadays hor, there are many young mothers. Those that are 20 plus, 30 years old. Because they want to take care of their children. Then this job, the timing is more flexible, so they join. So it's becoming a "younger" profession now. When there is a company gathering, we will meet together lah. Every year, during the Lunar New Year. A lunch one year, and then a dinner banquet the next.

When I first started, the company held a competition once a year for all the home delivery aunties. They had a competition where there was a target lah – it's quite hard to say what the target was, I'm actually not very sure how many packets you needed to sell to win first prize. I don't really know. But just nice, I've been doing it for many years, and one year, I got third place in the competition. For that, the company gave me a gold coin. Yah, the one with the queen. Another thing is that, for us, if we have been doing this for many years, after five years, the company will send a gift. The second time is after eight years. And the third time is after 15 years. So when I reached the five year mark, I got a gold coin, when I did eight years I got another gold coin, and when I won the competition I got one – so in total, I took three gold coins. They are all of different sizes. Then when I reached 15 years, because the value of gold increased, the company switched to giving cash. It was $300. I'm not certain if they have another one, must wait until I work 20 years then find out. [laughs]

Nathene Chua

Temple Flower Seller

I've worked here for 50 years. Ah, I'm 60 years old this year. I started helping my mother with this stall when I was eight, so I've done this my whole life. My grandmother gave this business to my mother to do, so I just helped my mother lor. So … those two generations, belonging to my mother and grandmother, they could burn incense. Later, when I first took over from my mother, the government had just changed the regulations, so then I switched to selling flowers. Last time at this temple, you could offer incense paper. You could burn kim zuah (Hokkien: joss paper) on the feast days of the different gods, the shen. Later, due to hygiene reasons, the government didn't allow most temples to burn kim zuah anymore. It's been a good 20 years since that happened loh.

Ah, so I have three daughters and one son, all of them university lah. Yah, they've all graduated loh! They're all working now. All the money I've earned here, all of it went to their studies. People say, "Wah, you work here you must make a lot of money!" Yes, there's enough: to eat, to travel, to spend. My life is can lah, just don't have money to save. All of them, I just helped them get that one important piece of paper, that degree. The rest, it's for them to walk their own roads lor.

My eldest daughter studied in Singapore Poly, then she went on to study in NTU (Nanyang Technological University). Then my other three, their grades weren't enough, so they went to study outside, in private universities. It's not like they wanted to study in private universities, it's so expensive you know. Singapore Poly, NTU and NUS ah, you need enough grades to get in leh. Not enough hor, cannot go in one. My eldest daughter is an architect. She studied this course lor, then she came out to work. She has four children. Thirty-eight years old, my eldest. So her job is like … like when those

Banglas have completed the building, she will go over to see. Inspect the buildings, to see if pass or not pass.

I attended English school one. I studied at Stamford Girls' School. Just down the road, now they use it for art things. No, it's not Raffles. Stamford Primary Girls' School. It was a girls' school, no boys. But later hor, this changed, so they had boys and girls. I sent my son and my daughters there. Because I was an old girl, you know? So I went to find my principal. I told her, my daughter wants to study here leh, can you admit her in? They can check the records for such things mah. So all my daughters and my son studied in Stamford.

I managed to pass primary school, yes, but when it was time for secondary school, my mother said, you don't need to study so much lah, six years is enough. Yah, I finished primary school, you know! Yes, of course I wished I could have gone to university. But my mother said – my mother had three boys and one girl – my mother said, I've already been so good to you by letting you study. You don't need to study one – you are going to get married, you will have housework to do. Let your brothers study, okay? It was like that in the past. Value the boys more than the girls. My mother said, "I've cared for you by letting you study in school for six years already." And ... I guess I'm content lah.

But in this job, even though I studied in an English school, I have to speak Mandarin so much that my English has worsened. In the past I could write and speak English. Now, even if I wanted to, I cannot write it. I can't do it anymore! You have to keep writing Chinese characters here, do you understand? Ah, look at the packaging here, it's all in Chinese characters right? There's no English letters here even. That's why my English has deteriorated.

Now my grandson asks me, "Grandma, your English can or not? It's really rotten leh!" [laughs] Even my daughter laughed at that.

I told him, it cannot be helped lah, Grandma only studied for six years. Six years! How much school is that? It's like kindergarten standard … in the past the primary school standard is like today's kindergarten standard. "Table", "chair", "apple", "orange" – like that only. Nowadays they learn all these things in kindergarten! So I told my grandson, don't laugh at me hor. Your mother and father studied in the university, it's different!

Ah, so a lot of people tell me, "Since your children all have jobs, you don't need to work lah." I say, "I've worked here for 50 years, what do you want me to do?" I like doing this job! The time passes very quickly: you come down, you set up the stall, you sell a few flowers, and then it's time to eat lunch. In the afternoon, you sell a bit more, and it's time for tea already! After you drink a bit of tea, then it's time to go home! So the time passes very quickly.

If you ask me to go home and just look at the four walls ah, I'll be bored to tears. I won't be able to take it! With old people, don't tell them to stop working, just tell them to work less. Do what you can. If you work too hard ah, then you'll have to go see the doctors, and give all your money to them. Doctors have a lot of money already, don't give them even more! [laughs] So that's why I tell my friends too, work part-time also good, do any work also good. Let's not compete or rush. We're past that already, let's just spend our time properly, earn a bit of money to spend. This way hor, it's good enough.

Start work ah? Well, so the temple opens at 6 every morning. Some people follow the temple, 6 o'clock. I don't, because my daughter only allows me to start work at 8. But in the past, when the children were younger, I would open at 6, because we needed the money, you see. Open at 6, close at 6. Yeah, 12 hours! Now that the children are all grown up, I don't want to do that anymore. Otherwise I will have to go and see the doctor too. [laughs] But life is difficult lah. Now that I'm older, engine will spoil one mah. [laughs] Like an old car, you know? There aren't any old cars around these days anymore, the government takes them … right or not?

But if you asked me what is the happiest thing about this place, then it's that there are so many people here who come to pray. All kinds of people come here: Indians, Chinese, they all come. Yes, there are ang mohs too. They are curious, so they will go inside to take a look. They don't come here to pray, just to take photographs. Because this street, there's a Hindu temple, a Chinese temple, a Thai temple. It's such a lively place. Full of people the whole day! If you sat at home, it would be so boring. Some days when there's no business, it's fun to look at this person or that person. What do you think she's praying for, what is he asking the shen for? There are just so many different people here to watch. That's what makes me happy.

People ask me, has this place changed? Yes, it's changed a lot! I think the changes in this place have been very good. Better and better. In the past, this used to be a two-way road. There used to be a temple around the corner, a small one. Then, after the government asked them to beautify this place, it became a place for walking only. You see ah, there aren't any cars here now, so it's safe. In the past, when cars were driving along this stretch, it was so dangerous. Last time, after kids came to pray at the temple, they would run out into the street eh, so dangerous you know? Now it's a lot safer.

You see, the government has helped people, so that there aren't any floods now. Last time, there were a lot of floods here. When it rained, very quickly, wah, this place would be full of water. Speaking honestly, if there wasn't Lee Kuan Yew, there wouldn't be Singapore. Lee Kuan Yew is PAP (People's Action Party) one, he controlled Singapore until very good. Everything also he control, so things got better and better.

Now there's also flats and shopping. Next street, there's Bugis Plus lah, right or not? Ah, when people come to pray to the shen already, then they can go to Bugis Plus. "You go and pray ah, Mama, I go to Bugis Plus and walk around, I'll wait for you there." Like that, where got bad? If you had to wait here for your mother to finish praying to the shen, it can take very long one leh. "Mummy, I wait for you very long already leh, I've waited here for half an hour." But if the children go to Bugis to wait, they won't feel it's very long at all.

Our licences are temporary licences. Where they tell you to go, you just go there to sell your things lor. No, you cannot just anyhow set up your shop one. Our numbers must follow one, we all have a number. It's not say, "Today I want to set up shop here, then tomorrow I change to that spot over there." The government is very law-by-law one mah! [laughs]

Hey, if our government isn't law-by-law, this place would be a mess. It's because Singapore has four races eh, four languages you know, right or not? Look at America, they only have two races but they're in such a bad mess already. Black people and white people: look at how they're fighting each other already. In Singapore, we have four. If Singapore wasn't law-by-law ah … last time, when the Malays beat up Chinese people, it was because the government wasn't fair, do you understand? Last time, this was the territory of the Malays leh. When Lee Kuan Yew took over, he changed things bit by bit, until we Chinese people had power, in the past it was the Malays who had the power leh.

Now the government is very clever, in one block of flats ah, there are only two or three Malay people, two or three Indian people – the government doesn't give them a chance to outnumber us. So the government control a lot eh. In the past don't have one. In our kampung, there were so many more Malays! If they said one, we couldn't say two! Now it's the other way around.

But we too need to be fair lah. Now our government says we all have to be friends. You can see this in any number of things. Ah, like for example, my flat downstairs, if there happens to be a Chinese funeral going on, and then just nice, some Malays want to get married, they want to use that space too. Well, if we wanted to, we Chinese can choose not to give way, you know. But we Chinese, we give in. You want to get married, it's a happy affair, it's a good thing, while we are doing funeral things, sad things – we can go to a funeral parlour mah! Malay people, you like to have your weddings at void decks, so we just give in to you. Like that hor, then they know that we Chinese people can be fair, we'll step aside, then the Malays will trust us more and more. You need to let them know! Fight here, fight there ah, we all die faster. Don't fight! I always tell people, cannot get along, then don't say anything. If can get along, then just say a few words.

Us Singaporeans hor, if can help, we just help. It's not that Singaporeans have no human warmth, no ren qing wei (Mandarin), you know. If they can help, they will help, it's just see how to help. Like, you can't just come over and say, "Hey you, lend me $10." Cannot lah! I don't even know what you're going to do with that money, take it to gamble ah, or take it to feed women, I won't know mah. Why would I give it to you?

Singaporeans really have ren qing wei, one. You take all these barbers. Every few weekends, they'll go to the old folks' home to cut the old folks' hair for free. If they had no ren qing wei, why would they do that? They could be at home watching television or drinking coffee, why would they go all the way to the old folks' home? It's not that people today don't have ren qing wei. Help if you can help, it's just how you help people.

Choo Ruizhi

Provision Shop Owner

My name is Kadir, 62 years old. I remember I come here from Bangladesh in 1994, working in plastic mould injections. After four years, the work also finish and in 1997 I start to open shops here. One here and one at another lorong. In 2000 I sell the other shop. For that one I get $23,000. Then I buy this unit here, the shop downstairs and the house upstairs. That one I get money from bank, $2.2 million. Now I already pay $900,000. So now still paying back, just work until die lah. [stops talking to give directions to a passerby in Chinese]

Twenty years here. Twenty years at Geylang Road. No off day. Seven days a week. Our shop here very long already. Last time from Lorong 40 until Lorong 1, maybe only one shop every 10 lorongs. So my shop feel like the only one here. Last time also a lot of companies rent house here, their Bangladeshi workers stay here also. So many will come to my shop. Then I open another shop two lorongs down. Because that time still have many customers. Some things I don't sell here – like soap, different vegetables, different drinks – I sell there. Because I cannot take care of two shops at one time, my sister become the boss there. Now she take care of the shop from start until finish. We now use different suppliers and sell different things. I only come to help if my sister calls me. She knows what she is doing.

I wake up every day at 9 o'clock. Makan, my wife cook for me. Then go out the house at 10 o'clock. Eleven o'clock I see my workers upstairs, then we open the shop together. I maybe go home afternoon to makan and to pray zohor and asar. If not, I also can pray upstairs. Evening, maybe also go home to makan and to pray maghrib. [two Sikh customers buy some cans of Red Bull and Kadir chats with them for some time in Punjabi]

If no more people, 11 o'clock I start close my shop. We cover the vegetables outside and tie the cover to the basket. Here have all kind of people, good people and maybe some thieves too. Sometimes they just take one or two onion or potato at night or maybe more and you know the next morning. [pats a rack with bread and other items] This one we push inside the shop then we close the shop. This other rack we put on my lorry. After that maybe I go upstairs and talk-talk with my workers, makan a bit then I drive my lorry go home.

You see, now no more business, no more queue. No more queue behind to buy beef. No more queue here to pay money. No more lorry queue wait for the Bangla men. Why? Because now so little Bangla men stay here. Now cannot stay Geylang anymore. Now must stay dormitory. At Tuas. So far. Who want to come here? Now also less people, but more shops. I don't know why still have people open shops. The shop opposite the road, they are also Bangla men. Last time they were workers also. But now they also no business. Now we have so much time to talk. Last time, three or four people waiting at the cashier. Now, you see?

I think the best years were 2005 to 2010. That time still have many Bangla workers stay here. For me, also easy. The foreign worker levy was $30. Now it's $650 for one person. Headache. Can you believe? Now next year they want to make the levy go up to $1,050. I don't know how next year. In Singapore, money is always running. See we nothing to do now, just talking. But you see the lights, the fans, the fridge? All money. Every minute, even if people don't buy anything, I still must pay.

[a customer walks in and gestures to the covered display rack behind the cash register. Kadir lifts the cover and after some back and forth the two are able to determine his preferred brand of cigarette] Now HSA (Health Sciences Authority) don't let us show the cigarettes anymore, this is what happens. Less business because less people buy cigarettes. Some want to buy cigarettes, also don't know the name. Like just now. So just point, point, point. Actually legally we cannot even lift the cover to let them point at the cigarette also. But we let them do it. If not, how to sell?

I become PR (permanent resident) first in 2000, then I become full citizen in 2010. What for keep Bangladesh passport? Singapore passport also can go Bangladesh. Now my two daughters, my family all here, more better to become Singapore citizen. More easier. Now I also stay HDB, resale flat. No, I am not sad. My wife is a Singaporean. I met her father at Geylang Serai Market before I start my business at Geylang. After that talk, talk, talk, then I marry my wife. My sister is PR, her husband Singaporean. I think she don't want to become Singapore citizen. Not so good also. At least she still have choice to go back if she want. Me? Must stay here and work, work, work.

Last year alhamdullilah my family went for umrah. The big Hajj? Oh no, I think that one you queue up 20 years, also cannot get. Because Singapore so small, one year only can send little bit people. More easy to go umrah, you can touch the ka'bah, less people. Like what I do. Syukur alhamdulillah, thanks to Allah, I can do it last year. Now my life, I have one big satisfaction already.

Now every last Saturday evening we help the mosque, help them cook and bring food. All the Bangla men will come. If you free, you also come lah. I know the imam. We always help him when we can. My workers and me also will help. Because why? Because from last time all the Bangla people will know our shop. Know me. So anything they ask and, if can, I will help.

From my kampung in Dhaka, people say this: when you still 20, you can do anything: smoke, drink, gamble, play, do all. When you 30, you start to get married. When you 40, you have children. When you 50, uncle, it's time for you to go back. Go back, uncle. So you know what go back means? Yes, that means anytime Allah can start to call you to go back. So when you grow old, your mind must change also.

Try Sutrisno Foo

Tissue Seller

I was born in 1949. I have seven or eight siblings. I am the second. Some die already. Old then will die mah. [laughs] I old already eh! I 60 something already eh! Cannot tell that I old meh? When I walk uh, my legs twist here, twist there. Sixty something already mah.

I sell tissue, no licence one. If want licence, must pay $120 a year leh! Later I never come then never sell, also must pay the licence money leh! Other people see us sell tissue then they also go and sell. Now a lot of people selling tissue. That's why now need licence. If not, don't need one! Those people got children got everything they also come out and sell.

[a passerby stops over to purchase the tissues. She hands Auntie $1 and Auntie offers her three packets but she only takes one] One dollar I give her one, $2 I give her two! [hearty laughter] Sometimes, people I got see before one will give me $3 or $4 and I will give them like this, one big stack. Now ah, coffeeshop $1 also cannot buy coffee. [picks up coffee and sips]

At night I don't sell. But morning have. Sell until about 3 plus then go home. Now seventh month (Hungry Ghost Festival) ah, don't want lah, don't want to stay late. I pantang (Malay: superstitious) lor. Earn a bit, can go home already, don't need to earn until how much, how much, then go. I got wear this bracelet so won't bump into those things (ghosts). I scared, early go back better … I never see before that thing. Choy, choy, choy!

You see my leg, [points at leg with multiple medicated plasters] inside here soft-soft one. Last time when I small never go doctor mah. Now, here soft-soft, no strength. When I walk, also will fall down one. So I use the umbrella to walk. This one hor, if never go doctor, later cannot walk eh. I now then know my leg got problem. I see the – not English (Western) doctor – the magic doctor.

See English doctor won't help one. Magic doctor got give me medicine. My friend bring me there one. One time, my leg cannot walk. Then the magic doctor was in other country. My friend give me money to go there. They bring me to take pills. This month I going again. Chinese doctor, the medicine cannot one leh. The god at the magic doctor will help us one. I pray to Buddha one. You pray to who? I got bring my pills. Come, I show you. This one very good one leh!

This one they bring me go other country get one, if not last year I cannot walk already. English doctor where got know how to heal? Everyone's body different, how they understand? This one is Thailand one. My friends give me a bit money to go see. Yah. I take this medicine. I take very long already. They will give you medicine and chant for you. Lucky they chant for my leg, if not I think I cannot walk anymore. After they chant, I feel healthier. Don't need eat those English medicine. Last time when I was young, I never go doctor, that's why my leg like this. If I had gone earlier, won't be like this already. Now this leg got strength already. Now I depend on this knee to walk.

I go Thailand for three or four days. The magic doctor temple is on the mountain. They all help me up, if not where got strength? This year gor ger chap gor (Hokkien: 15th day of the 5th month) they have big event. I am going. Go and let them chant-chant a bit. My friends ask me to earn a bit then go there. My friend's sister say that magic doctor very good at healing legs. They go there to treat leg before, got help.

This one ah, some people don't believe one. [points to church behind her] This church always ask people to go in one. What go heaven? Bluff you all one lah! Where got can go heaven one? You believe? You see my bracelet. This bracelet will bring protection. Let me walk properly, keep me safe. The magic doctor asked me, "How come you never wear any?" I wear these white strings is got chanted on before. Chant and keep me safe. Very good leh. Wear already, my business also better. If not where got business? Also let this leg got strength.

This church … they keep asking me to go in. I am Buddhist. Cannot! Cannot pray to Buddha and Jesus at the same time! We take joss sticks one, cannot believe in Jesus. Jesus is theirs, theirs! Jesus suit them, don't suit us mah. When we sick, Jesus also cannot help! Right or not? That Jesus: die already, where got anything? Those who believe in Jesus ah, when they die, they cannot eat the food outside. You know seventh month when they pray ah, the food they cannot eat one leh. That's why we cannot anyhow-anyhow mix Buddha and Jesus. You know there was this ah mah, she stays next door one. She pray to Guan Yin and then sometimes also got go church. And then hor, the god punished her! Made her fall down, waste money, go see doctor. Like this, warn her to not go church anymore. That's why, want to pray to Buddha then pray to Buddha, want Jesus then stay with Jesus. Cannot mix here, mix there. Cannot half-half one.

Actually, got a lot of people ask me to go find Jesus. But Jesus talk already will heal my leg meh? My doctor is do chanting one. Jesus where got chant? Jesus don't suit me. So I don't want lor. But Jesus suit others. Last time when I was small, 15 or 16 years old, I went with my friends to the church. Go there play-play lah. Then, never go already. Cannot lah, cannot. Buddha is better. If not uh, seventh month ah, next time I nothing to eat. [laughs] Very terrible, you know. They don't believe in hell but I believe! Aiyoh! By the time you believe ah, you reach there hor, too late already! [laughs loudly] That's why I don't want to go church. Many people call me to go. I just tell them no.

Last time when I was 20 something, I work in factory one. People in factory recommended me the job lor. They got make the T-shirt. Last time I young, I sew clothes one. In 1974, I worked in factory. I do random duties one. Got sew curtains, got tailor clothes. If they don't sew properly, we help to change. If they don't know how to thread the needle, we help to thread. Like this lor. Have machines also. All the jobs got people in charge one. One person in charge do random duties, one person iron clothes. But I don't sew for the boss. I sew for ourselves to wear one. Those sew for sales one, must be very nice. You know, last time this kind of T-shirt only a few cents, only 50 cents, 70 cents eh! Last time mah, last time 70 plus years ago.

Last time 1973, those times were better. Houses were bigger, money was big mah. Now, money so small. Now, no more that factory already. No business then closed down. The bosses also old already, don't want to do. Their son also don't care. At Geylang, Lorong 3, 1984 closed down. They run business very long already. Boss don't want to do, son don't want to do, they close lor. Then we all no more job.

After that, I go outside and do household jobs. Help people clean house, take care children. Wah! You don't know ah? I was 20 plus, 30 plus years old. I stay in the house, do work for them, eat there, live there. I wash children's clothes. Big people's clothes I don't need wash. They got hire another person to wash clothes, clean windows. I only need to bring children go out walk-walk, cook porridge for them, feed them. Like this lor. The children like three or four years old like this. Then the children big already, don't need me already. Every two weeks, I rest for one day, I can go back home. Like that lor. One month $15 or $20 something only leh. Now, no more. Now where got people need to hire this kind. Those times, very long ago already hor?

Then I also got wrap vegetables for living. Last time the people where got money to go school study? People will tell you what to do, how to do. Last time hor, no money one. Never study, everyone also never study. No money to go school. Government also never give money one. Where got people give money one? Never lah! Everything also don't have. Last time we want to take bus ah, 5 cents also no money. No money means never see doctor also lor. No money also never go school. Last time stay sua teng (Hokkien: rural area) mah. Stay that kind of attap chu (Hokkien: rattan house). The farming kind. Then we use wood to cook. Now change into Yishun already. That one last time is kampung one. Government keep chasing people to move house, move house. Chase already then ask us to go HDB. Our kampung attap chu, government got pay us a little bit and then ask us go buy HDB. Last time kampung got pigs, ducks, farm vegetables one. Never lie to you.

Now the people very xian nang (Hokkien: to have it easy; derived from Malay senang: easy) hor? Last time people very young, need to work already eh. Last time, people got money can go school but don't know how to study. No money ones never go to school, so also never study. That's why got a lot of people end up never study lor. Now the kids all good life hor? Last time don't have one. Very young, must work already. Some more don't have much to eat. Never work means nothing to eat.

Now the girls all power. They know to not give birth to so many. Give birth already still need to feed, need to take care. A lot of work one. Now government not enough people, that's why they keep asking people to give birth and then give them money. Last time people stupid mah, give birth to so many then not enough for the family to eat. You see now the Chinese families, all only have one or two children. If give birth to more ah, the han bao bao (Mandarin: hamburger) must divide into many pieces to share. Now eat anything also expensive eh, where got people want more children? Malay families are very big. I think next time ah, more Malays than Chinese already.

I never get married. Don't care lah! Ownself earn, ownself eat, enough already. Last time I got meet someone I like but I scared later not enough to eat then die ah. Don't want lah. Then I told him don't want. I told him next time our house need this, need that, and then need to buy things and then will start quarrelling already, then divorce. So we broke up. If not ah, if get married, later he no money, I no money then confirm quarrel one. Isn't that worse? Last time people is like that lor. No money, they fight. If fight, then each go their own way. I tell him break up then he said don't want, then don't want lor. Now I old already, take care of ownself better. At night also xian nang lor, got freedom. If not ah, need to take care of children. My mother got nagged at me but I didn't want to get married. Now, she die already. I live together with my friend, the one who brought me to Thailand. My friend divorced already lah! [laughs as if point has been proven] Yah lor, just like this. I have a godson. Last time I stay with him at Nee Soon. But he big already, got his own family, then never contact already. Like this, then I also don't want him already. He also don't miss me.

So I moved out and stay at Lavender. The rent is $50 every month. Electricity use more, pay more. If you have children, government won't let you stay. They press the computer a few buttons, they know already. Cannot bluff them one. I never take government's money. I will save, then slowly pay the rent. Sometimes, I lunch don't eat then go home eat. Not to stay sexy but go home cook, cheaper. I every day cook, like that better mah. Kopi? Wa kao! (Hokkien expletive.) So expensive. I come here sell tissue, will bring my coffee and bread. Save money lor. Sometimes eat out can lah, but cannot every day. Now, I ownself earn, ownself eat lor. Don't want to think about the past anymore. I don't regret anything.

Charmaine Tan

RECYCLING AND CLEANING

CHAPTER FIVE

RECYCLING AND CLEANING

Karung Guni Man

Well my job is nothing much lah. I'm just a waste collector. Collect rubbish one lor. I just collect different items.

Heartache. My heart really aches. My legs are really painful. They aren't able to carry my weight for long. Both my legs were previously broken. This leg, [points to right leg] there are titanium screws in it. My legs are unequal in length. One is long and the other is short. Walking requires a lot of effort, and I have take a break every 50 metres.

I used to be a lorry driver. One day while driving, I had to stop to shift these heavy metal pipes. The metal pipes dropped and fell on my legs. Thankfully, there were other workers who noticed that the driver in the lorry was missing, and came over to check on me. They called for the ambulance immediately when they saw me.

There are 7 litres of blood in a person's body, and I was left with just one. When they wheeled me into the operating theatre I was still conscious, and thankfully I woke up four hours after the operation. The doctor said that some people fail to wake up even after four days.

As for me, even though I woke up, it felt like my soul had already departed from my body.

The doctor gave me an MC valid for six years. And I have to take medication every day, even up until now. More than 10 types of medicine. But I received $40,000 in compensation. I was employed by a relative's friend, so thankfully he did give me compensation. After the operation I was unable to walk and kept lying down on the bed. This gave me bedsores. When I got better, I began to take on this job of collecting rubbish.

Such is life.... This is fate lor. In the past, when I was still schooling, our Chinese teacher got us to write a composition. And so I wrote, "I would like to be a road sweeper when I grow up." Indeed I am helping to clear rubbish now.

I collect items in this area every day. Usually I will work till about 5 or 6 p.m. To sell the items, I have to first classify them. It is really troublesome. For example, there are 16 categories for plastic. Sixteen different types! All the items have to be completely dismantled into the smallest parts possible. Only when items have been classified would we find buyers for these things. Otherwise, they will not buy from us. I sell my items at Defu Lane, to companies involved in the scrap metal business. Before that, I have to find a friend to share a lorry for transporting the items. Without a lorry, there is no way to transport the items to Defu Lane.

I collect newspapers as well, and after I have collected them I will split the profits with the auntie. Each of us gets half the profits. On Sunday, I will go and pick up empty beverage cans from another auntie. I pay her 70 cents for 1 kilogram of empty cans. And then I'll sell it for $1. I only earn 30 cents in profits from this transaction, but the auntie has an even more challenging time. She has to go to the coffee shops to look for cans, and then flatten all the cans so they don't take up excess space.

Everyone needs to earn a living, so I cannot sell my items at a high price. When I sell things to other people, they also wish to make a profit before selling it off again to someone else. And the transactions go on and on till the items are sold to a big factory. I'm not able to sell directly to a big factory, because it is located very far away, in Jurong. So I will only use the lorry to transport the items to Defu Lane – which is nearer – for sale. I don't exactly earn much each month ... at most $200.

I have three sons, and they do support me financially. I chose not to retire. If a person does not work, he falls sick easily. And the doctor has advised me to walk more. If not, my leg will get worse and it will have to be amputated.

Okay, it's getting late so I should go home now. Thank you for your questions.

Candy Lee

Part-time Cleaner

I'm Singaporean, but some people think I'm Malaysian. My parents are Singaporean. My father was born in Malaysia, but it was easy to get into Singapore back then. They had five children. I am the youngest. My father already passed away. My mother ... I don't want to go into it because I don't know how she's doing now. Very sad to say. There's a saying in Chinese, "Fate will bring people together no matter how far away they may be." Society nowadays though, when someone has money and you don't, there is a divide. Some people are very good, they don't care whether you have money or they have money, they would still keep in touch with you. But me, I haven't talked to my family in many years.

How old do you think I am? Over 50? Do I look that old? [laughs] I'm over 45. To be honest, my life is not very good. I have a lot of part-time jobs, cleaning jobs most of the time, because right now there's very few moving jobs available. They take a lot of foreigners for these jobs, for example, a lot from China or from Bangladesh and India. It's the locals that are cleaners. Some have been doing it for a while, and they continue to do it. But there's not that many young people doing it, because they have all been to school, they have degrees. Who would want to do such a rough and tiresome job? They would rather do restaurant and hotel jobs. They hire a lot of young people, I can't do it because I'm getting old.

As for full-time jobs, depends on what kind of jobs you're looking for, your level of education and skills. It's not that there aren't any. There's a lot in the newspapers, for example, there's a lot of ads looking for cleaners, jobs that people don't want to do. The pay is too low. It's gotten better this year because the government has said the wages must be at least $1,200 a month, but some companies still give less than $1,200. I've seen them. You can report them, but whether you will be successful, I don't know. Right now the Ministry of Manpower has been ... how to say? You can quit your job and report them, but how long you would have to wait? Can you get reimbursed? That's not certain. You can report them to the ministry but what will that do for you?

People ask me why I don't switch to full-time. I don't have a choice, really. I need money every day. I smoke, and I eat all three meals outside. If I had a stable job, I'd need to wait two weeks to get paid. If I don't get paid within three days I will have financial difficulties. I won't even be able to buy a pack of cigarettes. That's why I have done only part-time jobs for a couple of years now.

Take this pack of cigarettes I have for example, the government tax is about $7. This pack of cigarettes is $10, the government takes about $7. I've thought about quitting but I can't. I've been smoking for over 20 years. Before there used to be small packages, only 10 cigarettes, now they stopped selling those. It's all packets of 20 cigarettes now.

Sometimes, one pack is not even enough to last me a whole day. So, I need to do part-time jobs every day. Right now, I can get the money immediately after I finish my work. People say even if you work for 10 years like this, you cannot save any money. It's true. But I have no choice, I can only think about the present first.

To be honest, I'm not a very frugal person, not like some people. Some from China are very frugal, because they don't have a choice. They all cook for themselves and pack their own meals to work. They never go out to eat. Some of them will even be like, "Hey, you want to treat me to food?" They have to be like this, they don't have a choice. They have to mail the money back to their family, some have children. I don't have this type of stress but I still need to make a living. If you don't have a stable job, there will be a lot of tension between you and your spouse and you will fight a lot. It might even end in a divorce later, a lot of them end like this.

Us cleaners, we wait at a place for work. Do you know Little India? A little above Little India, some governmental blocks. You might have passed it. Do you know the neighbourhood police station there? It's just over there. There are two government buildings, we go over there to wait for jobs in the morning. We wait for the managers. I heard the others say that there used to be a lot of jobs – renovators, wall painters, movers. Now there are fewer jobs. There are a lot less in these few years, because there are a lot of foreigners working in Singapore right now. They don't need to hire so many part-time workers anymore. There are a lot of cleaning jobs there, occasionally moving jobs, but I can't do moving jobs anymore because I am getting old. Anyway, there the cars will pass by asking: "Do you want jobs?" I've been there for quite some time so I know a few managers. It's just the few of them. They will come every day. Some cleaning companies are very large, you might of heard of it, called ISS. It's an international company. Its boss is said to be a Westerner, but they seem to have a lot ... a lot ... how should I say this? For example they have little bosses, they're all over the world. There is a lot in Singapore, for example, the central hospital is theirs. Cleaners all belong to their company. Last time they come every day to pick up people; they can pick up more than 10 at once. They haven't come these two years.

After 8:30 a.m. there are few cleaning jobs left. We have to come very early. Sometimes when the car comes, all the people are waiting and they will ask the manager, "Is today alright? I want to do work. Do you need people? I can." There are few females there, not saying that there are none, but there are more males. Maybe females would feel a bit more embarrassed. To be honest, being a cleaner now ... if you need to look for jobs, open a newspaper and you'll find some. Why do I go down there to wait for jobs? Because I can get paid daily. That's the good part because I need money every day. Sometimes if I don't work for two or three days, for example tomorrow is Sunday, I don't work and I didn't work today, so I will need to wait till Monday. So it might be alright that I don't work these two days because I worked till late yesterday, I still have a bit of money. If I still don't work on Monday, then I will start to have difficulties again.

To be honest, if you asked me to do cleaning work back then, I would definitely refuse. Because being a cleaner here is the same as everywhere – it is the lowest class of work, the lowest. Except for those that beg for money, that is. Being a cleaner is the lowest class of work, a lot of people look down upon us. It's the same with those that wash dishes outside. They are all considered dirty work. Some people will even look down on you. People look down upon me, but what can I do? When I first started doing this work I was a little embarrassed, but now I'm used to it.

I studied in Singapore, where else can I go? I don't remember what I've studied. I stopped going to school after secondary school. How could I have gone to university? I did delivery and moving jobs after that. I also did waitering jobs in hotels. I was only in my teens when I started coming out and doing rough labour, because Singaporeans have to do National Service. Those with money can study abroad. As long as you have money, you can do this. Ever since I was little, my family was not well-off. I'll tell you this, I used to live here when I was a child, across from this building on the eighth floor. I've lived here at my current building since 2004. When I was little, my mum and dad also lived here. They've also moved to other places. Before here, do you know Bukit Ho Swee? We lived there. The buildings there were even worse than the ones here. They didn't even have toilets inside, it was all outside, very dirty. These buildings here were built in the 1970s. It's been a while, they are all very old. This one over there [points] is said to be here even longer, it's been here since the 1960s. Some people look at houses here and they don't even want to live here because it's not clean.

These apartments over here, they are rented. Now the government is encouraging people to buy apartments. It's not expensive to rent these apartments. Right now my rent is a little over $40 for a month, comparatively cheap. The rent has already increased quite a few times. It used to be a little over $30. There are no bedrooms inside, just one hall. For you rich people, this money is not even enough for meals spent in fancy restaurants, which costs hundreds. Plus alcohol that some of the big bosses drink.

There are other places like this in Singapore for rent. For example down the hill there. That side is a bit more crowded, because there are markets and restaurants. It's quieter here, because we're on top of a hill. There's a secondary school here, Outram Middle School.

There are homeless people in Singapore who sleep outside. For

example, I have a friend from my cleaning work, he doesn't have a home. He used to have a house, but he sold his house and got a bit of money. Some use that money to gamble, some use it on women. They don't really treasure the money and just kept spending it, gambling. In a few years, their money will be all gone. I don't even have this chance, to have a house to sell. If I did, I think I'd sell it too. [laughs]

To be honest, I don't even know how to use a cell phone right now. [laughs] Right now if you tell others you don't have a cell phone, they'll laugh at you. They don't believe me. When I am working, the manager will say, "I'll call you to contact you." I tell them I don't have a phone and they say, "That's impossible right, you can't not have a phone because it's so widespread." I say: "I really don't have a cell phone." They say, "If I need you for work in the future how can I contact you?" I say: "That's not a problem, if you give me your phone number I will call you." It's as if they don't believe me when I say that I don't have a cell phone.

I don't know how to do anything, all I know is how to smoke. How tragic. I've wasted a lot of time. The road is for you to walk, how you walk it, it's up to you. That's why happiness is in your own hands. If you haven't grasped your future while you were young, like me, now I can't find a good job, I can't earn more money. If I used more time when I was young to think about my future, maybe I won't be a cleaner now. But some people, due to various reasons may fall down. Some people may be a very high manager but end up falling down. But I am different. I didn't grasp my future when I was young. I am not the bookish type, but I could have done other good things, I haven't thought about it. I just didn't care too much, just did my part-time jobs. It's the same right now. I don't want to regret anything, there is no use in regretting anything.

Ting Zhang

Full-time Cleaner

Oh, first to introduce myself? Sit down, please, you can sit down. [indicates an empty table] My name is Xia. My family name is Wu. I never went to school, so I'm not sure how to write it; it's quite complex. If I had my passport I could show you. I'm 52 years old and I'm from Jinlin Province in China. I'm a farmer. I've farmed since I was a little child. You know, these days farmers earn less and less. And my family's financial situation isn't very good. So I went out for work. First I went to Guangdong Province and then I came here.

Before coming here, people told me that Singapore was nice and I could earn money quickly. Honestly, I'd never even heard of this country before. My …[considers how to characterise the relationship] friend asked me whether I wanted to come here or not. They asked me several years ago, but at that time I didn't agree. Then last year, they came to persuade me again. They said, "At home, you work. There, you work. What's the difference?" It seemed reasonable, so I agreed. My friend gave their company my information and they arranged a work pass so I could come here. I had to pay a fee, which was about 30,000 yuan (about $6,000). I paid for it in one lump sum. That's the same as a half-year's wages working here. After a few days of work, I felt regret. Working in China, I only need to pay for transport or sometimes for having dinner outside. But in Singapore, I have to pay the agency fee. So the truth is I work for half a year without actually earning any money.

I've been working in Singapore for nearly one year now. At first, I worked at a soybean processing plant. Depending on what had to be done, I cleaned the plant or tidied up the machines. We actually spent about four or five hours per day working. The rest of time we could sit down or walk around to see if there was something that needed to be tidied up. It was a very easy job. Not like here. Working here, my feet are swelling and numb.

Here, I have to work from 7 in the morning to 10 in the evening. I don't have any time to rest. It's very strict. And it's not just my manager who controls me. I can sit down here with you for a few minutes, but it can't be too long or else a customer will take a photo and make a complaint. Here, anyone can control me, even a little child. Who can bear that? Is it so wrong when I'm tired and I just want to sit down for a while?

The first thing I do after reaching here in the morning is to prepare my trolley. It's nothing much, really. Then I begin to walk around and clean the tables. Even if there are only one or two bowls, you still need to go and pick them up. And don't sit down. Don't. Sit. Down. That's it. You just don't sit down. If anyone catches me sitting down or complains, my salary will be deducted. It costs $20 each time. Once for $20, twice for $40. How can I afford that? Anyone can make a complaint on me. Everyone can control me here.

Sometimes when I get too tired, I'll eat something. You can't complain me for having dinner, right? [laughs] But we can't eat for too long and only when it's not crowded. Otherwise, you just have to bear the hunger. [looks around for her manager, then leaves briefly and returns with a pear that she offers to share]

There's a large gap between the Singaporean cleaners and us. I earn $2 or $3 per hour, while they earn $6 or $7. [eats a mouthful of pear] They work eight hours a day, while we have to work for 15 hours a day. We only have one day off per month, and we don't have vacations or overtime pay or insurance. Compared with here, working in China is much easier.

But life is hard for Singaporeans too. Look at the local cleaners. [gestures around the hawker centre] Some of them are in their 80s. Their government doesn't offer them social insurance, and they didn't save money when they were young. They spent as much as they earned and ate out all the time. And they like drinking coffee or tea, so a meal for them costs $5 or $6, doesn't it? If they don't work, they'd have to sleep on the street. And if they get sick and go to the hospital, it will cost them a lot. They lose not only the salary for the day, but also several more days of salary to pay for the medical bill. For us, we just use the medicine from China if we feel ill.

I can save $800 to $1,000 per month. Ordinarily, I don't spend money. The dormitory is paid for by the company as well as the bus that picks us up and takes us home. But the company doesn't cover our meals. There is some space for us to cook in our dormitory. Sometimes, I ask the stall owners for some vegetables that they can't sell, and then cook them for my meal. By doing that, I can save some money. If I ate out every day, I would spend my entire salary. If I lived like that, then what reason would there be to work?

There are not many people in one dormitory, sometimes four people or sometimes five. It's not too crowded, but it's really dirty. [twitches her mouth with disgust] People live there but never clean it. At the beginning, there were only cockroaches and mosquitoes, but later the bedbugs came. [puts down the remainder of the pear and rolls up sleeve to show strings of bites] I use some medicine from China, but it does nothing. And it's easy to lose your things in the dormitory. If you have something I like, I won't ask for it. I'll just steal it when you're gone.

In our room, there are all kinds of people, from India, from Malaysia, from Vietnam, and also from China. No, we don't talk with each other in our spare time. After we get back to the dormitory, we just wash our face, have a bath, clean our clothes, prepare the meal for the next day, and go to sleep. How can we have time to speak to others? You think we don't need to sleep? We have to get up at 5:30 in the morning, and then we wash our face, comb our hair, go to the toilet, everything. Even at 5:30 we still need to wait in the queue. If you don't get up early and all the people get up at the same time, you may not have the opportunity even to go to the toilet.

My husband and son are in China, but I don't miss them very much. When I have spare time, I might give them a call. I may not be able to write a letter, but at least I should know how to call someone. [laughs] Actually, I don't have time to be homesick. I haven't built a relationship with the other Chinese who work here. I don't really care where they're from; it's none of my business. We're not young anymore, so we don't care much about gossiping or making friends. We just do our work.

[checks to see if her manager is watching her, then sits down again] In China, I worked eight hours a day and earned 4,000 yuan per month (approx. SGD810). But here, I have to work 15 hours a day, and earn just 6,000 yuan (approx. SGD1,210). On top of that, I have to pay the agency fee. I really should have stayed in China. I'll go home after I finish my contract. And then I'll find a job near home. Maybe I can have spare time to walk around after work. Won't it be better than staying here? People who have never worked abroad all say that foreign countries are better, that the wages are higher. But they don't consider the higher prices or the working conditions. It is true that we can save money here, but that's just because we only have time to work and no time to spend.

Tan Zhuorui

Cemetery Caretaker

This is my one and only job here in Singapore. Most times I come here for 10 days. I usually come to Singapore nearing big festivities like Hari Raya. Sometimes it is because my kids need money for school. My work at Batam sometimes there is, other times there isn't. It's a contract job to build houses. That is if there is project. Therefore, sometimes we get income, other days it's quiet.

My wife works. They call it UKM (Bahasa Indonesia: usaha kecil menengah – small and medium enterprise). Every day she makes this thing called kerepek kari (Bahasa Indonesia: flavoured crackers). The ingredients come from the sea like gong-gong, udang. My wife works with someone and gets orders from them. If I want to rely on just that, especially to get supplies for my children's school, it's not enough. Hence, we sometimes come to Singapore so we can set aside some money for their food or school supplies. But alhamdulillah, that day when we came over to get for my children electronics such as laptop, I got to buy them. That explains why I come back every time to do these jobs like cutting the grass of graves, tidying up the graves for the families.

We don't want to target the price. We leave it to them. Any amount they are willing to pay us, we accept with much gratitude. We just accept their kindness. So, alhamdulillah every time I go back, there will be some profits. Working here for 10 days, we get about $400 or $200 or $300. At least $200, insyallah. That is sustenance from Allah. We cannot do anything much. This is all that we can afford to do. If we were to convert the currency, $200 would already mean millions there. Even if we were to deduct the ferry costs, it will still be worth it. Ferry costs barely $16. This is already very good. Sometimes I do get $500. Sometimes $600. In that 10 days. Depends if there's a lot of people, if they come and want us to tidy it up, alhamdulillah we get some money. But we can only hope for such luck during big festivities; other days sometimes when we come here it is not worth it. Like God has promised … what He desires happens if He wants it to happen. So we should leave it to the Almighty.

We only do these jobs here in Muslim cemeteries unlike those Bangladeshis. We are Muslims so we cater to just Muslims. While we do our job here, we want to do religious deeds too. We get sincere money from the people and blessings. The Bangladeshis do everywhere especially during this season, what the Chinese, call Qing Ming. They sometimes act like they're crying so that they get more money. Chinese are willing to pay a lot. But I do this job as religious deeds although I do get money from it.

Even when I am here, I face no problem surviving. I sometimes rent a place in Boon Lay or Masjid Pusara Aman. At the mosque, we will help with the upkeeping. For example, we sweep the premise and sometimes even recite the azan. In fact, there's not a lot of us nowadays. Especially with Singapore combining the old graves, there's less work to do here. These old graves probably have no owners anymore. But I wonder if they combine all the corpses or still have special exceptions for prominent people. I heard there are such exceptions given to government officials. Maybe one day Singapore should send their corpses over to Batam. Land is cheaper there and I don't have to keep on returning here. [laughs and shakes head ruefully]

I have two children in Batam. One is in secondary school, studying Islam. The other is already in pre-university – technical school. Sometimes, in this field of study, university education may not be needed. Even at this level, they are sought after by companies in Malaysia, Singapore. That time she worked for a company based in Taiwan to develop an app. However, my daughter does not own a passport yet. So, for her to go abroad for work, not so soon.

Even for me when I first came to Singapore it was try-try lah. This was in the year 2006. I was then 42 years old but it was my first time going abroad. That was the first time I had a passport. I felt a bit out of place until my friends introduced me to some grave contractors here. Then I realised that there were locals who did the same job as me. Just that they are under a company. From there on, we got to know each other and the bond becomes very close. There is no clear

demarcation of this area belonging to me and that belonging to you. But for most of us, so long as you are good to each other insyallah there's no jealousy between us. If we have the heart and spirit to be closer to God, there is no competition between us. But if we do bad with each other, want to eat alone, be selfish, of course locals will be angry. But all these won't happen if we are fair. Everything will be peaceful.

Ultimately, we Malays from Kepri and Malays from Singapore once shared the same roots, our ancestors were together. So, on that aspect we are not that different. [pauses] Just that of course now our economic status is different. For example, in Batam we don't have this service of cutting grass. We just do it ourselves. It is part of our visiting practices. It's also because of economy, I think. To compare Batam and Singapore, we just can't compare in terms of economy. If the people there were to pay for these services, they will be thinking, "I might be able to buy salt with this money."

I don't come to Singapore to be rich. I just need enough for my children to go to school without having to think about money. I want them to follow their aspirations. Unlike many of my people, I just need enough for my children.

Said Effendy

CARING

CHAPTER SIX

CARING

Maid

My name is Suryanti. I'm 39 years old and I'm from Jawa Tengah, Indonesia. I spent eight years working as a maid. Back at home, I worked … normally … like going to the farm and selling vegetables at the market. I got to know this job from the Indonesian maid agency. I want to work here because it's good and have protection from the MOM. So if anything happens, the MOM will protect us. I told my family I want to work in Singapore because I want to find more money to provide for the kids' education. So I want to work here as long as my body is strong enough and I can still take it.

I like this job, alhamdulillah. My first employer was a Malay … actually all the families I've worked for are Malays. All of them are quite nice. Except for one … but I still finished my contract. She was fierce like a lion. Her house was two floors and she's very particular about cleanliness. She feeds me enough though. Just that her mouth … talks a lot. If she screams, one whole block can hear. Always fight. But very fast okay. Sometimes the employer you get is not nice. I worked for a few not so nice employers before. Some of them like to scream at me until the whole block can hear. Some of them don't give me enough food. I need food to have energy to work mah.

I also had this employer who asked me to buy things using my own money. Sometimes they give me $10 to buy groceries but where got enough? I don't mind using my own money but sometimes I don't even have enough. Sometimes also they accuse me of not feeding the elderly in the house. When my employer's kids argue, also they like to point at me. I feel sad because it's like they're my kids but they're so rude to me.

I everything okay. Take care of old people okay, cook also okay, clean house okay, take care of kids also okay. Sometimes kids naughty and difficult to discipline. But what I like the most about here is taking care of the kids. It reminds me of my kids. I treat them like my own.

I was married and I have two kids. Now I'm divorced. I already had kids before coming here. My husband and the rest of my family also encouraged me to come here. I don't have parents. When I first came here my mum was still alive, but now I don't have a mother anymore. She fell sick. So when I go back I'll stay with my little sister. [pauses] I can't talk about my family much to be honest. [tears up] I can't talk much about my kids too. It's not that I miss my kids a lot … but I get reminded of the past and … quite hard to talk about it.

I keep in contact with my family via the phone. Sometimes Facebook, sometimes normal call. Usually we just use Facebook messenger. With my kids, I use WhatsApp. But I'm not really close to my kids. Because my husband has the custody of the kids and he's now remarried. My kids have grown up a lot. My daughter is 20 and my son is 14. I can't talk much about my kids … I will cry. It wasn't always like this; last time I was quite close to my kids when they were still schooling but after their father remarried we became quite distant. But I still give them money for school, buy for my son motorbike. I don't think my kids knew the exact reason why I got a divorce lah, because they follow the dad. I think they trust the dad more.

I'm divorced because my husband didn't trust me when I'm here.

He said all sorts of thing like I go see other man lah, this lah, that lah. I didn't even have a handphone. I gave everything I earned last time to him. I was stupid then. He wanted a motorbike and I gave him everything I had … it cost me four months' worth of my salary. I didn't even have an off day. But I gave him everything because I was stupid lah. When I went back to Indonesia, I stayed with my mum. My husband did look for me but I didn't want to see him anymore. Because he didn't trust me. So I decided I don't want it already. After that I came back to Singapore to work again. But I worked part-time three times a week, clean people's houses. I didn't work under a permit then. I was under tourist visa. Then I looked for agency and that's how I met my employer Ibu Sakinah, who was a trainer at the maid agency.

There are some Bangla men who want me but I don't want lah. Don't need like that lah, we are here to find work. Some of my friends want Bangla but, aiyah, I don't ask them why lah, I'm not that kaypoh (Hokkien: busybody). Some of the maids also smoke, drink … they're Muslims though. Sometimes I will take photo of them do indecent things and put on Facebook. [smirks] I posted one just now of a maid in tudung laying down on the Bangla lap. Come on lah, that doesn't look nice what. Not good. Might as well take off the tudung. This one wear the tudung and jubah. Some wear like artist, wear boots lah, wear miniskirts. I don't like people like that. We must remember who we are here. We are maids here. Just wear normally lah. Like me I just wear normal T-shirts and jeans. In my eight years here, I never even wear like that.

I love to play netball and volleyball at Kallang during my off days with my friends. Sometimes I go karaoke. I like. I got to know my friends from Facebook and the internet. Then we exchange numbers and discuss when to meet. I don't usually go hang out with the other maids at Lucky Plaza lah, City Plaza … I've never even been there!

I don't think people look down on our jobs. But, we maids, always say if you are Indonesian maid, don't work for Indonesian family. If you are Filipino, then don't work for Filipino family. I don't know, they will think that they are better than us. The pay also not that good. Amongst the maids also got class. First Filipino, then us, then I think the Myanmar. I think because Filipino maids can speak English, that's why they can also do retail. Sometimes their pay goes up to $700 if they work with Mat Salleh (Malay: Caucasian) or Chinese lah. Malays not so much. [laughs] They no money. For us, $600 is good enough.

Work here, last time and now also very different. The government stricter. If we come now, we must have more certification and it's quite hard. Last time easier. Ibu also say now is harder to come in. Now also got more protection from government and more rights. Last time, we don't have off day. If you're lucky, you get once a month. Now we have off day at least twice a month. And also have handphone. Some maids say they can work here without off day and handphone but after working for a month they start demanding for more things. Want handphone lah, want off day lah. This one is maid fault lah. But sometimes also employers' fault. When it comes to food sometimes also not enough. Maid never eat enough food but also stupid, don't want to tell the employer.

Now at Ibu Sakinah's house, I clean, sometimes I cook. But if she brings in maids to train for the agency, I will help her teach them how to do things. The commission (for bringing in new maids from Indonesia) is the one that brings in more money for me. I already bought land in Indonesia twice. About $8,000. [beams] Now no need to give husband money, so I keep everything. Except for my little sister and kids. Recently also I could contribute to pay for the korban (Islamic sacrificial ritual that is part of Eid Al-Adha) for Hari Raya Haji. My sir also increases my pay a bit – a bit every year. But pity him also because he has kids.

Sometimes maid have good ones and not good ones. Make problem. That time I brought in a maid – when I take a maid I will usually interview through phone first and tell them what the employer looks for and see if they're okay with it. Sometimes they say yes, can, but after two weeks she said she want to go back. I'm quite hot tempered so if maids ask to go back quick, I will ask them to pay penalty fee. So, for that maid, I threatened her husband. [laughs] I like to threaten, "If you don't give me the money, I will send your wife to Batam to be a prostitute!" I don't care. I get my money. When I interview maid, they call me ma'am. [laughs] I should open a maid agency there and partner with Ibu since I liaise a lot of things for the maids, it's like I work in an office! I still have 15 people on the waiting list to be a maid. But now maids not good. Not good like last time. Now they want off every week!

Got maid also want to kill themselves. There was a maid training here who wanted to jump down from the second floor. Like sinetron (Indonesian soap opera) lah. Cry got no tears all. She accused Ibu Sakinah of taking her money. Honestly, I don't like it when people talk bad of her or the agency. I dragged her from the window and threw her back inside. If she die, she die lah. I don't care.

Some maids also marry their employer. I got two friends who ended up marrying their employer. One of them – the male employer who divorce the wife and looked for her after. I think they had something going on last time lah, but he was still married then. But now they together. She PR already after a year. Now she is working as a cashier at Guardian. She's happy lah, the pay also more than being a maid. Her husband had three kids from his previous marriage – she also has one of her own but her husband made her send her kid back to Indonesia. He say there's no one to take care of the baby here. Quite bad.

Another one work for Chinese employer. They also had something lah. Then he went to Indonesia with her and married her there. But she still come back and work for him and the wife. The wife still doesn't know. Wah, I don't think I can live like that. If my husband kiss the wife, I will get jealous. But she say sometimes she jealous, sometimes she's not lah. She say the money is good. I don't think I can ever do that – share husband. I don't think I will get married actually … I quite old. I don't want marry younger man. But … if Singaporean want me and older than me, of course I want.

When I was younger, I wanted to be a policewoman. But my mum didn't have money to put me into the police academy. Now I have money but I'm old so they won't take me also. Maybe if I go back I will work in nursing home. But the pay maybe $300, here I work $600. Better I work in Singapore.

Nur Qistina Binte Ahmad

Stay-at-home Father

Was I destined for medicine? Well first, I wanted to be an inventor or a professor, and then I wanted to be either a doctor or a vet. My father convinced me that being up at 3 in the morning to see a sick cow in a field was less attractive than doing cutting-edge medicine in a hospital. And as it is, through these last few years I think being up in a field at 3 in the morning seeing a sick cow would be far more advantageous than working in a highly litigious occupation that people don't respect as they once did. But we make our choices and we make the most of them.

So yeah, my dad is a generalist within medicine, and now I'm an intensivist, a specialist in critical illness. In a sense though, I'm still a generalist, just within the most severe parts of health. You have to have a foot in each camp of surgery and medicine and infection. And that suits my mentality, because I get quite excited when things are very, very wrong and I enjoy fixing them, and then the longer-term, deep, critical thought I can leave to specialists. The joy of A&E is that you do 95 per cent of the detective work very, very quickly and then you hand a lot of the buffing and shining to other people.

Within medicine I consider myself a sort of high-end drifter. I've done the MRCP (Membership of the Royal Colleges of Physicians) medical examinations, the anaesthetic examinations, and the intensive care exams. Oh, and I've got a diploma in tropical medicine, and that's unusual with these other specialties. So I guess that makes me a high-end generalist in an era of super specialisation.

Why so many? I looked at who I was and I realised that what I enjoyed was world health, and I felt that people are very siloed in the UK, and that a lot of good can be done by doing health care projects in the rest of the world, and so it seemed like a good investment at the time. And it's also a break from anaesthesia, which can be very much a production line. Mainly, though, I was afraid of being pigeonholed into certain areas, so my investment of time in exams was so that I could have more freedom in the future to do interesting things.

We came to Singapore three months ago. I originally met my partner when I was doing a residency in Australia, and she came back to the UK with me, and then after London we moved to another city for my work. She's shown great generosity in her willingness to move to suit my will, and so when she got offered an amazing job here, we agreed that this time we'd follow her career and it would be my turn to put something together.

I've just been accepted to MSF (Médecins Sans Frontières, or Doctors Without Borders), so hopefully I can do a global health project with them sometime soon. One of the things I like about MSF is that they're an organisation that goes to a country and does health projects, but they also report how things are to the rest of the world. So you can improve things on a policy level, or at least be a witness. My hope would be to be based in Singapore, but do short-term placements abroad. Certainly, now that I've got a family, these short-term placements are a good option. And then later on, when my partner's job might be different, we can think about a long-term project somewhere else.

But you know the Eastern saying? The one that says you start off wanting to change the world but you end up just wanting to change your garden? I'm now approaching the age when you realise that changing global health is a massive thing and it's more politically and economically driven than a single doctor, and it's difficult to know your place within that.

I've also applied to NUH (National University Hospital). In the past, the Singaporean system was very open to expats. More recently they've realised that they have excellent home-grown doctors, so there's a move to fill jobs with their own people. So now someone like me has to prove I have a skill set that they need and that can't be filled by a local. While we're waiting to see how that goes, I'm being a stay-at-home father.

Our son goes to preschool from 9 a.m. to 1 p.m., so that means I drop him off and I can get a bit of work done, then I pick him up and he has a sleep, and then it's playtime until mum gets home. I very much like Labrador Park or Botanical Gardens, bug hunting or going to the play areas there. Sometimes we go for indoor stuff, but not much. Then my partner gets home and we have dinner together. It's never before 5:30, and sometimes it's after 7. Bedtime for our son is at 8, so she's always there to see him before bed. Her industry is famous for long hours, but she makes sure she sees him in the evenings on the whole. And then she may do some work after he's gone to bed. Or she's doing some work in the morning while I'm looking after him. But even if I'm primary caregiver these days, he does love his mum a lot, so whenever she's in the house he does tend to monopolise her.

She doesn't go in to work on the weekends, but sometimes I'll take our son out and she'll have to do a few hours of work here and there. But on the whole, weekends are quite free. Of course, we had lots to do in Singapore when we first arrived, but lately we've begun to stretch out a bit. So, a couple of weekends ago we were over in Bintan, and this last weekend we were in Angkor. And then next week I'm taking advantage of my freedom to take the little guy to see my wife's family in New Zealand. But for the most part we're just having adventures in Singapore, you know, a day trip to the zoo, or Sentosa.

The thing about caring for a child is how everything seems to be urgent and important. There's no such thing as patience with a young one. Everything has to be pre-planned, you have to have everything to hand, ready to go. And the number of different thoughts that you have to have, trying to micromanage someone who's potentially not looking after themselves, or doing dangerous things, is really wearing. It's like driving a tanker truck, you know? The constant stress, the constant need to make these tiny adjustments. You get to the end of the day and you're exhausted.

The other thing that you kinda stumble across as a parent is that it's not your job to tell them how to be, it's your job to be excellent, and they just model themselves on you. So there's a lot of self-improvement involved in parenting. We were in Angkor Wat two days ago, and we went out for the evening just for a drink and a bite to eat, and we took him with us. And there was a fishing game, and we were trying to feed him stuff whilst he's on the fishing game, and he looked at me very crossly and said, "I'm working!" So he's copying his mum in that he's prioritising what he thinks is necessary at the time, and his work at that moment was to get the fish on the magnet.

I'm kind of amused by the whole feminism movement. I seem to be participating in gender equality by being a stay-at-home father, but I've never really considered it important to me. I see myself as more of an equalist, really. I feel very proud when I'm walking around with my little guy. Sometimes I might get treated a little bit different, because people are amused to see a father out with his child, but it usually opens doors rather than closes them. That said, when I was deciding which preschool to send him to, it amused me how they would sort of say, "Well, when you come back with your wife then we can do the proper talking." As if only the wife can make the decision about where the child will go to school. And so they weren't taking me very seriously. And it can feel a little odd when we're at playgroup and I'm the only man there.

One concern about being a stay-at-home father is social isolation, because I'm an extrovert and I enjoy being around people, One of the things about Singapore is that as there are so many expats. They really tend to be open and willing to talk and to help. It's incredibly nice, actually. There's this Singaporean family that we know from my brother's time in university, and they're wonderful. We try to spend Sundays with them; we've gone to concerts with them, the Botanical Gardens, we were going to go camping in West Coast Park, so they're Singaporean. And then the variety of others, yeah, they're expat.

On weekends I go cycling with the ANZA guys (Singapore's largest cycling club, associated with the Australia and New Zealand club). Part of putting together a life as an expat is to take your interests and establish them in your new home as quickly as you can, so you don't have that hole. And for a cycling group I wanted a big one where they go out all the time. And the ANZA guys are great – you meet some amazing people. Different people with a huge variety of life experiences. I hadn't realised how many people have been in Asia for years. They've been in Hong Kong and then down to here, and they seem to fall in love with this region and know a huge amount about the area. And it's great: it's a mixture of social, with enough exercise to make you feel you've worked yourself a bit.

My partner's job came with a relocation package. That means they'll pay for your flights, extra baggage, some air freight, and some sea freight for the rest of your things. Then they put you up in a serviced apartment when you first arrive, and there'll be a couple of relocation people who show you around to the different areas you might want to live. Finally, an estate agent person who's paid by the company takes you around to see specific properties. It's kinda fun, going around and seeing different bits of Singapore. We'd been talking to our Singaporean friends, so we were primed for it.

The whole system is very different, you know? For one, the prices are through the roof. The second is the stratified system, where living in a house is seen as a luxury, and then condos being much more than an HDB. You kinda have to gasp a bit when you see the price of any of these. How much do we pay? Well ... I think it's a bit over $5,000. It seems like a lot of people don't seem to blink twice at paying $8,000 or so. And if you're looking at a house, some structural quality, then you're looking at $12,000. And people are prepared to pay it. But our condo is quite nice. It seemed like such a treat to have a pool, and at first we wanted to invite everyone over for a swim but then we realised that everyone's got one.

Life's changed recently because we got a helper. I was quite against it at the start, because I think the system of having a live-in helper is open to abuse and I didn't feel like I needed someone to do things around the house. And then when I said this, my partner stopped cooking and cleaning, and then suddenly a lot of my life was spent tidying up while running after a small child.

We're very keen to treat our helper well. When I look at the package we've put together for her, she has the take-home equivalent of a junior doctor in London, where you couldn't save so much.

So I don't feel too bad about that. And we are flying her home for Christmas, which I don't think she's done for years. I know other people who've paid for an education package for their helper as well. You want to give people opportunities, but at the same time you don't want to be paternalistic. We said, "Would you be interested in these courses?" And she looked at us quizzically and asked, "You want me to go back to school?" But even if she's not interested now, it's definitely a conversation that we'll come back to.

We had to do an online education course before we hired her, and it was a bit shocking. Because the stuff they were saying was reasonable, but the fact they had to say it wasn't. It was things like "Don't take their passports." Or, "You should give them a key to the apartment." Or, "Give them a day off per week." But then I was chatting with one of our Singaporean friends, and they asked us not to let our maid talk to their maid, because they didn't want her to know we give our maid Sundays off, and we pay her more, and she has a proper room. It gives you some insight, doesn't it? Maybe we are being silly paying more when we don't have to, but it just feels the right thing to do. And so far, it's working out fine. It's allowing me the time to learn some statistics, and possibly prepare myself to do some writing.

The way that we're looking at it, our income now with just my wife working is about the same as when we were both working in London. It's different in that income tax is lower, but accommodation is more expensive. Basically, though, we're trying to live in a way that sets us up for the future. Because business jobs aren't forever. And anyway, my wife plans to get a PhD and work in the non-profit sector someday, which will pay a lot less. So even though there's a relative increase in salary now, we're still trying to save so that we can have more flexibility in the future. You need the financial security so that you can choose the job where you feel fulfilment. I guess this is all the talk of the privileged. Because most of the time you're just trying to survive. I don't take it for granted how lucky we are to have interesting careers.

We came over here with the view that she'd do this job for a few years and then we'd likely go back to the UK, but then you put your feet down here and you start experiencing Singapore and then you realise this is actually a wonderful place to be. So now we're not so sure.

The progress here has been phenomenal, hasn't it? When I first came for a visit 20 years ago, there weren't any high-rises. My brother, about five years ago, six years ago, flirted with the idea of coming out to Singapore, and I didn't know anything about it, I thought it was some sort of developing country and I thought, "That's a bit ridiculous." And then you come here and you realise that the GDP has recently exceeded that of Denmark, and that the quality of life is much higher. And if you look at the West where they have all this isolationism and all this infighting with democracy, they've really hit a sticky patch, haven't they?

It's different over here. In the UK, the people who have a nice lifestyle are the high earners. There're my banker friends in London who have a babysitter once a week and they go out and they properly enjoy themselves. And over here, if you're set up with a helper then you can enjoy a quality of life like those people but on less salary. As expats in Singapore, we certainly have a higher quality of life than we did in London.

What do you make of the old joke about expats? The one that goes, "How many expat wives does it take to change a lightbulb?" Answer: "Two: one to ask the maid to do it and one to order the gin and tonics." I worry that the expat community are seen as super privileged and a bit spoiled. The term "ang moh", what does that really mean to a Singaporean?

Ng Shi Wen

Caregiver

My name is Pauline, and I'm 61 years old. I've been a 24/7 caregiver to Tai Ma for the past five years. I decided to quit my job as a cleaner in a law firm to care for Tai Ma because her health started deteriorating rapidly when she turned 86. We wanted to hire a maid to care for Tai Ma but she said she can only accept a ma jie (domestic helpers from China who worked in Singapore during the 1930s and 1970s) but you tell me, where can I find ma jies now? [chuckles]

After much consideration, I volunteered to care for her full-time because I am very close to Tai Ma. I was adopted by Tai Ma when I was a baby. My biological mother had too many daughters and when she gave birth to me, she decided to give me away because she could not afford to raise me. So when she heard from her neighbour in the kampung that someone wanted to sell her daughter, Tai Ma leapt at the chance and adopted me. Till today, I still feel indebted to her. I cannot imagine how different my life would be if not for Tai Ma. In the past, daughters were not valued at all. You know how people always say that daughters are po chu qu de shui? (Mandarin saying that daughters no longer belong to their parents after they get married, lit. once married, a daughter is like spilt water and cannot be taken back.) But Tai Ma was different. She not only brought me up, she also gave me the opportunity to go to school and receive an education but, of course lah, I stopped going to school after Primary 4 because I was playful and didn't take much interest in studying. After I stopped studying, I stayed home to do house chores, take care of Tai Ma's grandchildren and pick up cooking skills from Tai Ma. I learnt how to make many traditional Hokkien dishes.

I feel that I have to take care of Tai Ma in her remaining years. You know what is yin shui si yuan? (Mandarin proverb about showing gratitude, lit. think about the source when drinking the water.) I

cannot ignore her when she needs me the most. In fact, I don't even have anything to complain about being a 24/7 caregiver to Tai Ma because it is something that I want to do even though I don't get much money out of it. It is not just some job I sign up for to earn money and take people's orders. I feel that this is the best way I can repay Tai Ma for her years of upbringing.

I really have three roles as a caregiver: a maid, a nurse and a daughter. My daily routine is like this: I have to feed Tai Ma six times a day because her appetite is really small. Her breakfast includes soggy plain biscuit soaked in coffee so that it's easier for her to swallow. Then I wheel her out to the living room to give her a change of environment rather than staying in bed the whole time. This is good for both her physical and mental state. About two hours later, I feed her soft-boiled eggs and Milo before feeding her first dose of medication. For lunch, I will feed her porridge with fish at 3 p.m., followed by two other different types of medication at exactly one hour after the meal, before she takes her one-and-a-half-hour nap. I have to do all this while ensuring that the food cooking in the kitchen doesn't burn. The routine I just described isn't fixed though, because there are days when I have trouble getting Tai Ma to eat. She will push away the bowl whenever I try to feed her because she says it's painful to eat, so I try to whip up her favourite Hokkien dishes, especially mee sua. I will cut the noodles into small pieces so that she can just slurp and swallow it without much chewing. I realise that she eats more whenever I cook her favourite food. So maybe, after all, I made the right decision to care for her because I am the only one who can still cook authentic Hokkien dishes that she taught me when I was young.

Between her meals, I will massage her limbs while having a conversation with her. That's why the room smells strongly of medicated oil. Can you smell the feng you (Chinese medicated oil)?

Tai Ma's skin is easily bruised because she is very weak now, so I massage her in circular motions whilst ensuring that I do not exert a lot of pressure lest I bruise her even more. I don't just care for Tai Ma's physical needs but her emotional needs too. I will chat with her whenever I give her a massage. Her words are often slurred and unclear. I don't really understand what she's trying to say sometimes but I try to guess. One thing for sure is that she always tells me to look after Ah Hock and Ah Ma after she passes on. She has repeated this many times because I know she finds it difficult not to worry about Ah Hock. Buddha teaches us to be able to let go of mortal burdens towards the end of our life journey, and I sincerely hope she can put down her worries before she leaves.

The most tiring part of my job is when she needs to use the toilet. Tai Ma is too old to walk and sit up straight so the doctor warned against taking her off the bed to prevent fractures or broken bones. I tried putting on diapers for her so that she does not have to make trips to the toilet and risk fracturing her fragile bones but Tai Ma is too strong-headed and she feels embarrassed to use diapers. Even after trying to help her get used to diapers for two years now, she still refuses to use them. She just grimaces in pain and demands that I bring her to the toilet when she gets urgent. [sighs] This is very troubling for me because I try my best to take care of her, but if she does not cooperate with me and insists on doing things her way, I feel torn apart. It's like I want to bring her to the toilet too, so that she can be comfortable, but I will feel very bad if anything happens to her under my care. No one will understand how I will feel if something untoward happens to her. [pauses] I don't even want to imagine the possibility of it happening. I feel stress because of this every single day.

When Tai Ma is resting on the bed or napping, this is when I can do household chores and cook meals for guests who come to the house to visit Ah Ma and Tai Ma. Sometimes, I will just use

10 minutes to go down to the supermarket to buy ingredients and come back as fast as I can. I know the supermarket so well that I know where to get the items. Even when I am doing grocery shopping for a short while, my mind is still worrying because I don't know if Ah Ma can cope if Tai Ma needs something. So grocery shopping feels like a competition for me.

I'm thankful that my nieces and nephews are nice enough to give me a bit of money every month. They understand that it is tough to care for Tai Ma and that I am only working during the weekends so I don't have much income. During the weekends, I work from 9 a.m. to 2 p.m. as a freelance cleaner in various homes. While I'm out working, Ah Kim takes over my caregiver role. I want to work as a part-time cleaner on weekends because I have to be independent also, right? If not, very bu hao yi si (Mandarin: embarrassing). Plus cleaning is very relaxing for me; I can just put on my earphones, listen to Hokkien songs and start cleaning. I treat it as a break from my role as a caregiver. I can also do some quick shopping before I head back.

Tai Ma only has a few years left to live, so I try my best to make her as comfortable as possible. I see myself having the privilege – not everybody has the capability and willingness to care for an aged person – to care for Tai Ma in her remaining years. I am mentally preparing myself for her departure too, because before I know it, she may be gone. I will definitely care for her as long as she lives and for as long as I am able to.

Tseng Yi Ying

Funeral Director

You not pantang one right? Because I just pang gang (Hokkien: got off work), haven't shower with huay zui (Hokkien: flower water, to remove bad luck). Okay, okay, so you know right, the funeral industry gives the impression that only ah bengs (Hokkien: gangsters, hooligans) work in it, at least for Singapore, Indonesia and Malaysia. Why? Because last time during the Qing period, it was the scholars that arrange all the funeral one. Because a funeral requires a lot of knowledge, you must know all the traditional rites and custom to be able to arrange a Chinese funeral. If you illiterate, you do not know how to write the Chinese characters, you think I want to engage you to take care of my papa, mama, meh?

So now everyone got go to school, everyone knows Chinese and a little bit of English, so who want to take up this job? Confirm the ah beng one what, then they take up this job and try to push everything down your throat. Like you must buy in as a package and they blur you with things that you don't know. Like if you are a Buddhist, do you really need to burn paper house for your beloved? If you are a pure Buddhist, you don't need to burn any paper money and paper house. But because a lot of the funeral director, they call themselves funeral director lah, right, actually they are just pure businessmen, they just want to tan lui (Hokkien: make money). So actually, I cannot blame people for this mindset, because really the industry portrays a very ah beng image and not very professional.

You know right, after we ORD (operational ready date, the end of National Service), I went to work at a design firm. It's a family business lah, small company, all family members but they all sibei ho (Hokkien: very good) one. So after working for four months ah, one day I just tell my boss, I quit, I want to be an undertaker. [laughs] Because I always tell my boss my dream is to be an undertaker, because when you young you watch WWF, got the wrestler Undertaker and you want to chokeslam people and then put him into the coffin. No lah, joking, joking.

But yah lah, I always very interested in the undertaking business. When I was 16, I join a lion dance troupe because like sibei cool but people in there mostly ah beng, so I very sian because I'm not an ah beng and I don't like to fight and all that. So I join a few months and quit because I don't like the people there. Then I join a Taoist temple because they got tiao dang (ritual in which the deity possesses the body of the medium), like very cool. Wah, also a lot ah beng in there you know. Then the adults there introduce a job to me, to be a night caretaker at funerals, to jaga the things there, the coffin and watch out for cats because they say cats like to climb on top of the coffin. Yah, so when I doing night watch at different funeral managed by different funeral companies right, it was sibei boring, then I walk around and see the Buddhist altar. So I got very interested in wanting to know what are they for and all the Taoist/Buddhist stuff lor, like why need to use lotus candle, why for some funeral the coffin is placed vertically and some horizontally.

Sorry, I sidetrack a lot. Yah, so that day I quit my design job, my boss very brother one. He asked the finance woman, which is my lady boss, to issue me my pay straightaway. Wah, then I walk out and it hit me, I tomorrow boh gang zoh and my mother will kao peh kao bu (Hokkien: nag) at me why I quit my job. So I Google and called up 40 over funeral companies. You guess how many funeral companies there are in Singapore! Wah, yah, how you know ah? Got 100 over companies! So after calling 40 over, my current company accepted to interview. Heng ah (Hokkien: lucky)! I was about to kill myself liao, call so many companies, no one really want to hire me, some more I'm so young, 24 years old only at that time and no experience, sibei heng this company accept me.

Now I'm working here for more than two years already, and I can tell you: I am working for the passion. Everybody in the industry will know me, you ask them who is the best they will tell you it's Jason. Really, because when I work I do everything swee swee (Hokkien: beautifully) one, I put myself in the family's shoes. Then the family will be very thankful and tell me, thank you for helping to serve my papa or mama. Because you just lost someone so precious to you, then you want someone to anyhow come in and do the arrangements for you? I cannot, I will feel guilty one, I see how others do it, I want to hit my head I tell you, they don't care one, just want to faster finish, faster go back and lepak (Malay: relax). Go back also nothing to do, also sit there at the funeral parlour and wait for calls, so might as well do things swee swee. They always anyhow do things, for example, sometimes they never ask the family to chant Papa hou hou gia, kia tua chu (Hokkien: Papa, leave well and in peace, come and stay in this big house) when they sealing the coffin. I feel it is very zek aak (Hokkien: frustrating), you know? All this ritual things, if you never do properly, what if the spirit of the deceased get lost or doesn't rest in peace?

So I hope one day, the government will learn from Taiwan, you know in Taiwan the funeral directors or undertaker, all certified by zeng hu. Wah, they really professional, look presentable, very calm, very friendly. That's what families want. If you cannot present yourself well, who are you for me to entrust my beloved to you? So in the future, I hope zeng hu can do the same, make all the undertaker go through a course then certify us. Like that we also got more pride in the job and people will not see this industry as dominated by ah beng, ah seng.

Even though my company is not the cheapest, but we are not the kind that will want to earn a lot from you and got no morals one. My company has this no angbao policy. You know in this industry because you work with death, so it's something like a suay (Hokkien: unlucky) thing, right? So the family members are supposed to give the undertakers red packet to ward off the bad luck. But my company don't allow us to take the angbao because our company feel that we are just doing our job, and although the angbao is custom and tradition, it will breed greed. Because after the first day, the family member gives you angbao then you go to the toilet and open, you see only $2 inside, you will feel like, wah, this family member so stingy, I'm not going to do my job properly for you. So my boss set the rules, if anyone caught asking for angbao, he or she will get fired immediately. Ah, okay yes, so if the family members die-die want to give you angbao then we will accept it and declare it to our boss, then our boss will compile all the angbao received by the family and donate it to charity under the family's name, then we will email them the donation receipt for the family to keep and for them to know that they have done a good deed. I think this policy is really very good and can change the image of the industry.

So two months ago, I received a call when I was working, my dad called me to tell me my aunt might be passing away soon. I work long enough and I was very calm, so I just told him okay relax, I will come down when I finish work. So after work I went home to get my aunt's identity card, because when the worst happen, you will need it. So when I got home, they called me to tell me that she passed away, so I went down to the hospital, pass the nurse the identity card – if not, they will not release the body for embalming. Unless your surname is Lee then maybe you can backdoor lah.

So I was thinking siao liao (Hokkien: madness), because my company is not the cheapest. But I also don't trust the other companies, because their facilities I know one. The embalming place, so dirty you know not, it's like a rat's hole. My facility at least I know because I will always clean it and I know it's clean. I don't want to decide for my family, you know? Later every Chinese New Year my relatives will nag at me say, "Wah lao eh Jason, why you ask us to engage such an expensive funeral company for auntie's funeral?" Wah, very stress you know? So I told them, I do not want to set the decision of which company to engage, but for now, let's invite auntie back to my company embalming home to do just embalming. So yah, in the end my aunties, uncles just decided to let my company take charge of my aunt's final journey. Which was good because I can rest assured that my aunt's final journey was well taken care of.

I really love my profession, but to be honest, the pay doesn't really justify the long hours and sacrifices that we make for the job. Sometimes I don't get to go home because I'm on standby and there are a lot of cases. You can't control when you got case, right? If that person choose to go at that time, even if it's nearing the end of your shift, you just got to suck thumb and do your job. My pay is comfortable enough for me, but I just feel that it is not fairly compensated. This job takes a toll on our health, you know? Sometimes we have to skip meals, sometimes we have to work late at night or some days it's so quiet that we just sit at the parlour and smoke cigarettes to pass time. The longer we wait, the more we smoke, what to do? I tell my boss already, the pay is not attractive enough to retain staff. You see, the staff here ah, come and go one. The turnover rate is so high, young people don't want to do this job because of the pay and the job is not very respectable. Older people with family, need to take care of family, where can be on standby, work until so late? Actually, other company paying a lot higher but if I jump there, I won't be happy because the working culture not good, they are all very unprofessional and they don't have the passion and compassion. So now I just cin cai (Hokkien: be easy-going) lah, when I have a girlfriend in the future, need to BTO (built-to-order, applying for a Housing & Development Board flat) or touch wood ah, shotgun (wedding) my girlfriend, then I jump company lor.

Bernard Loh Meng Chin

Pet Crematorium Worker

Are you the 3 p.m. appointment? No? Okay, then why are you here? Ask questions ah? What kind? Okay, but how long, I got work to do. Okay, sit down, sit down. No, no, I'm not the boss, the boss doesn't come here often. They have an office but it's not here. Actually I also don't know where it is because I have never been there before. I have been working here for one year plus already, over here, got me and two foreign workers. I cannot tell you their name because if you want to know, you ownself ask them. You also cannot anyhow put in the interview project my name, okay? What if my boss see leh? When you write your interview, cannot write where this is, the name of the company and take photo, okay?

Yah, so this company has been here for 10 over years and the space here is rented from the farm at the front. We don't have a toilet or pantry. So we have to go over to the farm and use their toilets. We bring our own water for the day when we come to work. We don't have much here, we have a roof over our head, but no air con. But this place is open air, so fan good enough already. All we really need is just water, food and cigarettes because it is so quiet here, so many trees and birds and every day just passes by peacefully. Before this job, I was working in manufacturing at Woodlands and I live in Woodlands. Easy for me to go to work, go home from work. Now this place also not say very far, but good thing is the company got arrange transport for us to come to work and go home. This place is too far from any MRT or bus stop, the nearest bus stop is 25 minutes' walk from here, yah, 25 minutes and that bus stop only got a few buses. So we bring our lunch from home or get someone to dabao for us lor.

No lah, I never quit the manufacturing job. The company say want to shift operations to Johor, what to do? They say we can go over there, our pay will be the same, we will still hold our job. But who will want to go over? Bring your whole family over? Go over yourself? This is a huge thing and although I don't have children but my wife would not want to leave Singapore. How will she find job there? The pay there not good. So I resigned because they say you still have a job but if you don't go over you have to resign. So resign means no compensation or anything. After I resign, I went to look for jobs, other manufacturing jobs. But the economy not good, very few jobs and most of them need people who have N Level and above. I don't have, so they never even call me back. So I flip the newspaper, found that this place hiring, so I call them and they tell me come and try one month.

Actually, very easy to do this job. You just need to learn how to use the machine, the cremation machine. Learn how to warm it up before the cremation, learn how to see if it is cooled down, learn how to put the ash into the urn. So after a month, I decided to just take this job, because the pay also not too bad. I cannot tell you how much lah, but yah got more than $2,000. But we work six days a week. Every day got cremation one, public holiday only we don't do business. We rotate the off day with each other, that means most of the time Saturday, Sunday, we will be working. No choice, you go anywhere to work now, everywhere also like that.

Twenty years ago, there's so many jobs for manufacturing at Tuas, Boon Lay, Penjuru area. So easy for me and my friends to get a job. They will teach you how to do things there and you slowly learn. Now they don't seem to be very willing to teach you their line of machine. They expect you to know or at least they expect you to pass some technical test, then they hire you. How to pass? So easy to pass? Simple English I know, but you ask me to study machine and what, engineering? I fail so many times, waste how many months. So in Singapore, manufacturing is not so easy already. We are replaced by machines, stronger smarter machines that they need ITE or poly people to operate.

Okay lah, now I am also operating machine, just a very special machine that uses gas and diesel. We got around seven to eight slots for the pets, so one time we can do that amount. Most of the time they are cats and dogs, but you will also see people bring their pet fish, pet hamster, pet tortoise and all those. Our company got a special service, which is we can go and collect the pet, bring over, then we cremate and send the urn to you. So just need to call us, 24/7 for collection.

Cremation is every day if it is not public holiday. Since we deal with dead pets, of course AVA will licence us and make sure we know how to handle them safely. The whole process will take around three hours plus, because cremate takes three hours already, then we have to cool the machine down and put the ashes into the urn. The urn they can choose the colour and the shape. Depending on the size, we charge them differently. Cats and dogs minimum size $250, hamsters $120 to $150, fish will be slightly cheaper but I cannot remember. All the payment and order, the office side will settle. We just get told what time the pet will come, put into which urn.

Sometimes the family is very close to the pets, they will be crying while their pet gets cremated. Especially the young children, they will cry so much that it will make you feel sad also. Some family are so religious, especially the Taoist or Buddhist, they will get the priests or monks to come for the cremation. They will do the prayer rituals or chanting before and after the cremation, not cheap to hire them! Easy, easy, a few hundred dollars to get them to come and chant but it's people's religion, so need to respect. Buddhists believe in reincarnation, so maybe they hope their pets can get a better life with the monks' chants? Me, I have no religion, so I don't know how that feels. No lah, I got no pets now and I don't feel the need to have one even when I work in this line. I just want to have a simple life, just me and my lao po (Mandarin: wife), don't need to have kids or pets. Why go through all the trouble to take care of others? You see, it is so hard to raise a child now. Also it is very expensive to have children, baby bonus also not enough.

Okay going to 3 p.m. already, my next family going to come already, you done yet? No, no, cannot-cannot, cannot stay here and watch. You know how to go back right? Remember don't put my name inside ah. Bye bye!

Bernard Loh Meng Chin

LEARNING

CHAPTER SEVEN

LEARNING

Student Care Teacher

My name is Xin Yi. I'm 23 years old and I'm from Guangdong, China. I stay in Singapore for four years already. But not all four years I work. I studied for my diploma in early childhood for two years before working. Now I'm working as a student care teacher. You know, those kind, after school I take care of them until about 7 p.m. when their parents pick them up. Very poor thing, you know! I just help them with their homework, teach them some spelling and just give the centre activities. Centre activities ah? Got character development, sometimes I bring them downstairs for line dance or those games.

Hmm, I enjoy this job lah. I enjoy the time with my students. Of course there are things I don't like but it's just those normal things. They're seven to eight years old and very naughty. Like when I scold them, they get unhappy, won't listen to you at all and will talk back lah. Some of the students here also got ADHD so it's really hard to control them. Some of them also have dyslexia so they can't do work fast. Like right now, right, I'm taking a Primary 2 class and each class only has one teacher to take care of all students. When we get students like that, it's difficult for just one teacher to take care of all students. I feel that the company doesn't look out for us lah, our centre is not trained to handle the special kids what. So why do they take the students? Maybe parents pay more lah. The students here are all rich. Stay in condo.

I feel that students in this generation don't know how to respect teachers. Not only teachers lah, just no respect in general. Like their parents or friends. It's like "So? So what? I just do what I want to do lah!" Maybe because they're too pampered? Their parents won't really scold them when they do something wrong. They'll just, "Okay, this is wrong. Don't do it again." Wah, in our generation if we do something wrong our parents will say, "Watch out, you'll get it from me!" [laughs] If my kids behave like them ah, I will really slap them ah. So rude! Really stress you know, in my class most of the students aren't even scared of the teachers, not even supervisor! And you must know that my supervisor – he's a guy. But they're not scared of him! These kids so good at arguing and will give you a lot of excuses. But cannot scold also because they won't listen to you. How like this?

Working environment ah? Hmm, my colleagues are nice, just that sometimes I don't really appreciate or agree with their way of working, like how they handle things or how they talk to other people. Like my supervisor, he like to scold us after we did something he asked us to do. It's weird, you let me do something but after we do it you say that we handle it wrong. You know, you need to teach students the correct things, right? But he doesn't even teach us how to deal with it in the first place, like talking to parents. This job may look like there's nothing much to do but actually, when you're in this position, it is quite stressful because every day you need to plan. Every. Single. Thing. The supervisor just let us do it like how we want to do the class but we don't have training on how to plan the curriculum.

It gets harder the longer I stay here. [sighs] You know, the other centres don't need to finish the centre worksheets but at our centre, we have to push students to finish it. Our supervisor … it's like he wants this centre to be the best! But it's impossible because students have a lot of work to do – their parents' homework, school homework, tuition homework – where got time?! He always say that, "When I was a mentor, I always do this and this." But not all the students are the same right?!

Last time, it was easier. When I first came here, my supervisor – woman. If anything happen she will take care of the mentor first. She will really see both sides. Is it the students' fault or is it our fault? She won't just protect herself, but now, sometimes, it's quite unfair for us. We have to do everything and everything is wrong. Sometimes I feel that it's easier to work with female supervisor. Must put your employees before you. Like we take care of our students but we need you to take care of us. But yeah, I guess he also got a lot of problems and parents nowadays demand a lot of things and complain a lot. "Why the lunch is like this? Why the class is like this? I wait so long already where is my child?" But you cannot just because you are pressured, you come and pressure your employees. Maybe it's because he's a guy?

My colleagues also. At first got a lot of problem because half of them Malays, then half is Chinese. Like got groups lah, that's why we don't talk to each other much and only talk about work. Actually, between the Malays and Chinese, we feel that Malays are very lazy. Like they like to talk between each other and come to work late and don't do their work properly. Actually before working, when I first came to Singapore, I also heard that Malays are very lazy. The first few days I work in Singapore, my colleagues from China also told me same thing. I think that is true also lah. Sorry ah, maybe except you because you're in NUS. [laughs] But yah, I also feel that the Chinese people here don't … actually like the Malays? Like Singapore Chinese, I feel got some tension between Malay and Chinese. Won't mix with each other.

I was forced to study here because my family wanted me to study overseas. And because most of the Singaporeans can speak Chinese, it won't be that hard as compared to other countries. But most Singaporeans don't like us. I feel lah. Because, how to say ah, most of us Chinese people they're not really polite or something lah. I also sometimes feel angry at them because, you see, they talk very loud, like to cut queue. All this most of them is Chinese one. When they know we are Chinese from China, they have different feelings to us. Of course not only in Singapore lah, I think everywhere people see us that way. But China is a big country, there are different parts, so different level of education. To some of them, maybe they think manners are not that important like, "I have the right to do what I want to do." But for me, Singaporeans never rude to me but it's okay, also I know most of the time it is our fault. You know Singaporeans call us China people: China people. We are also Chinese like them but I feel that people label us because we are not good enough like the other Singaporean Chinese.

Lucky for me, I'm quite educated so people don't treat me that bad. Singaporeans are actually quite shocked that I can speak English quite well. When I told them that I'm from China they get quite surprised because they always tell me, "Your accent is not as heavy as the other China people." Also, since I was hired as a Chinese teacher, I can still use Chinese to talk to parents. You know Singaporean kids now, their Mandarin is very bad, I think that's why they need more Chinese teachers from China to teach. Even in the school, the MOE (Ministry of Education) teachers are also from China. I feel that Singapore Chinese is very different from China Chinese. Actually Singapore Chinese is not as pure as China Chinese. I feel that if you want to learn proper Chinese you should learn from the China Chinese.

Of course, there are times when I wanted to quit my job because actually my salary is only $1.5K and it's not enough for me to stay here. I need to pay rent, I need to eat and pay for transport. I don't even send money home, but my parents are okay because they know it is expensive to stay here. I rent one room and just share toilet, like that already $800 but we stay two people in one room so $400 each lah, but that is still a quarter of my pay. Then you know lah, we are girls right, we need to buy new clothes lah, new cosmetics, and some more I got boyfriend now I need money to go out.

I met my boyfriend through a dating app. It's like Tinder but for Chinese. We dated for a few months already but sometimes I feel like I'm not good enough for him. Like I said, I'm from China. I'm scared that his family won't like China people. Actually yah lah, his father don't really like China people. We still talk to each other but … whether this person is real or fake, can still feel it. I mean, even though I got Chinese boyfriend, it's still different. The tradition here and there quite different, so sometimes I don't know what to do when I follow him to family event but he always reassures me that everything is okay. My boyfriend works at a hotel so his pay is quite good … almost $3K. I think after meeting my boyfriend, I want to stay longer here. You know, the most stressful moment of working here is that you are always alone. You have no one here. When you are sick, sad, or something happen to you, nobody can take care of you. So yeah, have to be independent. And actually my parents are worried about me. [tears up] Sorry, sorry. Family is hard. All my family and friends are in China and I'm here alone. Like most of my friends are just my colleagues but my workplace take a lot of part-timers so everyone have their own life and they just come and then go. I don't have a fixed group of friends. It's sad when they leave the workplace.

Anyway, I think I will stay in Singapore for maybe at least two more years. I like this country. I feel that this country have more opportunity. In China, if you got no experience and no connection, like your family or parents not rich or influential, it is very difficult for you to get a good job. So now I'm trying to get PR because I have a boyfriend and I want to stay here longer lah. But it's quite hard because I have to get the S-pass. You know, the lowest is work permit which is mine, the second is S-pass and the highest is employment pass. It's actually not that hard to get employment pass. It's quite strict to us because I think there are too many Chinese here. And these Chinese don't like to follow rules in Singapore lah. Actually not only in Singapore lah, Australia and Canada also. Like last time if you stay here more than four years you can go apply PR but now everything change. Last time a lot of Chinese people marry Singaporean just to get the Singapore passport, then they run away. Now, you can't just get it by marrying. Unless my partner's salary and education and my one is high, then can. Last time people come here just to get married but I will apply it on my own. I don't want my boyfriend's family to think that I am only with him to get the Singapore passport. That's why I want to get my degree. I'm looking at SIM (Singapore Institute of Management) now. It's part-time for four years. The course is in Chinese and must work in Singapore lah. The course fees about $40K total but why take loan when my family can pay? [laughs]

If I have to choose between Singapore and Chinese passport, of course I will choose Singapore! Singapore passport convenient leh. It's something like the most powerful one, right? It's important to me lah, because I like to travel. China passport must apply this, must apply that. Actually, I will feel like I want to make my child study here too. It's better here. English now is important in China but still not good. In Singapore, English is your official language. English can use all around the world. That's why in Singapore can learn both languages well. If I PR and my husband is Singaporean, then my child will study cheap. Singapore also more safe than China.

China is too big. The police and government not that strict also, but in Singapore it's different. I mean everyone here will follow the rules and laws ah. So I want to stay here long lah.

Nur Qistina Binte Ahmad

Primary School Teacher

My name is Adila, and I teach in a neighbourhood school. I teach a Primary 4 class, my kids are about 10 years old. My class belongs to the lower stream, which means that most of my kids have serious school problems. These are either caused by learning disabilities or their background. Many of my kids are Malay; so they come from poor economic backgrounds or have single parents.

I have 36 kids in my class and most of them have special needs. I don't have a teaching assistant nor a specialist for retarded kids – there is only me and I don't even have a special education for learning disabilities! Of course I asked for some assistance but the school does not want to give me. "No money," they said. So I have to find my own ways to cope with that situation, which is quite new to me. Now it is my second semester with these kids.

The motivation level of my kids is very low and last semester the absence rate in my class was very high. Sometimes a third of the kids will not show up for school! Some of them would skip class for several days! I knew that I had to do something, so I talked to the kids because the parents will not listen or have another way of thinking and are just not interested. So I told my kids that I don't want them to miss school again this semester and – so far – it worked!

I really try to work with the kids on their motivation and to make school a good experience for everyone. Nonetheless there are sometimes situations where I feel incapable as a teacher. For example, some weeks ago I did an exam with my kids and literally the whole class failed except for three students. Their grades were about three out of thirty, zero out of thirty and so on. And this moment I panicked! I thought: "What is wrong with them?!" I discussed with them and asked them what the problems were but they couldn't answer. Then last week, I did a re-test and at least three-quarters of them passed it, although I simply changed the numbers! I saw in their faces that they were proud but also surprised about their improvement. Seeing this made me think: "Whatever it is, push them!" Of course I have to stay realistic – my aim for them is not to get a 100 out of 100. First they should just pass and then they can aim higher.

I started thinking about further ways to motivate them and I started to give them stickers to reward them when they do well. But the first time I did this they were shocked because they didn't have this before! It is those little symbolic things that you think don't really matter to them but they actually do. I also realised that using emotions is effective. I say to my class, "I am very upset with you!" Or I ask somebody, "How would you feel if I would do this to you?" Sometimes I also use my religious side to manipulate the kids in a way.

For example, there is this boy who lives in a children's home because his parents left him. He used to have anger management issues and got in trouble every single day. One day I asked him, "Why are you so angry all the time?" And I told him, because he is Muslim too, "Do you know who you are following by being angry? You are following Satan! And do you want to follow him?" I got to know him better, I asked him what he was doing during the weekends, and about his family. And I told him that I am gonna help him with school when he shows me that it is worth the time putting in my effort for him. So now he is listening in class, he is improving and the anger issues haven't come up at all. I hear from his friends that I am like a mother to him. But I am afraid that I am too attached to him and that when another teacher comes, everything is ruined and he will turn back into the original self.

I also cannot change what is going on at their homes, but I can try to create a good atmosphere in class. But still, whatever you do in school has to be brought back home. So this year with this bunch of kids I wanted to try something new, I created a WhatsApp group with their parents. This is my way to contact them immediately. I created this to inform them on what is happening in class. I send them pictures of their kids to show them that they are safely in school. I also use the platform to get things back: homework, exams or worksheets. But I will only message them till 5 p.m. Nothing personal is in it. I use my private phone number and so far – thank god! – I got no strange calls during the night.

It helps to get in contact with the parents and to get to know the kids' background. So this semester I decided to spend the breaks and lunchtime with my kids, which is not included in my official workload. My number of working hours is not even written in my contract. Usually I start work at 7 until 1:30 or 3, then we have meetings and remedial lessons, that's another hour and a half. Makes 32 hours but then I also have to mark papers etc. It really depends on the school how much you have to work, but this year is crazy! I usually leave school at 5 or 6 and besides I am still studying. My lessons are three hours, my travelling two hours each way, I am taking two modules that makes 14 hours extra work. This year I am really tired. I just want to get my degree and my pay increase!

Since I only have a diploma, which is the lowest grade, I get a lower salary than the degree holders. The difference makes at least $1,000! We can step into a higher salary level and get a higher performance bonus if we perform well in the annual rating through the MOE. To reach a higher level you have to take a lot more workload and your students have to perform well and so on. The more things you do and the more the school sees it, the more money you get. But it is never enough! You always end up having to do more. That is also the reason why we have a very high turnover rate – the people are just leaving after the bond, which says that you have to work for three years for the MOE. It's also very competitive and I don't think I earn the money that I deserve. In my opinion the whole system is totally fucked up! Unfortunately we don't really have a choice since this is how the system works. I really hate it!

Besides there is also a lot of ranking going on: the kids are being ranked, the teachers and the school. Previously my school was very badly ranked and we didn't have a very good reputation, but our new principal brought in a lot of change. We now have a lot of things going on in school. We went through building renovations and have more facilities, bigger sport rooms and a bigger staffroom. We also have a lot of events going on where we invite ministers and other people to our school or we send some of our teachers to other schools for sharing. So the school's name is being spread out. You have to make things bigger! Unfortunately these changes go on the workload of the teachers too. With the extra tasks you must really learn how to manage time. Nonetheless at the end of the day I still have to bring work home. But since I have very nice co-workers, I really enjoy my time there and definitely want to stay there after my graduation. Although the work days are sometimes very long and exhausting.

Carmen Ferri

Tuition School Owner

I started working when I was 14. My first job was McDonalds at Shaw Centre in Orchard. At that point in time, my dad had to support all of us … with me, there's six of us. He's the sole breadwinner and he only sold curry puff. I don't know how we survived, honestly. But anyway, my brothers were independent and went out to work at a very young age, so I followed suit. My first job was the fries station ... I thought it was tough. [laughs] I mean it was hot and I was young. But I needed the money so I didn't think much and just do. I was good at following orders and half a year later they promoted me to crew leader. I was 15 then and not long after, they posted me out to McCafé. I guess that's how I stepped into the working world. I stopped working at McDonalds when I went to poly.

After secondary school, I had a very strong interest in sports. At that time, only two polytechnics offered courses related to sports – NYP (Nanyang Polytechnic) and RP (Republic Polytechnic). NYP offered Sports and Wellness ... very technical. The one I entered in RP was Sports Business. Anyway, when I was in poly ... same thing: I needed money to fund my studies and pocket money. Since I was 14, I never took pocket money from my father. It was tough lah, but good experience. McDonalds' pay was too little so I worked in a gay shop ... I mean the pay was good. It's not exactly a gay shop ... it's a metrosexual shop. They hired guys who look good and got figure one. [smiles cheekily] Funny lah, the bosses will touch you, hold you and somehow your pay increase! So yah, I did that during my poly days. After the third year, the shop closed. When they started, the hype was crazy and I think the boss expanded too fast – he had 20 over locations in town area, you know? One shop rental about $20,000. Crazy ah, that's why have to close down all 20 of them.

After working there, my next phase in life was army. I was thinking, what can I do before entering army. I didn't think much about making money lah, but just being independent. So after poly, I wanted to continue my studies but money is always a factor lah. My dad ... my mum ... I didn't want to depend on them. I mean they probably just had enough for themselves. My siblings also I don't know lah, we are all very independent. I got into the tuition industry before army and worked for this tuition centre which only had one branch in 2012. Half a year later, I had to leave for army but still had a close rapport with the boss. I got into OCS (Officer Cadet School) in army … and the only takeaway is you will never die, you only get stronger. I just followed orders lah … I follow orders very well. [laughs]

Halfway through army, my boss contacted me to ask whether I wanted to join him for tuition again. Today he has 16 branches. So after army, that's when my real career started. I wanted to further my studies right … and I had intentions to do locally but there was only one university offering a sports-related major but it was too technical and it wasn't Sports Business, which I wanted. There's one course in Western Australia: Sports Management. But I had to go overseas, right? So I think, think, think. I thought I wanted to take a bank loan then come back, pay off. But then, I weigh my pros and cons and told myself how about I work for two years then go. I shelved my studying plans and focused on my career. When I came back to the tuition centre after army, the boss offered me franchising! Franchisee rights eh … I have to pay $20,000 to use his name, replicate everything to another location then find my own students.

I ended army in October and if I were to franchise, it will start in the beginning of the next year. I had two months to fork out that $20,000 or just settle for a normal salary worker in that tuition centre. Twenty thousand dollars, add a bit more only, can go overseas study. That time nobody really cared, so I didn't have advice so I just listen to myself and see what I think is the best for me. Very risky thing to invest in something I'm not sure of … but I thought to myself: what is life when it's so boring and monotonous?

That two months ah, I worked like crazy to the point ah … people work eight hours a day, I work 16 hours a day. I was holding two jobs – daytime is tuition then nighttime I work in a construction company.

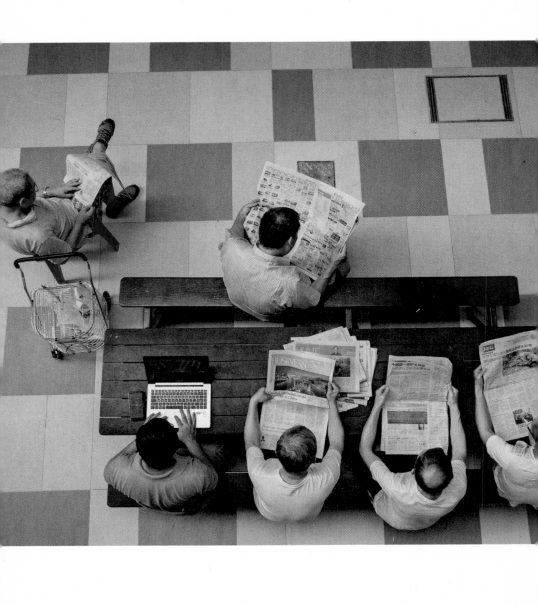

My colleagues all Bangla. You know those roadshows in malls? Who's gonna set up the carpet lah, the board lah … it's the Banglas. They assign you to an events management company with a lot of foreign workers. Why they get me in is because with one Singaporean, they can bring in six foreigners. I'm that one Singaporean. I work with them and learn a lot about their culture. I tell you, Bangla workers … they are the best workers. Why they don't take Chinese workers ah, is because Banglas are really damn good at following instructions. You tell them like that, you tell them by hook or by crook I want like that, they will give you that. They don't talk so much, they don't complain so much, they just do. I just followed them around. That time we were working at Plaza Sing, we slept outside Plaza Sing. In the morning the driver will come. Night shift usually 10 p.m. to 6 a.m. Then I sleep till afternoon and go teach tuition. My whole day crazy ah, just to fork out the money. The Bangla mindset is to come here, work hard, then invest back in their country. In our land, they are just construction workers. In their land, they are successful businessmen. I was inspired.

Anyway, December ended and I told my boss, I got the money already and I'm going to join you. That was my first flagship. I had to fork out a lot lah. Not just $20,000 – your teacher's salary, monthly rental and all the hidden-hidden costs I didn't know of. That time die already lah, I give everything already. But cannot die lah, so I went to think of ideas. Before the new year started, I went to do my own marketing to save costs. I print out my own flyers and personally handed them out. I work through the night. Midnight I start. I don't want to give flyers in the day … doors are opened and I feel a bit paiseh. I don't want them to think: "Wah, the tutor doing this kind of job." Macam (Hokkien: like) this centre no budget. I wanted to maintain the professionalism so I work after midnight. I took the last train every day after I finish, I wanted to save money so I didn't take the taxi back home. I slept at the playground to wait for the first bus and woke up early morning. The sun so hot, wah, the heat will wake me up. Then I take the bus home. I did a lot of planning ... source out for a lot of teachers and post on a lot of forums like JobStreet and Gumtree. I did this for a month. Supposedly my tuition centre start in January but I no student, no teacher, so I pushed back the opening time.

Three or four weeks passed, still no calls. I stress already. That time I got girlfriend lah – Alexia. She saw everything. She was my pillar of strength because I wasn't close to my family since I'm always out working. She kept encouraging me but, wah, really no calls, I very stress. My head botak (Malay: bald) already. Money all I throw. One week before opening time, the first parent called. Then wah, suddenly whole floodgate open and everyone started calling. My phone was ringing so much that I had to have a separate number for tuition enquiries. On the opening day, parents were queuing up all the way and I was like, what? My hard work really paid off, man. That time I no cash already and every day before that was torment for me. When registration day came, the entire centre was filled. I counted all the students ... each time I count, wah. Two days my centre open, you guess how much I made. Twenty thousand dollars. But I wasn't complacent lah, and I worked hard. I was confident and wasn't scared already ah, I had my own team. That year, at the end of the year, I bought my first car ... normal car.

After the first year in tuition, I thought I had enough money to go study already. That was the plan, right? But I think, think, think, I don't want to stop there. I felt the thrill of doing business already. Year end, I opened a photography company. My first business was a tuition centre franchisee. Anyway, all these things I do are the things that I love to do. So I did tuition and photography. I was thinking we always bring our students out on outings and excursion, but we didn't really have any memories lah, like no one taking photos. So I set up this photography company and my first client was my tuition centre. Anyway a few months after, I clinched my first deal with this marathon event: I was their photo booth provider. After that I entered into government, y'know those people who take photos during bursary awards? A lot of CC (Community Centre) events, D&D, presentation awards, PAP dinner and all that. Now my main clientele 90 per cent government. That year really ended with a bang. Wah, I had my tuition centre and I had my own photography company.

I thought, okay lah time to study already. That time SIM came up with Sports Management and Physical Education. Remember I said I wanted to go Australia to study? If I go there, I must leave all my barang-barang (Malay: things) here. All gone lah, die lah. So aiyah, put that aside and just nice SIM got the course, so I got in as a part-time student. While schooling, I realised I want to roll my money again. So what did I do? I opened a car rental company … on top of my tuition centre and photography company. I needed transport what, for my tuition barang, for my photography barang. A lot of logistics, so why not open car rental company? That's how I got my BMW! I don't really fancy luxurious lifestyle but cars ah, I will splurge. Bought my first BMW, then buy another BMW, then SUV, bought MPV, bought a sedan. I bought everything then rent … roll the money ah. This kind of thing need lobang (Malay: connections). Car dealers mark up prices one, if not how they earn money? If you got lobang, you can get it at a decent price. So that time I had three jobs and I was studying part-time. I was also involved in networking events. Wah, they see Malay, they look down, y'know? My name card was initially Ahmad. I change to Sam then they started taking me seriously. I also have to thank my dad for opting Chinese as second language for me instead of Malay. Usually businessmen call me and say, "Ah Sam ah, let's meet to discuss." And when they see me they're like, "Eh, you Malay?!" They like me even more lah, because I can speak Chinese. So in the working world, I am Sam.

This year … I already told you my biggest interest is sports, right? My dream is to open a sports academy, that's why I study sports. So about two months ago, I started something related to sports. I'm doing community sports now. The thing is ever since I started working, my health went down. I was 86 kg because I don't really work out. I was only on my laptop – replying emails, always in meetings – hardly even move. So I thought, why not start a sports business then I can work out and keep myself fit also. Work out alone very boring, so why not community workout, right? My main objective is not exactly community sports. I want to enter schools to be a trainer … like for CCA (co-curricular activities). CCA will run all year one, and Singapore so many schools. Stable and big money. But before I enter there, must build portfolio first. It has been a good two months. I have four jobs now. It's crazy lah. People who don't really know me will say, "Eh Sam, you change car like change shirt like that." But they don't know the shit I went through. Bad times they don't know, good times of course they got eyes, can see.

I always tell my friends even when they are studying right, go and work. Don't care what job, just gain experience. You don't know where this experience will bring you. If you just study … I always tell them you're like a domestic cat and I'm a wild cat. Domestic cat ah, basically you're at home and not exposed in the jungle or wild. If you're a domestic cat, when you finally go out, how are you going to fight a wild cat like me? The wild cat will eat you until finish. Yah, you have the cert and it's for your level of entry but experience is a whole lot more. That's what I feel ah. I work for 11 years already so I gained a lot of real experience. I hit a lot of things also – so many obstacles. If you really want to carve something for yourself, start gaining your experience. Singapore is damn crazy and I don't want to be part of the rat race. I don't want to complain about my work, don't want to complain about the competition … I just want to do what I like. I want to be a datuk (Malay male honorific title) at 45 and retire. [laughs] I don't want to continue working at 50 or 60. At that age, it's man and God already … time to prep for my next life. [smiles]

Siti Nurfatin Binte Raja Ali

MOE Scholar

When is this ah? Let's see if I remember. I was about 18, 19? Back then I was trying to choose whether I should do law, or whether I was going to study lit overseas lah. Cos I really liked lit, and also law lah actually, to see how society is structured, and also I thought if I know the law, then I will have a lot of power, I mean knowledge is power, right? Then I will know how things work and I can tell like, "Oh no, you can't arrest me for that shit" or "Yeah, this shit can get me into trouble." So that was me when I was very, very young lah. I applied to do literature in Cambridge, and then I also applied to law lah, and I got places for both. But I didn't have the money to go to Cambridge to do my degree. So after I got my place I started to look for scholarships. The problem with lit is that no one's really that interested. So I think only MOE offered. After a bit of hemming and hawing, I took the plunge and said okay lah, okay lah. I give them six years of my life. I think I wasn't not open to the idea of teaching … I thought it would be interesting, and it wouldn't be something I hated and that has proven true over the years.

Why I chose lit over law? [pretends to sob] Passion! Stupid lah, haiyah! [laughs] Okay lah, no lah, I say that flippantly. There are definitely times when I look back and think, aiyah, if I had just taken the more conventional path then I'd be earning more, right? Then again, how much money do you really need? And I think I really wanted to go overseas as well. Young, you know, then you get very frustrated with authority, supposedly sick of Singapore at 18, so I really thought I wanted to go overseas to broaden my perspectives. And at that age, also a bit kena colonised lah, I suppose… thought I wanted to see the West, the West is good, cultured, you know? I remember my interviewers in MOE were asking, "Oh would you do a lit degree in Singapore instead? So if we offered you a local scholarship instead would you take it?" I was like … no? And then I thought okay, okay, I cannot be unprofessional about this. How do I give them a reasonably professional answer? So I told them I wanted to study lit, and I wanted to study it in the country where the language originates … it's all bullshit, really. And they bought the answer, so I joined lah! The bond was supposed to be six years, if I studied in Singapore it would have been four years. It was a good deal, because if I signed up on my own it would have been three years anyway.

My parents were … hmm … not very supportive actually. I think generally my parents don't really try to dictate what path I take. But they also are not very supportive lah. So I had a lot of problems with my scholarship because my parents refused to sign my bond. I think we were going through a very tense period lah, okay, it's still pretty tense. But at that time I had more or less come to terms with the fact that I was gay, but I was obviously hiding a lot from them, so I go out late, and if they asked me where, I was probably quite shady and shifty with the answer, so there was a bit of a trust issue. So the way the bond works is that there are sureties to sign it, and these sureties are liable if I disappear, so if I fuck up or if I don't come back, they will try to get the money back from me. If they don't get it back from me, they will try to get it from the guarantors next. By right that would be your parents, right? But my parents don't want to sign.

So even after I accepted the scholarship after my first year in NS,

I was still trying to get someone to sign and this was very difficult because you need two sureties, right? And people would be like, "Sure, I can do it, if one of them is your parents." But then I have to be honest, right? So I told them, "No, my parents won't be signing it." And they'd be like, "What's wrong with you?!" In the end I got one of my ex-boyfriend's father to sign it. Yeah well ... they knew me well enough to sign it. If I were them, I wouldn't have done it [laughs] but, yah lah, they are Malay lah, so they are not so calculative as the Chinese lah hor? The other was the boss at a gay social media company I was working at.

Being away ... that was the first time I stayed alone. It was great! Independence! I come from a fairly ... uh ... my mum's Peranakan, so that says a lot if you look at stereotypes. Very controlling: my house, my domain type. Also quite emotionally manipulative. When I came out to her she started crying and saying, "What did I do wrong?" And so I thought I would play along and told her, "Oh, you know that masak-masak toy you bought me when I was a boy?" She immediately recovered and said, "Eh, you don't come and blame me." [laughs] So anyway, there was very little room for me to kinda carve out my own space lah. Little things like doing my own laundry, buying my own groceries that kind of stuff – I quite enjoyed that. There's also the environment. At Cambridge it was a really intellectual kind of environment, so you could really talk about all kinds of things and you don't need to worry about whether people think you're geeky or what. Met a lot of new people too. But I struggled a bit with identity there too, because the UK is where I discovered what it means to be a racial minority. I had to actually think about what it means to be Asian or Chinese, how people view me, how to play the racial stereotypes sometimes for acceptance, or how to reject it when it's just fucked up, things like that.

But over there being gay was not quite an issue, in fact it made things a bit easier, got more social cred lah. Gay culture is very uniform one lah across the world. It's fucking like Kylie everywhere, and like the mannerisms, the queeny type of mannerisms. You can tell one, lah! Then people know how to relate to you. Then you make jokes about – back then it was *RuPaul's Drag Race* – so it was easy for me to plug into stuff like that lah.

So over the years I came back for summers and they would make me do school attachments, my first year I taught in a neighbourhood secondary school, then after that an elite JC (junior college). So an attachment means two months in the school lor. So when I came back I had to go to NIE (National Institute of Education) first, and at the end of that you know there is the practicum lah hor? So by then I knew I didn't want to go to just any school, and I wanted to choose my own school. They do allow you to ask schools to take you in. So I went to ask a JC and also heard about this specialised school, so I approached them lah. I got offers from both schools on the same day. I chose the specialised school in the end. I knew I didn't want to go back to RI (Raffles Institution) that's for sure, those kids already so smart, you teach them for what? I thought okay maybe these schools because the kids already quite motivated to want to do well already lah, you just need to help them get there. Aiyah. Educational low hanging fruit lah. [laughs]

Teaching was very scary at the start. My mentor would just sit at the back of the class and stare impassively, like, make joke also no smiles, no facial feedback from her whatsoever. But she did help me improve. I think the hard part about teaching is not so much the content – I mean they're kids, what do they know, right? You study all the way up to a degree already, this stuff is very easy. I think actually don't even need a degree to be able to teach secondary school lah. I think it's actually the management of your class that's difficult. At that time when I joined the school it was quite new, so it was still quite experimental. There was a bit of a blank canvas to design the curriculum, which most teachers don't get to do.

The whole ministry is actually just this HR machine that is very concerned about successions lah, you know they assign you this thing called CEP (current estimated potential). So after your first year, your principal is supposed to assign all teachers this thing lah. It is supposed to estimate where you are likely to be at the end of your career if you stay in the civil service. So I feel like this specialised school was a bit of a career suicide lah, because the principal didn't really care. As part of the system they give scholars higher CEPs and more high-profile projects, partly to stretch them and also to see if they live up to expectations, to groom them to eventually take over leadership positions. That didn't happen at this school. So being a new school, somehow we just fell off the grid, a lot of times HR even forgot I was there. I think they didn't give me the kind of opportunities I was supposed to get. Things like design curriculum right, doesn't really register with the ministry because they are like, "Design what? It's already designed!"

Did I feel different as a scholar? Yes lah. It's very paiseh to be a scholar one lah, generally, people always look at you. So apparently before I entered the department, the HOD (Head of Department) told everyone, "Oh, we are having an MOE scholar coming in." So back then in NIE, I was really getting a little restless lah, you learn all this theory but I really wanted to see how it would really work, how to feasibly apply all of this lah. So I asked the HOD if I could get a tour of the school just to meet the kids and see what they are like. So she goes into the department meeting – and my colleagues tell me this a year later when we become friends lah – and she tells them, "Oh! And The Scholar wants a tour!" So I think when I came in there was definitely this suspicion lah. So people always think when scholars come in they always yaya papaya (Singlish: an arrogant person) lah, they want to change this and that even though they don't understand how things work. I think some of these are of course warranted ... you know sometimes lit departments, fucking bitchy one. So when I came in I was very cautious lah, something go wrong, just keep quiet. After a while when you get a bit more clout then you maybe make a recommendation.

So as part of the progression eventually I was posted to HQ (MOE headquarters) lah. Usually they let you teach in school two, three years, then after that they move you to HQ. It was interesting for me lah, because usually in schools you complain, "Aiyoh, what is HQ doing? They don't understand what's happening on the ground." But when I got to HQ I saw it lah, they do understand. So what I did in HQ was actually to try to bridge that gap.

And when I got to MOE HQ, you could tell that the difference was even more stark lah. I literally got opportunities for free one. First year, wah! How come I get to do all these things ah? You have to manage the tensions with colleagues who have been here longer and didn't get the same opportunities lah. So first year I got to be involved in policy changes, I got a lot of policy portfolios. It's a bit unfair lah. Most people have to work at least one year first, prove yourself, then you get it. Scholars get it in reverse lah. You get the opportunity, then if you fuck up, then they don't get anything else, people just damage control for you. Systemically it works lah, MOE needs to ensure succession and they want to retain their talent. But person to person it causes a lot of friction.

In HQ the work is definitely less immediately fulfilling. I mean teaching is fun lah, every day you go in, you teach the kids, they become a bit smarter, every day you give them work then you happy lah, you think, "Wah, I made this stupid kid become a bit smarter." So it's very easy to see the results lah, and of course kids are very unpredictable so it's exciting and fun. A lot of teachers miss that in

HQ. But I really appreciate that at HQ they aim to be more objective and fair. They try to take the personal out of the work. What do I mean by that? Okay, so in schools, you report to who? Your HOD alone, right? So at ranking who's going to talk for you? Your HOD, right? What if your HOD doesn't like you? Then you're fucked lah! But at least in HQ – with my department lah – you report to different bosses. So when they do ranking, they get all these people you worked with together to talk, so it prevents single-person bias lah.

I think it is a fairly well designed system, although it can be frustrating when you want to do one thing, also must clear four, five times. In schools I feel it is more political because everyone is more emotionally involved, so people can't just let go. I mean, people always say that they are doing something for the good of the kids. How do you even argue against that? I mean everything is fucking good for the kids! Don't teach them is good because it makes them happy. Assessment difficult is good for the kids because it makes them smarter. Assessment easy is help them build confidence. Anything is good for the kids so there is a gridlock, and politics comes in lah.

I'm gay and I'm fairly open about it. Not to my students, I will only talk to them about my boyfriend and stuff after they've graduated. So things like smoking also lah, I can accept that in every profession there are some bits of yourself you have to kind of cut off lah, or at least shave off a bit. But ministry or government as a whole hasn't made up its mind whether homosexuality is immoral or not. For the large part, they just fucking don't give a shit. So at the start of this year I talked to my boss lah, and I asked her is being gay in the education service going to be a problem. So essentially her answer was that "it's not a problem until it becomes a problem" which is shorthand for yes lah! And so what I gathered from that conversation was that the ministry does not have a stance on homosexuality yet. You know in teaching they have this thing called the ethics and code of conduct for teachers right, and one of the tenets is that teachers have to be role models.

So yah … I can't entirely disagree with that principle, but I cannot entirely agree with it also. At a young age I would accept that I am an undue influence on the kids. I mean they're so young, they follow what other people do. So if I smoke in front of my 13-year-old charges – I personally would find that wrong. You wouldn't be able to rationalise to them: look, this is bad for you, I pick up bad habits over the course of my life, I am only human. That doesn't work on 13-year-olds. Maybe on an older kid it might work lah. When they're older it should be about critically thinking about what's right or what's wrong, why it's right or wrong. And all this is tricky when people haven't decided what is a good role model lah. So this is what happens when it comes to being gay lah. Her point was that when you become more visible, the public will start to notice. That time when my colleague did the arts festival (and was involved in a controversy over an R21 film) parents were asking why you let a pervert teach our kids. Teachers also kena blackmail by one of the kids' parents! The parent threatened to write a letter to the press saying there is a gay teacher in the school, and what kind of values are the school imparting to the kids, unless the teacher raised the kids grades.

So this role model thing. Role model for how long? Twenty-four/ seven one what! So let's say I completely conceal it from the kids, but I'm out on the streets and I hold hands with my partner and maybe a photo online will surface of us being affectionate to each other, then how? So my boss she tried to downplay it lah, she was saying, "Huh? But girls hold hands also what?" But I am not a girl. "But Indians also what?" [makes exasperated expression] No, but I'm not Indian! So I think it leaves very little room for doubt, right? But even for herself she says when she goes diving, she thinks about whether she is revealing too much skin, whether she should post this photo on social media ... so we all have to make some sacrifices for our profession. We just have to decide if it is worth it lah. And for me I said no lah. I think if it were just me then maybe I would reconsider, but I also have to think about my partner, who is a very affectionate person. But also the way I work – I am a fairly open and genuine person, and I don't think I will function very well if I have to keep hiding. So for example when I first entered HQ, of course I hid it at first, must see what the environment is like, whether they are open, and they were. So after a while people were asking me, "Oh, are you seeing anyone at the moment?" I don't want to lie so I have to say yes. Then someone else will ask me, "Do you have a girlfriend?" And I will say no. Then people get confused and they think I'm being shady, but ... I can't talk about it! So eventually we talked about it and, yah, it's not like there was discrimination or anything from them lah. So people think public and private can separate, but no, it's not so easy lah! Honestly, I know she was trying to empathise, but I was quite irritated with my boss also when she said, "Oh, I have to hide my skin when I go diving" because she doesn't see ... this is woven into everyday life for me.

It's very interesting because I actually have colleagues who wear white (as part of a campaign to promote "traditional family values"). Which is very like, what the fuck, right? So at first I wasn't sure if I should be open, but as we worked together I think I earned some trust and respect and I also got more comfortable and more certain of my standing ... and I just don't care already, right? And I find that these people they are not as demonic as they appear to be online. So when I told one of them why I would be quitting my job, he was actually very upset, he was like, "This is not right! You should not be discriminated against at your workplace because of your sexuality!" And this is the wear-white one ah! But he was very like, "This is not right, these things have to change." So I think the problem with campaigns like Pink Dot or Wear White is that they don't see the people. I mean, what I've learnt is that – okay there's this person who says things like he wants me to burn in hell – but let's try to be friends with them. It's tricky – it's really difficult but it's the only way we can get anywhere, to try to break down these barriers, to let people realise that what they are hating is not just an abstraction, but a real person. Someone they might work with, someone they might actually like, who knows?

So I don't feel any resentment towards my colleagues lah, resentment maybe towards the system but certainly not towards people I've met. Yeah, so one of the reasons why I quit quickly after that chat with my boss was also I was very afraid. What if I get stuck in teaching? Dunno what the fuck else I can do, right? Then one day they will decide, "Oh, you are gay. We are going to move you into some invisible role in the ministry so you can't be a comms risk to the public." Then I will be stuck there, and I cannot do anything else outside. Maybe in the future I'll join the dark side and join a tuition centre. There is a lot of money there. But I do think one day I would like to go back to teaching again. So maybe when I make peace with the fact that I cannot progress, and just do it as a way to give back to society, then I might go back to teaching.

Ng Shi Wen

Academic Ghostwriter

I'm 23 years old and I'm currently an undergraduate at NUS. I used to work as a product manager for a local defence contractor, but currently I work as an academic ghostwriter. As the name suggests, I write anonymously on behalf of academics, students and people generally in the university system. I've been ghostwriting for … let's see … five years now? Part of it is you write for people who are …

people who contact you tend to be people who know you because there needs to be a high level of trust. So yeah, I have written for personal friends before. So normally when someone approaches me with an assignment, firstly I ask for all his materials for the semester. That means either he passes me all the material by email or he'll give me access to his student portal and student email so I can communicate with his supervisor or lecturer. We'll go through all the questions I want to ask his supervisor and give him the exact phrasing so he can copy it and paste it to the email and send it to the supervisor, or I will actually use his student email to communicate with the supervisor myself.

Most of my clients tend to be very wealthy. They're mostly foreign students who come to Singapore to study in private universities, hoping to get the credentials, but they do not really want to work for it. In fact, they can barely speak passable English and they enrol in these private universities, like, well I won't name names but we all know who they are; and they essentially want to go back with a foreign sounding degree. University of London or … Greenwich … or some other English-sounding name, right? And when I say wealthy, it is really wealthy. It's the kind that, well … for one of my clients, for her 16th birthday, she got a Bentley, so I am talking about the top 1 per cent sort of wealthy; because, for my services, 2,500 words is $250 – three essays costs you an iPhone! So especially the China Chinese community in Singapore, they tend to keep coming regularly. Another group that you see is Singaporeans who are desperate to get a good grade, you know, they're really stressed and they come to me for a quick fix.

My clients tend to be a mix of males and females. They tend to be from China, but I have had students from Sweden as well, I have had students from the UK. They come from a wide range of disciplines and backgrounds, like law, sociology, finance, economics, history, business management. But there is a sort of a biased profile towards a certain nationality, particularly Chinese. And wealthy, because it is costly, right, to hire an academic ghostwriter.

What you are getting is original, but it's not yours so it's technically plagiarism. But it's impossible to catch – no amount of software can detect a ghostwriter. There are cases where some of my clients have been sort of, like, suspected by their supervisors or their lecturers but all the lecturer can do is kind of like, "Okay, it doesn't sound like you are capable of writing this, I reject it, I want you to submit a new one." But in the end he still has to accept it because there is no way to prove that it is not from the student. There is an entire shadow army of people like us, you know. In many universities, you shouldn't be surprised to find that many of your competitors on the bell curve aren't actually your classmates, but rather us ghostwriters.

There are agencies, online agencies and all these sorts of things through social media, but for me, I tend to get my clients through personal networks, because ghostwriting takes a lot of trust. A recent client from a UK university depended on me for 100 per cent of her module grade, and that level of trust just doesn't happen through a website. But there are services online and people do use them. On the websites there is a grade that they promise and a price that comes with it. They of course tell people that these are meant to be just model essays, that they are not meant to be used for plagiarism, but of course we all know what happens. I personally don't guarantee my clients grades, I guarantee them minimally a pass, and then I work together with them so they know what they are doing. To date, I've written three honours dissertations. Their supervisors had no idea what's going on, they think they're talking to their student when in reality they're really talking to me, and the student just keeps track of the progress and makes it seem like he or she is the one who is doing all the work.

For me, the point came when a friend referred a client from a local university. He had forgotten he had two essays due that midnight and he came to me begging me to do it since he really doesn't study and goes out partying all night. I said okay I'll do it, I charged him double, of course, because the work was insane, and he actually got an A. It turns out that the module was actually a really difficult module and he was one of the top in the class for that paper. So my friend got really really upset, [chuckles] because he really worked really hard for his A, whereas this guy just paid for the service.

It kind of made me think for a moment that, okay, maybe I am kind of like killing what education means. But in another way, I realised that education is already dead, that in systematising education with standardised testing and tuition schools, we've made it easy to game. In Singapore, the tuition we've received just because our parents could pay for it, all the extra advantages we had that other kids may not have had, it's all part of a whole industry. And as long as you have a system like that, you will have wealthy elites who will game the system at the expense of others.

The ironic thing is, I got into ghostwriting because I really love learning. But at school all you've got is standardised tests, and I never did well on them. You know, my JC lecturer told me not to read outside the syllabus because it's not tested. I wanted education to be something more. Then when I didn't do well for my A Levels, I just went into the army. So while I'm doing my NS, one of my friends, she was studying law at the University of Bristol, and she decided that okay, for one of her assignments she would let me have a go. What drove me to do it was the fact I refused to believe I wasn't good enough to enter a foreign university. By then, I had been rejected by 13 different scholarships and taking that assignment was my way of rebelling against the system. And I managed to pass four law modules at the University of Bristol. Okay, so maybe I didn't do exceptionally well, but the fact that I managed to pass four modules from one of the best law schools in the world, to me, showed that education was about more than doing well on standardised tests or getting into some famous university.

So, I guess, the moral dilemma is sort of like, not really there for me. Until you stop the army of bureaucrats who want to impose standardised testing, you will never stop this army of ghostwriters. But even if you pay your way through, ultimately it's what you get out of it that matters. So I consider myself an intellectual rebel, if you will, and ghostwriting is my way of saying education is about more than just a grade.

Ng Li Ying

MOVING

CHAPTER EIGHT

MOVING

Flight Attendant

My name is Nisa. I'm 21 years old and I work as a cabin crew in Singapore Airlines. The interview to get this job wasn't easy. It differs for each person: some of them have to read passages, while some of them have to debate. Yes, I had to debate, I'm serious! I don't know what they were trying to look out for when they asked us to debate. Apart from our interview, we also had our height and weight taken, and also we got checked on whether we had scars or tattoos on our body. If you have scars on your arms, legs or back, you cannot get the job. You can say that they are very strict. Let's say you have a small scar here, [points to hand] you cannot get the job as long as the scar can be seen by the passengers. There was once I was just about to sign my contract, then this girl – I think she fell or something or played sport – so she has this small scar on her hand. She could have used a concealer to cover that scar. Maybe she didn't cover it because she thought she already went through the interview. But when the interviewer saw it she didn't get the job. Just because of that small scar!

My interview was a group interview consisting of eight or ten people, I think. Basically, they asked questions like, "What colour best represents you?" or something like that. It was the most nerve-wracking thing because you can see that everybody there was so tense. But I remembered what my friends told me: just keep smiling! So I did that. But I think they don't really care about your answers for that interview. Rather they wanted to hear how you speak. Then I went to the debate round. And the question was, "Do you think the man is the king of the house?" My team had to disagree. Right after that debate round, they had another round where they asked us questions and we had to answer individually. The question for this round was, "If you had a million dollars, what would you do with it?" My answer was I think the most honest answer I could give. I said that my family is not very rich. I will use the money to support my family first then maybe donate it, or something like that. The other girls gave very different answers. They were also quite honest. Some said they would use the money for shopping.

After all the questions, we had to take our height and weight. I just got through the height minimum which was 158 cm. Can you imagine, they were like whispering, "Aiyah, I think we just give her a chance lah…." They then told me that they will email me for the last interview.

My last interview was with the management and their question was, "What was the lowest point in your life?" I was like, "Damn … what's with all these questions?" I was thinking of the time when we got kicked out of our flat because my dad got bankrupt. That was the lowest point of my life. My family had to stay at the void deck for the night and that was the point where we felt so lost and so helpless. Since I am the eldest, I had to bring my family together and put up a strong front. Even though at that point of time, I was actually tearing apart. Anyway, they also asked me about school and, right after, we just had to wait for the management for further update. They called a few names and then you could see a few girls walking away because they were rejected. Then they called my name. That was not the end of it! We had to do a catwalk with our kebaya.

So we had to find our size and then wear the kebaya and the sandals. And after you change, they will check your legs, your arms and check your back and even your face. One of them even said to me, "You have a few bumps here, [points to forehead] you better be careful okay?" Then they checked our height and weight again. So they stuck this tape on the wall and it was supposed to mimic the height of the cabin and I had to stretch to reach it. I had to really tiptoe to reach it. When they took my weight, they told me to eat more because I was too light. I was just like, okay.

So after that they told me that I was 90 per cent through the application process and the final stage was the medical check-up. They checked my eyesight, my stomach and I had to go through urine test. I have a history of gastric pain, so I had to go another round of check-up and get the memo from the doctor saying that I am fit to fly. I had to wait for a few weeks before they told me I could go for training. My first interview was in March and I was only accepted in May. I had to graduate from polytechnic first, before I go for the training. So in the end, I only began training in June.

I've been cabin crew for a year now. It has its ups and downs. There were some good flights and bad flights. But I truly believe that my colleagues make a huge difference. Like, even if you have bad passengers, you would just let it go and think of it as normal to have bad passengers. There are many passengers who take too much alcohol, especially the Russians. They drink alcohol like water. But it really depends on their alcohol tolerance. Most of the time, we just keep giving them the alcohol until we realise their speech is slurred or their eyes are bloodshot; then we have to tell our leaders on board. Sometimes we just have to take precautions because there are very different types of getting drunk: some are happy drunk, some are angry drunk. If they're an angry drunk, they might disturb other passengers. One thing we do is to dilute their drinks. There was once a passenger who realised we were diluting their drink. They got angry and punched the crew leader. Then, the captain had to come down from the cockpit and give a warning. If they continue to give us problems, we will just tie them up ah. [laughs] We call it the restraint kit. That means that the person cannot move anywhere, not even to the toilet. We have to do that if the passenger is violent. So far, such a thing has never happened in my flight. If it ever happens, the police at the arriving destination will be informed and they will take the rowdy passenger away before letting everyone else out. We always ensure the safety of the passengers first.

There are a lot of stories I heard which are really scary. There was this passenger that didn't tell anybody he was taking sleeping pills. So I think the flight was shorter than he expected. When the flight was arriving at its destination, the crew tried to wake him up, and I think at that point of time he had a weak pulse or they could not detect his pulse. The crew tried to do CPR on him, but he did not react so they thought he was dead. They put him in a body bag. We have the body bag in case any person passes away on the flight. So when they landed, the passenger woke up and was shocked to realise he was in the body bag. That's when he explained that he took sleeping pills because he has a phobia of flying.

There are times where I don't want to go to work, especially after a bad flight. By a bad flight I mean when the superiors scold you or something. There was this guy who really brought me to my lowest and I felt so helpless because everything I did was wrong. He kept telling me the things I do was wrong. He was saying that I was very slow and if the flight was to Jakarta, we would have already landed before I finished my job. I felt so pressured. And all these things make me stressed. I tried talking to the steward but, you know, he totally ignores me. Sometimes, I feel sad for him because I feel like he has no love in his life, like he constantly wants to instil fear in his juniors.

But you can also meet very nice people on board. There was this Singaporean lady, she asked me whether we had some toys, so I said yes. She told me she has a son and a daughter but the toy was more for her younger son. For me, it was a light flight; we had a lot of toys so I gave her more even if she did not ask for it. She was so pleased with it, it surprised me. So in the end, she wrote a complimentary letter for me. That was nice.

Some crew, they expect to receive complimentary letters. For me, when I receive such letters, I will just hand it to my leader and it depends on my leader whether they want to write it down or not. Some crew expect their names to be included when another crew is praised. Some crew would just give the compliment letter to the passengers and ask for their opinions. There are also some passengers who would verbally compliment the service and some crew would ask, "Would you like to pen it down?" So these complimentary letters help for promotions. That's why some of them die-die want the letters because they want the promotion.

Actually I love a lot of things about this job. The travelling and simply being away from everything, being alone and doing your own things. Other than that, meeting new people is fun. If the crew is a nice bunch, it makes the whole trip fun. I also feel that this job is not so stressful unless you are a junior and the other crew do not have the trust in you. It is a good and a bad thing to be a junior. Good because they allow you to ask questions and they know that you are learning. When you are not a junior, they expect you to know everything. But other times, as a junior, you get bullied. When I was a junior, they asked me to do everything and I could not do my own duties. Honestly, you just have to suck thumb if you are a junior. The politics can be quite bad sometimes. But the best part is you don't see all these people every day so it is nice to get away from some people.

Many of them who are staying in this job are because of the money and also the lifestyle. Because you don't have any homework and you are only working when you are on board. You also don't require that many skills and you are basically doing the same things over and over again. Sometimes, it becomes rather brainless because you are doing the same things. Personally, I really like the travelling and seeing different parts of the world. But what I like most is what I get to learn. I take it that every flight is a learning journey: there are different situations on every flight. This job also teaches me how to speak to people and it also made me very confident. We always have to know the right choice of words when talking to the passengers, and how you react to certain passengers. Most of the passengers, when they don't get what they want, they just want to know that the crew is trying their best to do something. For example, some family members get separated on board. It is not our fault but we have to handle it. Sometimes they want to change, but they cannot change because there are not enough seats. So we have to learn on how to be courteous and polite, but at the same time be firm with our answers.

The job of a stewardess is very important. We are skilled and trained, and if anything were to happen to the plane, in terms of emergency evacuation or crash landing, we are the ones who are trained in what to do. That's why, before we go on a flight, we are always reminded that any other thing on the plane can be spoilt or whatsoever but we must always take care of ourselves because we are the most important people in the plane, apart from the pilots. If anything were to happen, we are the ones who know what to do and who will be responsible.

In the future, I see myself being a teacher. It is very different from being a stewardess. Actually, I don't know … I have always wanted to teach and I have always found joy in teaching. But then again, I wouldn't know really whether I would enjoy it. Because my current job is the total opposite of teaching, with the homework to mark and having to bring home work. But I also think this current job is not for me. The crew culture always makes you insecure because people are always judging you. So I tend to be paranoid because sometimes I know people are judging. And you know, they say if you cannot beat them, you join them. Even if it's not for me to judge, somehow, I think if I stay too long, I will be influenced by the culture. Some of them tell me that it is good that I want to be a teacher and tell me to go for it. Because to them, the longer I stay here, the more I will get stuck and I will not be able to get out of this job. So yeah, it kind of stresses me out because sometimes I don't know what I want to do and I'm afraid that if I take too long, I'll be stuck in this job.

I don't think people know what being a stewardess is really like. I'm not trying to say it's a bad job, but I think the job is not meant for everybody.

Nur Nadzirah Binte Abdul Halim

Aircraft Maintenance Engineer

My name is Dave and I work in SIAEC (SIA Engineering Company) as an aircraft maintenance licence engineer. Where do I even begin with my job? Basically, what I do keeps the airport running. [laughs] No lah … we are the people who identify problems in the aircraft and ensure the airplane is in certified flying condition before it goes out again. We need to sign off to make sure that all the airplane's parts are fit for flying. Everything from the engine to the windshield is under our jurisdiction.

There are two sectors of work for us. Firstly, there is the hangar. Here the aircraft is powered down and we do our more long-term maintenance of the aircraft. If we need to strip the aircraft, here is where we do it. If any aircraft parts are expired we change it here. If a bird hits the windshield, for example, this is where we replace the windshield.

The more exciting stuff is in the second part. Here we work on the aircraft itself on the ground. A normal regional aircraft lands and rests for about eight hours before it flies off to its next destination. So once the aircraft crew steps off the plane, that's when we come in. There is a computer which gives the flight report and here we are able to see what's wrong with the plane and work on it to rectify it. Here is where you see a lot of things.

As a passenger you take a lot of things for granted. You think that you can do whatever you want onboard a plane. One example I can tell you is about this time where we received complaints about a choked galley. A galley is where the flight crew who is clearing liquids from your drinks is supposed to pour water down only. This water vaporises at high altitude as it goes out of the plane. There is a filter fitted on this galley. So even if you pour down tea or coffee, the sediment can still be filtered out. So these stupid galleys kept getting choked. When we opened up the galley, there was this weird pink coagulation that looked a bit like yam paste. Wah, it smelled horrible leh. We informed our superiors and there was a full-fledged investigation launched with the flight attendants and crew. Turns out it was a mixture of wine and milk. So after many flights up down, up down, the calcium and fruit had hardened and that pink pasty thing formed! So we had to remind the SIA service crew of how to operate the machinery and remind them that the galley is only meant for water. So I mean that's the main point. If you adopt the layman's approach that is what is going to happen. But once you know how the system works, you do what they call a "trend analysis of failures", you are able tackle the situation.

Basically that is our job, we are the sort of middlemen between the manufacturers – our main aircraft carriers are Boeing and Airbus – and our main customer Singapore Airlines. We also work with international carriers when they transit at our airport. That's us playing on an international level, and they really do respect you when you can solve any problems their flights have when they stop over in Singapore. So whether there is a problem with cargo, the cockpit, galley, seats or in-flight entertainment, we need to be the relay between the manufacturer and the customer in terms of education on how to use the equipment or troubleshooting. I think you kind of realise after a while that using the aircraft has its limitations, that it's not a flawless piece of equipment.

As a trainee you are not really involved in the decision-making processes. This is good in a way, because you are really focused on the crux of the engineering job. Work-wise you are basically doing the same thing as a senior engineer. We normally work with a senior engineer who is really there to supervise and assist. There are all kinds of senior staff here. So you have those who would be really helpful and those who are not really. But overall these years are really important to make sure you take in as much as you can, familiarise yourself with all the different systems and to take initiative to learn from the senior engineers. One problem I face is that because my batch of apprentices is the first batch of degree holders in this apprenticeship programme, they really expect a lot from us. In the past you only needed a diploma for this job. As a result, there is really this social barrier where the senior engineers expect you to do something in 45 minutes for which they give others an hour to complete. So you are living under this weight of expectation. But I mean, I am a third-class honours student and the job market is very uncertain out there.

I don't really have any complaints or regrets about my job. Anyway, the best part about being a trainee is that we don't have to stay back and do paperwork! On a good day we can actually have lunch for 25 to 30 minutes in the staff canteen!

Speaking of lunch, while we don't normally eat lunch with the senior staff, we do get to have lunch with the technicians. The technicians are the people who get their hands dirty. There are different kinds of technicians. Full-time staff that has been here for 30 years and also short-term contract-based staff. You get to learn a lot from these people, but ultimately you learn that no matter what grievances people have with their jobs, or their relationship with the company, everyone has to work together to get the job done.

I'm currently working on a shift schedule. One day I work 9 a.m. to 9 p.m. day shift. The next day I work a 9 p.m. to 9 a.m. night shift. After which I get two days off. At first, night shifts were very tiring. But after a while I got used to it. Night is when there is the highest volume of planes. So night shifts are really important. I also have to burn my weekends, which sucks. But I do get weekdays free which means I can spend time with my wife, so can't really complain lah.

Moving around Changi Airport, one thing that happens without fail is that people always asks me for directions. Just because I have a lanyard and have the Singapore Airlines logo on my shirt right, I am always being asked for directions. I have improved my engineering skills as well as my knowledge of the airport. So if you are looking to find your way in the airport you can look for me, I can provide that service! [laughs] Working in the airport is really very interesting. This place is always under construction. It's good for tomorrow, but for today it's really like, "Oops, we can't use this escalator today. We've got to use the other one." It's a fascinating place, always changing.

Working in SIAEC is pretty good. Before this I used to sell light bulbs for a small company. This is bigger and you can feel the difference. There is this sense of organisation. You do get unions to represent your needs. I feel I am in a company stuck in a mode of operation of the '80s but is still remaining competitive. You know right, my father and grandfather used to work here also. Yes, technology might have improved and whatnot, but the way that the job is structured, our mode of operation, I feel it hasn't changed since their time. In a sense that things here are quite old-school, so I don't really get what most of my friends in other jobs talk about job hunting or moving jobs. Job security here is pretty high. What I love now, which I hope will last but I know it won't, is the fact I am at the stage where no one is really looking to climb the corporate ladder or wayang (Malay: theatre performance). Because we are all trainees, we are really able to fully concentrate on our jobs. To learn as much as we can. Overall, I'm happy where I am and I'm excited to see where the future takes me.

Samuel Devaraj

Able-bodied Crew Member

Have you eaten? If you want, let me get something for you. Rice? Coffee? Let abang (Malay: older brother) Donnie treat you. Okay, Mas, one coffee for my adik (Malay: younger brother) here. I was scared you were lost. Because only fishermen and boat workers know where Platform 2 is. So when you told me you know this place, I wasn't sure you really knew.

Oh yes, about my work. I've been with the ferry company for a year. I just celebrated my 48th birthday – on the ferry. We're a passenger ferry. Not some cargo vessel. You can walk around with a black face when you carry cargo. But not with people. It's all about service. Sometimes the heart of a bad passenger beats more dangerously than the worst of storms. That's why we always have to please them. Passengers can write into the office and our lives can change. Sometimes you also have those super religious women who don't want men to touch them even without skin contact. It's hard especially when we are told to help passengers on and off the boat because the waves make the ferry bob up and down. Sometimes passengers fall and we get complaints.

But we are not always at their mercy. Complaints come in all the time. But we are protected by CCTVs. Last week, one stubborn passenger was carrying a large luggage. We offered to help her with the luggage but she said no need. A few days later we got a call from boss saying one woman hurt her back because no one helped with her heavy bag. And her items were broken because we mishandled her bag. We got the HR boss on board. Get him to watch the CCTV footage. And all clear.

So the ferry is like our playground. We can do anything we want. Bosses only check the CCTV when there's a problem. And they skip footage not related to incidents they're investigating. They also know how bored we can get. Rules get relaxed after our last trip. This is not Singapore or Indonesia's land. Even though we carry Singapore's flag. After work, we raise our own flag. [laughs and pulls out the waistband of underwear] Like every time we dock, I play this game with the police officers – usually the nice ones. Because their job is to check the ferry, but sometimes they get lazy and just ask for a crew list. So we play this fishing game where they will extend a fishing net and I just drop the piece of paper into their net. Plop. So easy.

Our bosses are quite nice. If you don't give them reasons to nitpick. Our big boss has two sons and they always take our ferry and mingle with us. They are very relaxed people. But they care about our reputation. See, we are one of two ferry company plying the Singapore–Tanjung Pinang route. So the junior bosses always tell us to skip the lifejacket and safety video at the start and quickly play comedies on the TV. So that we don't bore the passengers. It's not right. But we just follow lah. So far no complaints. Anything the junior bosses will explain themselves. But because they care so much about image, sometimes without you knowing they are scrutinising our appearance. One captain from another ship got his bonus cut for not ironing uniform. Another captain, second-time offender for not wearing his shoes properly – he wore his shoes like slippers – got his pay permanently cut by $50. All these to prove a point. That they want our company to be the ferry of choice.

But we are sometimes in cahoots. You know how every time we come to Tanjung Pinang, the ferry makes a sharp turn? We do that to avoid a coral reef. One day during bad weather, we had to avoid a small sampan which suddenly appeared from nowhere. So when we trying to avoid it, we hit ground. Technically it's a shipwreck. We called the bosses. The bosses said MPA (Maritime and Port Authority of Singapore) will kill them. They said to do whatever it takes to get out of there and we will pretend none of it has ever happened. And true enough, after that day, nothing happened. No warnings, nothing. Even the captain offered to resign but they did not accept his resignation and he felt guilty. He even passed over a job opportunity waiting for him at the end of this year. The damage was a lot. About $400,000 went to repair the ferry. That's about eight years worth of the captain's pay.

Speaking of pay, compared to many of my crew members I don't earn as much. I'm the newest. And the company has been through several hands. They have changed owners at least two times in last 10 years. Last time it used to be owned by Singaporeans. Now, believe it or not, by Indonesians. Part of the reason why our boss is so competitive with the other company is because the other company is also owned by an Indonesian. Both from two neighbouring districts somewhere in Sumatra. So kampung rivalries also brought here.

Anyway, those who used to be under the older bosses didn't get their pay changed when the new bosses took over. So if you earned $2,000, you still do. New people like me earn between $600 and $800. I'm an AB, it's short for an able-bodied crew member. So I don't have any specialised function like the chief engineer does. Other ABs from the period of the previous bosses all get slightly above $1,000. Given my rank and my certification I'm satisfied with my pay. It's been enough to support my family of five.

The thing is, my current certification is a Class 5. The next highest one is a Class 4. I want to go to school to get my Class 4 but that will take time. And money. If I leave the job to get a Class 4 there's no guarantee they will take me back. I will have to wait around for another job. Have you been to the Seamen's Mess in Batam? It's filled with people looking for a job. I don't want to be there while my wife supports our two daughters and son.

I also cannot go to school because my eldest is two years away from university graduation. So we take turns to go to school. Once she graduates, I apply for Class 4. It's either she studies, or I study. It's not right for me send myself to school when the outcome is not guaranteed. Look at my daughter. [shows daughter's profile on Facebook] My daughter has gone to Bangkok for a choir festival. Can you imagine our family's pride? We always send each other pictures of our travels. Then I will post them on my Facebook. Imagine if I pursue my Class 4? Who is going to pay for my daughter's school expenses? Will we get to enjoy this pride?

Actually, if I work in Indonesia I can easily become a captain. One of my previous jobs in Indonesia was as a captain. But I'm working as an AB because I have less responsibilities. You see, that's why I'm so happy. Yeah, maybe I don't get to visit my family so often, it's been eight months, but as the lowest-ranking officer here I usually have to wait for my turn to take leave. Working on a passenger ferry is also better for the health. We have regular sleep hours. Not like my previous jobs on cargo ships where you have watches at irregular hours.

My work is just to make passengers feel good, tie the rope every time we dock, take out the trash. Actually you know what's the worst?

When passengers don't properly flush the toilet. I'm the one cleaning. But it's alright, not something I cannot do. Already used to it. So the toilets in the ferry can make or break my day.

Another thing that can break my day is the Singapore immigration system. Last time, every time we dock we can just stay on the ferry and wait for the next group of passengers. But now, we all have to go through immigration. So instead of staying in the boat, we chop passport to enter Singapore and chop passport to leave Singapore again. It used to be easy because we have the seamen's book, we don't have to go through such things. But now we have to. You know why? One day I asked the immigration lady. She told me one seaman from another ship entered Singapore but until now has never left. So there's a missing foreign seaman somewhere in Singapore. He could have slipped out of Singapore. But we never know. So because of that one man, all seamen in Singapore now under more scrutiny.

It was not easy for me when they made the change. For some reason I'm always held up at immigration. Even though they have always seen my face, every time, without fail, I get held up. They won't disclose why. So one day when I ask the very kind ICA (Immigration and Checkpoints Authority) lady, her name is Jenny, she's the nicest because she always ask me how I'm doing and whether I've eaten or not. I think she likes me. But I'm married. And I'm not interested. But I be nice to her because she's immigration.

So Jenny told me it's something to do with my name. Maybe it is weirdly spelt or that it matches a person with bad records in their database. And that affects my work because so many times our ferry departs the ferry terminal late because they keep holding me back. And then we get complaints. So one day Jenny told me to report to ICA headquarters at Lavender. I asked my boss for permission to be away just that one day to go to Lavender. I went there and met one Malay officer. A few weeks later…. [unlocks phone and shows wallpaper] Yes, people normally have their family photo, a nice beach or their pet on the screen saver. I have this email from ICA. [laughs] But this has saved me a lot of trouble, now I don't have to get held up. I just have to flash my phone. And I can go through. I feel like a VIP. All thanks to Jenny.

You get all kinds of people working here. Our company's biggest source of money are mainland Chinese tourists. Yeah, they are loud and noisy. We know the passenger is Singaporean or Indonesian if they are not troublesome. You can learn so much about Singapore from the ferry. You meet regulars. Like every month Singaporean men who've settled down in Tanjung Pinang but still keeping their Singapore passports, clear Indonesia's immigration to get another month's stay. Some have second wives. Some have secret families. Not all are men. Some woman also do the same. Some have interesting pasts. Some were former generals in the forces. One of them even said he works for the intelligence division and still reports news back. Sometimes you meet fishing buddies. Sometimes families taking short holidays. Young couples who want cheap holidays also go to Tanjung Pinang. These are all usually people who either want a cheaper way to Bintan resorts or want to avoid it all. All kinds.

What's next for me? Actually I don't know. I'm actually over-qualified for the job. My degree is in financial informatics. But because I could not get a permanent job last time, I went to sailing school and got my Class 5. Back then my mother-in-law gave me her gold earrings, necklace and bangles to pawn off to pay for my sailing school. She told me I don't have to repay her. I personally don't feel pressured either. But I am forever in gratitude to that wonderful woman.

Once my elder daughter graduates, maybe I'll go to school to get a Class 4. In fact, my captain told me he would vouch for me a place in the company if I pursue a Class 3. But that is if he stays in the company.

Ah, coffee's here. It's cold tonight. It feels like I never left the ferry. Even under this jacket. Are you not cold? Look at that. The steam rising from the coffee. It's one of the best things to watch when it's cold like this.

Try Sutrisno Foo

Bus Captain

I'm a bus captain. I've worked here about four or five years lah. Is the job good? Well actually … I'm just here on a work permit. Before this I worked in Malaysia. Yes, every day it's a back and forth commute. I personally feel that this is a job I'm extremely satisfied with. It's also not really that difficult. I belong to what you would call the short-distance routes, so it's still pretty decent.

No, I don't have to come in the morning. I only start work in the afternoons. If outside people look at us, they would think it's pretty good. But actually, if you want to put it crudely hor, we come and go back with our motorbikes, we are actually risking our lives, okay? You see, when I come over, it's noon. When I go back, sometimes the jam at the Causeway is so bad that I'll only reach home at 2 or 3. Yes, that's 2 or 3 in the morning.

Actually, in the past two or three years, it wasn't so bad. But now almost every night there will be a jam. It's to do with politics lah. Relations between Singapore and Malaysia. All the grievances, they all come out here lor. You just go and take a look at the Woodlands checkpoint at 10 p.m., 10:30 p.m. lah. It's a world-class spectacle alright! A traffic jam of motorbikes that can stretch to maybe 3 kilometres, imagine that. To cross Customs hor, sometimes you need two hours. It's like that lor. Especially on Fridays. Friday nights are terrifying.

And then when you're coming back at that time of night, you have to be alert too, in case you get robbed. There was a period of time, a

lot of my colleagues were getting robbed. Yeah, on their way home after work. There are other things too, when you're so tired. You ride a motorbike so late at night, you fall asleep, and the next thing you know you collide with another vehicle. Then accident, then die. All these things have happened, it's just that nobody talks about it. Yeah, so there's danger even after you're finished with work! I travel back and forth like this every day lor. There's no choice lah. If I could avoid this, I wouldn't want to do it this way too, right?

Then why I chose this job? It's the closest there is already. Work in Malaysia? [long pause] Of course, I've considered it. I used to work in Malaysia. That time, everything was still good, I could still feed my whole family with what I've earned. Now the economy … it's just so bad that you can't do that anymore lah hor. So I can't feed my family working in Malaysia lah, no choice. That's why I ended up here in Singapore lor. I got to know about this job from the papers. I was thinking, "Drive a bus? I've never driven a bus before leh. Wonder how it feels like. Let me try it out lah?" And then after I'd tried it out, I was like, "Hey, it's not bad!" And then the salary – it's also okay, quite okay ah. So now … it's just that I can't spend as much time with my family lah. Yeah, I do feel a bit guilty for that. I have four kids. Two of them are in college, one is in secondary school, one is in primary school. Johor Bahru lor, the college in JB.

This here ah? No lah, I didn't cook it. My wife cooked this, she says it's for me to eat a little healthier. This here, I call it my ai qing can, my "meals of love". She cooked and packed it for me. You want to take a look? [shows lunch box] This is my lunch hor, and over here – ah, this is my dinner, for later. Yeah, so she will cook and pack my meals for me every day. That's why I say it's my good luck, I married such a good and caring wife.

Look at the others here, they dabao their food from outside every day, and it's so oily. They buy it from outside. Yeah, of course you can buy it from the canteens nearby, but there's no time, you know. If you come back late, you only have 20 minutes, where are you going to have time to go out and buy the food?

The bus drivers here … well, I think I can get along quite well with them. As a person, I'm quite easy-going lah. Every day I'll brew a pot of tea, and place it here. You all want to drink tea, just grab a cup. My reason is … you know, I see so many of these bus captains all the time, they'll always drive until they are so tired. When they are tired, they will drink Red Bull, all those energy boosters, it's not good for the body lah. I feel that if you drink all these Chinese teas, it's a lot better. So, every day I'll brew a pot. You don't have to pay for the tea leaves, it's my contribution. It doesn't come up to much anyway.

Yeah, we have to undergo training, of course. We have this training school. Then you have to sit for an exam, and then only when LTA (Land Transport Authority) gives you a pass, then you can start driving. You need at least two months of training. Yeah, two months and then you can be a bus captain.

Actually driving buses isn't such a stressful job at all. It's still okay lah. Our greatest stress actually comes from … management. Not the passengers. Even if we are late, as long as we explain ourselves, most times the passengers will accept our explanations. I've done this job for four years, and from my first year at work until now nobody has ever complained about me. I personally feel passengers are very reasonable. If you explain, they will accept. At most just a few passengers lah, they will complain. But we also have to understand them. Imagine if you're one person just waiting for half an hour and there's no bus – you'd be so pissed off too, right? So we try to be understanding too lah. When they board and say a few things, we just go, "Oh, so sorry." And then carry on driving lor. Yes, that's right, it's not like anybody wanted this to happen mah.

The thing that left me the most touched ah … so there were three aunties, when I started working the afternoon shift. That time, it was the Chinese Lunar New Year. It was the third or fourth day of the New Year, so everyone's back at work already. When they finished work, they specially waited until my bus arrived – then, after getting onto the bus, they gave me an angbao. And then still said thank you. "Waaah," I said, "Auntie, I'm really very touched!" Although there wasn't much money in the angbao, that gesture ... even until now as I say it, I'm still very moved.

If you must know, there's a lot of focus needed when we are driving. You just slip up one moment – and there you go. So you know why sometimes hor, you see all these bus accidents ah, why are there so many? This is the reason. Tired, yes. Because, if you think about it, you're driving for two hours at one go, and then the whole time, your mental focus needs to be very intense. Especially during peak periods. Old people, young kids, hor. Even if it's not a pedestrian crossing hor, they assume that you've seen them, so they just cross, just like that. A lot of times, that's how accidents happen. I've had a lot of close shaves myself. Ah, that's just how things are.

So ... you know, all these problems, management knows about them, it's not like they are unaware. They just pretend they don't know about it. Rest times, break times, it's okay if we miss them, you know? The most important is our lunch time. Half an hour? It's not definite. Sometimes they give you 20 minutes, hor, 25 minutes. But then, who knows? The next break after that is 10 minutes, 8 minutes, and then you're running again. Yeah, it's like being in the army, that's right! To the minute, go, go, go! That's just how it is here.

Sometimes hor three, four rounds, I'm just going and going, even though I really need to pee, I just hold it in and keep going, just keep going. Until I finish my fourth round hor, okay break lah, got five or six minutes, okay quickly go for a piss and a smoke. Rice ah? No need to eat already lah. Eat what? No need to eat lah. So for those of us that work in this job, most times lah, always have one illness: that's stomach pains. All of us have stomach problems. There was once I was driving this route, then never eat. Stomach pain lor, until it flared up, and I had to be warded in NUH. Pain until I couldn't drive. Pain until my hands and legs were trembling. That was last year. No lah, it wasn't so serious, I just stayed for one night in the hospital.

Actually ah, another problem that we face here … well, a few bus captains, including me, we smoke. And in Singapore … yeah, the cost is one thing, but there aren't even many places you can smoke. You should give us a place to smoke, at least. No such thing. Here? Well, actually you're not allowed to smoke here. If we wanted to take a smoke legally, wow, do you know how far we actually have to walk? If they catch you smoking, they'll cut your bonus, it'll be on your record.

You know ah, after I finish driving one cycle ah, it's okay if I don't eat, but I need at least to have a smoke. Because if I don't smoke, I'll be very drowsy, and it's very difficult to concentrate. Even half a stick will do, because then at least I have some energy, some focus. So sometimes ah, this supervisor of ours, even when we're running late, he'll give us a few minutes to smoke. Upstairs, the management, they'll say, "Hey, time's up, you must go immediately!" Yeah, they'll scold you! It doesn't matter if I have a full bladder; I really need to pee ah. But our supervisor will help us to hold them off for a while, so we have a few minutes.

No, there isn't management here at the terminal, but there's a telephone. Which is to say, we are still under control lor. Under telephone control lor. On the buses, there's also a line, if they need to say a few words to us. But this place, there isn't anyone bossing us around lah, it's just a place for us to rest, yeah. This is just a small little terminal. There are fewer buses here. It's definitely more relaxed here, because the people here are also more easy-going lah. They aren't so anxious.

I've driven this route for … nearly a year now. Almost a year.

No, they won't change me already. I've reached the point where I'm confirmed in this route liao. So for all the routes hor, after you've been driving for eight or nine months, the company will arrange for you, they'll ask you what route do you want to drive. Yeah, I chose to come here. Why? Because I've always believed in the saying "tian gao huang di yuan". That means if you're far away, the emperor can't see you. [laughs] Our supervisor here, he's really easy-going. He was once a bus captain too, so he understands. It's not like management over there, you know.

But I have to say, towards this company, I really like it a lot. I'm really satisfied. I'm still willing to work very hard for this company. But the management.... So many of these accidents ah, too many of these accidents are happening. It's not because we are bad bus captains, or that we are lazy, okay? We are professional. We are bus captains hor, we are trained to a very high standard. All of us who graduate from the school, it means there is absolutely no problem with our skills. If we had problems, we wouldn't even have made it past the training. It's really more to do with the kind of conditions – the problems – we face.

It's really a contradiction. The company stresses that safety comes first, hor, but then over here, what does the management demand of us? Punctuality. This is a conflict lah. They keep stressing us. The first shift I go, no problem. The second round, I start to have problems. By the third shift, you still rush me like that, it's very difficult lah. So that's why, a lot of the new ones hor, just come in, just come out from their training, those bus captains hor – accident. This is why. So you know, you hear in the news, someone got killed ah, all those accidents? This is also a problem of the management, not just the drivers themselves. Their internal organisation isn't even coherent, then they put all this pressure on us, put all the blame on us. They don't want to accept any responsibility. All these accidents where the buses knock people down – who would want to knock anybody down?

That time when I had an accident, it was also because of this pressure to meet the timing lor. That was when I'd just arrived. So back then ah, I was really nervous about these things. Because I was running late already, you see. It was at night, I wanted to go back already, I was so hungry. Because they had given me 28 minutes to eat, and I was already running late by 14 minutes. Once we go into the bus park, we still have to line up to park the vehicle, still have to wait, by the time all this was done I would be left with only five or six minutes….

"Go lor. Go!" That's what the management there said to me. "Time's up, go, go, go!" Yeah, "go" until I had the accident.

That was my only accident. After that, I slowly got more experienced. Don't need to stick to the schedules so tightly, just running and running, non-stop. Now: late ah? Okay lor, at most just don't rest, just go on lor. That's how we cope with things here. Yeah, so don't need to be so panicky.

So you see, the higher levels, they're way too high up, they won't ever see such things. All our schedules, all the adjustments, it's done by them, but they've no idea what we're going through. They'll say, "This is your own problem. If other people can meet the timing, why can't you?" Once they use this question on you, there's really not much you can say. You know that saying, "If you have bitterness, just swallow it yourself?" This type of hardship we just have to swallow lor, there's nothing we can do.

Choo Ruizhi

MRT Station Usher

I'm Nancy. I'm a service ambassador at an MRT station. I work from 7 a.m. to 11 a.m. daily, ushering passengers in and out of the MRT carriages, giving directions to the elderly and those people who are lost. I also help people at the ticket station if they don't know how to buy tickets.

I applied for the job after I saw a notice on the boards at Yishun MRT station and decided that it is something that I want to do. On that day itself, I brought my birth certificate, identification card and all the paper to apply. I used to be a Chinese teacher for 10 over years, but I retire already, so I got nothing to do in the morning, so I thought it's better to find a job and do something, because afternoons I give tuition. After I retired, I got nothing better to do, so I went to do my supervisor course, English course, service course to improve myself. I take the course so I can speak English and talk to passengers, if not later very paiseh when passenger say things then I cannot understand.

This job is okay lah, not a bad job if I don't think so much. I'm not fussy and I don't go and listen to what people gossip about. Some people ask me why I change from a teacher, to work in this kind of job. So I ask them what do they mean, this is a good job after all, can help people and it's part-time. [a passing uncle waves and exchanges greetings] True lah, passengers don't really care about us. Sometimes they see our job as lowly and feel that it's a dirty job. Just the other day, the train stopped at Ang Mo Kio and all passengers have to alight. I blow my whistle, then this Indian man suddenly shout at me, ask me to shut up. But I just be nice and explain that he has to get off, then I walk away. I work in the morning, then afternoon I can do my own things, go out, give tuition, meet my friends. I cannot complain.

I like the job. My colleagues are like my friends, we can talk and joke with one another. Actually that is how I got to know more about the job. I have heart problem, so I often go to Outram Park (National Heart Centre) there was a lady who work this job also, we used to talk. Then I saw her here at Ang Mo Kio and she ask me, "Wah, why you not teaching?" And I told her I retire already lah, now I'm working here. [laughs] You see the lady just now, [points to another staff member] she treats me very well, after work she will ask me to eat lunch with her. I made a few friends while working here, sometimes we go out together also.

I do meet nice passengers too. There was once when I just started out, there was a lady, she forgot to eat breakfast then she collapsed. Luckily I was there, I'm fat, so I can catch her and bring her downstairs to rest. After her husband came to bring her home, she kept thanking me. It's my job what, so I told her it's okay. Got another time, there was an ah pek, the Indians and Malay cannot understand what he said, keep saying he want to go to Dhoby Ghaut. You also know lah, all the old people get angry very easily, he keep shouting. So I went to help him, then he said he want to go to NTUC, so I bring him to the escalator to NTUC. That day, the supervisor say I good. That time also got one old auntie, she wanted to go Aljunied. By right, need to change to Circle Line, but old people cannot walk so much, so I told her to take bus and bring her to the interchange. That day the supervisor also tell me I good. [shrugs and smiles] As long as I do my thing properly, I don't care what, good or bad.

Of course not everyone is so nice. Sometimes we maybe have conflict, when emotions are not so good, then sometimes will quarrel. My supervisor when I first started, he forced me to do what was beyond my job scope because he is higher than me lor. There was once, I reached the station at around 6 a.m., because I'm usually early, then the lift spoil and my manager insisted that I had to go up to the platform to start work. He tell me, "You! Go up now! Start now!" I was having my breakfast and he just shout at me. He was a man and I am a woman and he just raise his voice, of course I not happy, but because he is my supervisor, so I have to do what he says. After I tell my colleague, some of them say I have to apologise to him, but I don't agree. This is not necessary because it is not even my fault, he should apologise to me. I studied service, and if he need help, he should say "please", "excuse me", cannot just shout at people. It's very rude, but what to do, he's the supervisor, if I want to work some more, I just keep quiet. Aiyah, better don't talk so loud, later the other people say I gossip.

You see, all the people here all dark-skinned, not many Chinese. They always side each other, you know they same race, so a few of them stand there and scold me if I do something wrong, but then I just keep quiet. I just ignore because I want to work here, so I just don't care about them and do my own things. I'm also new and I work here to pass time. I told my children what happen and he say, if I can take it then just continue to work, if I cannot take it then he will go down and tell my supervisor and I don't have to work anymore. But aiyah, I don't want to cause so much trouble, just quietly work to pass time, I also don't need a lot of money, and I don't want to have nothing to do also.

But I want to work, so I won't think so much. About nine years ago, my husband had an affair. I came home and caught him in bed with a China woman. I was so angry. I call my children to come home. My children gave him two options, either to leave the China woman, or to leave the family. You guess what he chose? He left. If I not strong, I think I die already. Lucky my heart can still take it also, you know I got heart problem, my heart got five balloons inside, the balloons never burst already very good. After that I take the time to learn English, and take courses so I don't lose to people. I told myself that I cannot go into depression just because my husband left, if my husband see that I cannot survive, he would think that without him I will die. So I need to be strong and not think so much, even my siblings also say I very strong, because if it were them, they long ago die already. That's why I say education is important, if last time I never go to school like my siblings, I think now I wouldn't be standing here.

I'm just thankful I have this job. I'm already 64 years old, ah mah already. My grandchild is 13 years old and my oldest son is already 40 years old. Cannot really tell, right? Because I eat lots of fruits and vegetables. I got heart condition, you know, I still need to take medication and go for check-up. You look around, a lot of aunties working here, maybe because now Singapore got more old people. But I tell you, men are not suitable for this job, women are more motherly and patient, so we last longer. If more men work in this job, I think every day we'll have fights. [laughs]

I only work for three months, but I always make sure I say, "Good morning, how are you?" and put on a smiling face. You make people happy you also make yourself happy. Last time I tell people to move in, I shout, but nobody care, so now I try say, "Please kindly move in for passenger," some will move a little. So talk to people need to talk nicely one. [laughs] Got some passengers, they look at their phones like looking at treasure like that, but I always talk to them, then sometimes they would come and greet me like a friend. That's why I want to work here longer, because I got good relationship with passenger and I get to know more people. The job keeps me busy, so I won't think about this, think about that lor.

Charmaine Pang

Postal Worker

My mother gave me the title "Al-Amin", which in Arabic means "trustworthy". I also not sure why, but my guess is so that I will be a responsible son, always caring and looking after her after my dad passed away 10 years ago. I am the eldest son in the family. I will always visit her at least once a month, or more when I have more free time. I will be 58 years old this November. I have three sons and my wife is a housewife. All three of my boys still live with me. I am

thankful lah, that I am able to provide for my family until they are all grown up now and successful.

I have seven other siblings, thus I started working at an early age. I did not manage to complete my formal education since I have to work and earn money to support the family and ease the burden of my dad. He was working two, three jobs at once. He was rarely at home. Life was tough in the past. It was not easy to work and study, both at the same time. At night, I was tired and sleepy and could hardly concentrate when in class. So I stop my education when I was in Primary 6. Actually, I fail the final examination three times. I gave up studying and did part-time work during the day and attended classes at night. But still no formal education certificate. I did various part-time jobs before. Cleaner. Sweeper. And even selling kueh (Malay: cakes) around the kampung last time. That is why now I always tell my children to study hard to have good education and lead a better life, work a better job than what I did. Do not be like me. Do hard work, get paid little. That is why I regret that I did not take my education seriously. If I could change the past, certainly I would have studied harder and get good qualifications.

Now I have been working as a postman for more than 35 years already. Before that I was job hopping. I was lucky to be able to land this job even though I had no education. Being a postman is hard. We have to cycle while carrying heavy loads of letters, parcels and registers (registered mail). Thus you need to be healthy, fit always. I cycle a bicycle and not ride a motorbike. The company used to offer me chance to get a motorbike licence, but I refuse since my mum was against that idea of riding a bike. To her, it is very dangerous. No one in my family rides a bike. The bicycle that the company gave me is a lousy bicycle. Seriously, how can they give me this kind of "piyo piyo" bicycle which is so old fashioned and not strong enough to carry my daily loads of letters, parcels and others which can amount to 15 or 20 kg? Front and back of the bicycle! Of course the bicycle will wobble! But I still prefer to make one trip rather than two trips. I do not like to waste time. I do not know why the management so stingy one. Least they could do is to provide a good bicycle so that I do my work more efficiently and better. Even if the bicycle got problems I have to repair it with my own money. The company would not account for this matter.

I will wake up every day at 4 a.m. Wash up, perform my prayers, eat a light breakfast. On days that I wake up later, I will pack them lah. Usually my wife prepares them for me. But if she is too tired or unable to wake up, then I make the breakfast and drinks myself. I will leave house around 5:30. I take bus to work and reach my workplace by 6:15. I would pray again, the first out of the five mandatory daily prayers in Islam. The official timing to start work is actually 7:30, but I start by 6:30. I will need to sort the letters first. Each postman has to do this. Some are lazy to do this sorting of letters. Sometimes others are jealous because of my work style. But I am stern when it comes to work. They cannot disturb me when I am doing my work. Once they was some PR postman who would scold me for not sorting all the letters. I am a senior postman so I know my responsibilities. I gave that PR guy a good scolding. I wake up his idea and told him that he should sort his own letters himself. After that he kept quiet and shut up. I find it unfair that these PR postman, mostly from Malaysia, when they start work here, they earn as much as I do! They will double the money when they bring back Malaysia, you know. They will profit. I took 35 years to get the amount I earn now while these PR when they just arrive they earn quite high already. But that is why you need certificate and paper qualifications now.

I will cycle around the Tanjong Pagar area, Robinson area and some parts of the CBD to send the letters. I hate to see new buildings being developed around my area. This means I got more letters to send. More workload. But still same pay. That is why, do not be a postman. For registers, the client need to sign on the letter of acknowledgment. If the office is closed they will need to collect it from any nearby Singpost offices. I had bad experiences before. But some are funny too! [laughs] For those who slow to open their door, I would force myself in. Yes! I did it a few times before. I hate it when they are slow. Delay my work. Then the workers will give me a surprise and shocked face if I do that. [giggles]

I like to do things fast. I hate to waste time. That is why my superiors and friends call me "Superman", simply because I will be the first to finish sending the letters before anyone else. What is my secret? No secret. Just do everything fast-fast. So people get jealous. It is normal. I cannot change my style because of others. My supervisors keep on changing. Some are good, some are bad. I like those who recognise your hard work and performance. Not to boast lah, but I always do my job fast and well. Less complaints from clients. No troubles. But sometimes I get mad when I get lower bonus money than my friends who are more terrible than me. Plus I worked in the company for a very long time! So it is so unfair to me. But I cannot do much. I cannot complain as I am the breadwinner for my family. I am thankful for this job and do not want unnecessary problems. I only voice out when they gave negative comments or remarks about my work. Then I will talk back and defend myself. Now my supervisor is not so good. Usually I end by 3:30 p.m. After that I can straightaway go home. But under this new person now I can only go back home at 5. So I help my friends, those who have not finish sending their letters. Even so, I still come early every day to work. That has been my daily routine and change of management styles will not affect it.

I used to not taking MC when I sick lah. Be it fever, diarrhea, or body ache. I will try my very best to go to work. Because if I take

MC, my friends have to cover my work. I don't want to burden them with extra work. Some more, taking one day MC they will cut $25 from your pay. I already earn less than $2,000, even after 35 years of working. So I cannot afford to have lesser pay. But now since I am getting older, I take MC when needed. I need to rest my body. My sons also encourage me to take MC when I am sick now.

Problems? Have lah. I lost a registered mail before. But that was not entirely my fault. When that happens I need to make a police report. Police report because some register are confidential items or documents. Thus making a police report save myself from further troubles and I have to inform the office when that happens. Luckily only once so far in my career that happens.

What else ah? When I just started working, I would cycle very fast. There was this one time when I need to make a sharp left turn. My speed was too fast and the load was too heavy. So what happen? I panicked when I saw a car coming my way. Thus I jumped out and throw the bicycle away. The car stopped and the driver look at me, feeling a bit guilty. My bicycle was on the pathway. My bag of letters were everywhere. I needed to pick them up. It was a humorous incident. I was a newbie back then. Now I have no problem cycling fast or making a sharp turn. I need to use road when cycling, but so far no dangerous accident occurred.

Now the retirement age is 62. I still have a couple more years to work. My only worry now is what can I work as after I retire, since I have no qualifications. Or maybe I will sign yearly contract to work as a postman and work till my body cannot work anymore. I do not know about the future. But for now, I will just continue to work as a postman and provide for my family. I always wish and pray that my sons would not have the same fate as me. And I pray that I will have good health to continue working for my family.

Muhammad Fathul Ariffin Bin Ayub

PROTECTING

CHAPTER NINE

PROTECTING

Police Officer

How did I end up working with the police force? Well, when I did NS, I was assigned to the police for two years. And at the end we had the option to continue on a part-time basis. So then I started university and I was thinking, like, if I could do this whenever I'm free, like weekends, you know, Friday, Saturday night, then why not lor?

We work a 12-hour shift, so we start at 8 a.m. and work till 8 p.m., or 8 p.m. till 8 a.m. But usually it drags on, so in reality it becomes a 15-hour shift. Because there's always stuff that needs to be resolved. Let's say we arrest somebody, we have to finish up the paperwork, right?

Whether the shift is intense or not really, depends on a few factors, like, definitely the timing. During daytime you have different kinds of cases compared to the night shift. Or it depends on whether it's a public holiday or a festive period. Because, let's say it's Christmas: you obviously get more drunk people than on a normal day. But it really varies. There are certain days when things start happening and they never stop, and other days when you're just driving around looking for something to do.

We work in four-men teams, because one police car can put like three to four people. I'm attached to a team that patrols a tourist area. It's quite demanding, because with four men there is only so much you can do. You know, we've got sex crime – prostitution – because I mean naturally when you have a tourist area, the sex tourism comes along with it. You have the massage parlours, the strip clubs and bars and stuff, and then that is where the underaged part comes in too. Policing this can be really challenging.

The job isn't really physically demanding – in Singapore no one really tries to run away from the police – but emotionally it is. You get domestic violence calls. Or stuff like child abuse, parents who are alcohol or drug addicts; they would physically or even sexually abuse their children. Some days you have to interview a victim of abuse and you can't really ask the child a question like, "Have you been sexually abused?" You have to really angle the question in a harmless way, and that is the part that really saps you emotionally. Because even after you finish your shift you still think about this child and you ask yourself, "Did I do enough? Did I do it right?"

My first day on the job was a suicide case. So I had to go through the body – or whatever remained of it – to look for his ID card. The person jumped off a roof, it was very messy. That was quite a heavy experience. But with time … I wouldn't say you learn to deal with it, but you have to go through it and then … work is work. You sacrifice your emotions, lock yourself down and tell yourself that you don't have time or use for that now, because, you know, you have a job to do and you have to get stuff done. So, that is partially how you deal with it. There is nothing much you can do. Often, when the police come, the damage is already done.

One day that I particularly remember was a few years back. There was a riot in Little India. A foreign worker was run over by a bus, so his friends got very upset and started burning buses. So it was a full-scale riot on the streets of Little India. That was one of the few times where I did really feel scared. Because, if you imagine Singapore, you don't exactly expect riots on the street. But for that day you had dustbins and bricks and objects been thrown at you as you stand there with all the cars burning. And you are like: "Shit, what am I doing?" That was pretty heavy.

I mean, it was scary, but it was also the most exciting thing in my life. To be honest, I think after four years of doing this I've developed an appetite for adrenaline, in the sense that I need to have a minimum amount of drama to excite me. After a while you get kinda numb. Nowadays when I deal with a case of death, there's actually not much emotion involved, because I kind of see it as a daily occurrence. If it happens, it happens.

Still, dealing with these things isn't easy. I guess everyone has their own way of dealing with emotional stress on the job. Me, I turn to music. So basically I plug myself in and blast a lot of songs to carry away the negative energy. And religion helps too. But I know we also have a lot of people that turn to stuff like smoking or drinking to cope with the stress. That's the not-so-glamorous side of law enforcement that no one really talks about.

Every month we have a review with a superior to assess not only our performance but also our mental state: are you emotionally ready to take on duties? So if you say maybe you are not up for it at the moment, then maybe you will just take a break for month, or you get a referral for psychiatric help or whatever is necessary. All so that the appropriate help is given to people at the appropriate time.

That's the theory, anyway. Because of course you can fake your answers, you can tell people, "Yeah, I'm fine," or "There's no issue." Because for some people, they depend on this for their livelihood. For me, I'm a part-timer, so there's no harm in being honest. But for people who are doing this as a career, right, when you are off for psychological reasons, you get a pay cut. So some people just lie, because they need their salary for their families. This is a loophole in the system that they are trying to plug, but I don't think … I don't know whether they'll be able to do it, you know? It's a pervasive mindset in government. They sort of put the onus on you. They take your word for it, and then, if something happens, they will blame you and say, "Oh, before you said you were fine, and now this is your statement." So it becomes like a double disciplinary issue now. In a sense, they just wash their hands of the problem.

And the other thing is, you know … like it or not, the uniform service is a male-dominated environment, so there is a lot of pressure to sort of put up a front, especially with all the guys around. So, in that sense even when you have a problem, they will basically just tell you to man up. It is a very alpha kind of dominant mindset. You know, when the newcomers come in they are sort of indoctrinated into that sort of mindset, and after a while people are too scared to ask for help. Because that is the culture, that is the way the organisation functions.

In terms of ethnicity, the police has hands down the most amount of Malays. It was like this the day I entered and it's still like this today. I guess it is due to their employment conditions. Obviously, when the government recruits for the services, when they are screening people to join this career, they will definitely take into account the educational background and stuff like that. But in Singapore, race is a very sensitive issue. So there are even certain events when the force is made of teams only consisting of non-Muslims, so only Chinese teams. Things like security for national events, certain areas.... Officially it wouldn't be called discrimination, but they rather use the broad term of policy. Basically this is – how they say? – that policy dictates certain things. But I leave it to you to draw your conclusion.

We have a fixed team that we're assigned to. As a team we are really close. I've been with the same team for four years now. One

thing about the uniform services is that we train to a level where we know we can trust the person next to us. That means you can place your life in his hands. One of the basic things they taught us is: "If you fuck up, another person dies." It is not like oh, this is like a scenario exercise where I say, "Oh, can I go back to the drawing board and let's start over again." No. If you screw up and someone gets injured, that is a very heavy responsibility. So when you train, you have to know your stuff, right? That's why we know we can depend on each other completely. We support each other, and by now we can sort of read each other's emotions. So you know when somebody is having a bad day and you step up for him, or today he knows I'm not having a good day, and he'll fill in for me. We're really a tight-knit group.

I identify as bisexual. This makes some people feel uncomfortable. And I don't really hold it against them, because in Singapore a lot of people just haven't had to deal with this sort of thing yet. I mean, in Singapore people are used to a guy and a girl walking, holding hands, and maybe a girl and a girl. But the moment they see two guys holding hands they get freaked out. I can understand it. It doesn't bother me professionally, because the way I see it is: work is work. I don't think anyone's gender identity, or family background, or race should affect how we view each other.

I've come out to my team as bisexual. They may not agree with it. But I guess there remains a degree of mutual respect, in the sense that: "You may not agree with what I'm doing; but that doesn't mean I'll impose my values on you." But there are still certain people who, I wouldn't say they are against it, but they're just confrontational. So they would try to find chances to … I wouldn't call it bullying, but to casually mention stuff, just to … make you feel uncomfortable. Like, they would say things like: "Oh, so-and-so has been back to see his boyfriend." And they will say it in a very sarcastic way that tries to put you down. [laughs] You just learn to deal with it.

There are other LGBT people out in the force. Lesbians especially. The thing is, it's easier for women to be out than it is for men. I've got female co-workers who are lesbian, and people are a bit more accepting. So for them, they sort of have it slightly easier ... not exactly easy, but just slightly easier with co-workers.

When I first came out, I guess people were a bit fearful to sit next to me. Suddenly they didn't feel comfortable. But I mean, if I didn't tell you, would you even know? I guess in Singapore sexuality is still seen as something that can be influenced. I keep telling them: "I cannot force you to like a certain ethnicity; I cannot tell a Chinese person to only like a Chinese person. Same goes for gender: I cannot force one particular gender not to like another gender." [laughs]

And I guess after a while people realise you're still someone who does their job, you're still someone they can count on, and maybe you're not that bad after all. But you definitely need a period of time to gain their trust again. If people have an issue with you, it's a very subtle thing. Sometimes things can get very awkward, because you can be sitting in the car next to each other for hours without saying a word. [laughs] Or after work, right, they will just go off, part ways. You learn to deal with it. For me this took about one year plus. Yeah, for these 12 months it was a more difficult journey.

Yes, the law specifically criminalises acts of gay men. But the way I see it, our job is to enforce the law, it's not our job to debate whether it's moral, right? One thing about the military and law enforcement is that you do not question an order. If you begin questioning: "Why do you do this? Why do you do that?" Then eventually people will get hurt, people will die. You need discipline so that everything runs smoothly and no one screws up. Because even if in a personal sense I may not agree with it, but in a professional capacity, when I'm wearing the uniform, I have to do my job. That is where I have to draw the line. Of course I will not go out of my way to arrest anyone, but if the order is given, I will definitely do it.

To be honest, the perception of uniform jobs in Singapore is actually quite poor. So when you tell someone you're in the uniform service, especially when you are from university, you get questions like: "Why can't you find a real job? Why don't you do this other job?" Everyone is running off to the private sector, you know, wants to be part of a bank or a consultancy firm. "Why would you want to wear a uniform and do 14-hour shifts, and burn your weekends and public holidays?" That kind of stuff. Even my parents, they ask: "Why do you spend all your time doing that stuff?"

At first, this negative public perception made me question my decision. But I thought about it, and I realised that for me, being on the police force is really another kind of social work. The number of people you help, the kind of people you help – broken families, kids, victims of violence, people like that – you can't place a dollar figure on the value of the work we do. It might sound idealistic when I say this, but I'm doing this job because I feel an obligation to serve this country. When I think about all the people who have served before me, I feel like it's my turn to give back to Singapore after living here for the past 22 years. You don't get freedom and security by doing nothing. Someone has to step up and do the dirty work.

Jona Jannis

Investigation Officer

I was with the police force for almost seven years. Since I graduated from school till 2016. I was an assistant investigation officer with the financial investigation branch under the commercial affairs department of the Singapore police force. It was a huge enforcement agency, all controlled by the Ministry of Home Affairs. After I finished my National Service I worked here. There was no training prior, they hired based on qualifications. So I was a polytechnic diploma holder, and based on that they hired me after the interview. But there were quite a few tests, they will check your National Service records, and I had to do psychometric tests, and one more test, can't remember what it was called.

I didn't want to work in the police force, but I couldn't secure any other interviews at that point in time and I wanted to start working quickly. I decided on civil service because that was the only thing available. I finished NS in November and started working here in January, after medical checks and background checks and nobody knows what else.

I didn't exactly hate my job, I could do it because it wasn't that hard. But I told myself that I wasn't going to stay for a long time. It gave me a fairly good pay, and that was the enticing part. It was rather interesting, for someone like me who majored in communications and was freshly out of National Service. I got to go out and conduct investigation, and ... solve crime, for a lack of better term for it. But if you ask me if I liked it, no. Back then I thought it could get a job in the private sector doing advertising. Something creative. Or in public relations sector. But I couldn't secure a job paying more than an intern's pay. They expected us to basically be an intern for more than three months.

So my job is like ... not every day, but sometimes we go to do a raid. We surprise them at their homes and basically tell them: we need to go through your home because we have received a complaint against you that you are involved in alleged crime. For us it's financial related crimes. We search their belongings, and I've done quite a bit of searches throughout the seven years. This is not every day. Most days it's actually desk-bound, when you have to go through tons of bank statements. I also have to take statements from them and then plough through their statements to search for evidence to see if it is sufficient to proceed to charge them.

When we show up at their place, they are surprised and can get a little hostile. So far I have not seen any violent cases, and I get accompanied by police officers who are armed and trained. We do prepare for worst-case scenarios. They are somewhat shocked and most of the time wondering, "What am I in for?" So they are quite cooperative because they don't know what has happened. So they sometimes have a lot of questions and can be very defensive and intimidating. Yes we do arrest them too, and if the evidence that they have provided in the interview is insufficient we can detain them, the law allows us to detain them for up to 48 hours, then out on bail thereafter. They can contact their families and their workplace to explain why they are not at work. I think the treatment is quite humane; when we arrest them we try to be discreet. We don't arrive in police cars, and we try not to get the neighbours' attention. So I think it's quite respectful.

Sounds exciting, but it gets to you after a while. It can get rather repetitive, and you don't see the progress. A case can drag on for a few years, so it cannot be resolved fast. This consultation back and forth with the Attorney General's chambers is a very long and thorough process. It's not like what you see on television – cannot solve so quickly, it can take years. And at one time we can have 40, 50 cases unresolved on our hands, all in different stages. The evidence we deal with is really tedious because we are dealing with fraud and other financial crimes. We have had cases where we send boxes of interview transcripts for the prosecutors to plough through. It takes us about a year to prepare those, probably. So it's really extensive and tedious. It's not like, say, a murder, where there is the knife, and a dead person. No, we have to gather the evidence and make a case. The paperwork is crazy and it makes the bulk of our work.

It was crazy, I learned so much about money laundering. Prior to this job I had never even heard of it. It's very prevalent in Singapore, because Singapore is a financial hub. There still are a lot of loopholes, so much money being transferred in and out of Singapore. Some of the companies that money is being transferred to are fictitious, and we find out when people make reports. There is a suspicious transactions reporting thing … it's a whistleblower lah, basically. Singapore implemented in 2003. Financial institutions like banks and remittance agencies will know this. For example, someone transferred $3,000 to some account in the Philippines, they need to declare their particulars. If someone doesn't earn that much, and they transfer a lot of money, then that's suspicious and our office will pick it up.

Very often we deal with small fry: someone has been duped into transferring money and they believe it. Like maybe someone told them their relative is sick and they need to transfer money into an account for medical fees. It's actually the syndicates behind it. They may dupe 10 people in a scam, and when we find these individuals who make suspicious transfers we find out how complex the case is. These suspects are actually also victims, they don't even know they have been scammed and implicated in a crime. Once the money goes out of Singapore we have to work with Interpol and the suspicious transactions offices elsewhere in the world can share information with us.

In the years I've dealt with a lot of high-profile cases, involving religious institutions, listed companies, individuals who … can be Googled. The investigations into religious institutions I think is the most tormenting. Because people fail to see that it's not the religion, it's the people. Yah, I don't want to judge them, you know. I realise that people abuse their power when they are in a position to lead or in a position to gain people's trust. Wealth is very corrupting lah, people who have some, they want more. It's just human nature, greed and wanting more. It has nothing to do with their religion. They think that by surrounding themselves with people who agree with them, they are right.

In my department it was predominantly Chinese, I would say 80 per cent? Initially when I came in I thought it was a bit intimidating, but I realised afterwards it's because I was the only junior officer who was Malay. I think it wasn't a problem lah. But you know what was weird for me? There was a trend that when there was a minority officer who was transferred out or resigned, there will be another minority who is hired. So there is a racial quota. We kind of get used to it, but it's still a problem. I mean, Singapore majority Chinese right? What do you expect? But I don't think race is a problem for me. I think at work, it's always your performance, there is always a reason, I have never felt discriminated. I think the only people who claim to be discriminated against must stem from a personal conflict or a misunderstanding.

Why I speak Chinese ah? [laughs] My mum is the reason lah; I think all mums are amazing role models. She likes to watch Chinese dramas. I think honestly Channel 8 is the only channel that makes decent dramas. So we learn by reading the subtitles and linking in with whatever that was being said. Soup is tang, and meat is rou, then we progressed to harder words, then after that phrases. I think you learn best when you are young and you are not being forced to learn. I realised I could pick it up after a while. Plus living in Singapore you hear it everywhere. Now even when I encounter new words I can figure out the meaning from the tone and the context. I can even differentiate between PRC accent and Singaporean Chinese accent and the dialects. I use my Chinese at work. There were a lot of times when I had to make calls, and when I had to go to homes and offices when we have to bring evidence back, then sometimes there were

those cases where the person or family member just didn't speak English and I can just say, "Wo men shi jing cha" (Mandarin: We are the police). I just think about the Channel 8 police dramas lah.

Sometimes at work I hear my colleagues gossiping about other colleagues in Chinese, then I will eavesdrop and tell them, "Wo zhi dao ni men jiang shen me" (Mandarin: I know what you are talking about). I think I've been quite a good colleague lah, I haven't heard anyone bitch about me.

But I think being a Malay in Singapore is unfortunate. So many non-Muslims think that every Malay Muslim is the same, and have the same level of belief, and they think that if they have a colleague or friend who is a Malay Muslim, then they think that every other Malay is the same. When even among us Muslims we have different tendencies. Me, for example. I only started praying recently and I started doing it because … yah lah, I want to be a better person and I want to be at peace. And I feel that it is such an individual and important aspect. And I discovered it through my own journey. So this is my religion lah!

Unfortunately everyone thinks that all Malays should be the same, and they should all behave the same, and worse still, should behave as all Muslims do in other countries. I give you an example. Say, they see that some women are wearing full niqab. They will come and ask me, "Eh, why are women in Singapore not doing that?" Am I a preacher? This really angers me when a colleague or a friend expects me to answer. I mean, what do you know about my religion? They do not ask with respect. I will immediately shut down the conversation because it will not lead to good things. They take me as the token Malay to answer all these questions. So how come my religion, how come Islam can be so easily discussed and everyone can come and ask me these questions? I don't go around saying, "You Christian, you do this? You Buddhist, you do this? In

Myanmar, this is happening, how come?" Then these people come and give me all the specific countries, Indonesia, Middle East, and ask me, "Why Islam like this?" This is really a trigger for me. I expect more from them because these people, they are grads, even dean's list, but just really ... Chinese privilege.

So now I've left the police force. I had a good opportunity to volunteer with this madrasah in Indonesia, a two-hour drive from Jakarta. So since 2010, I've been helping them with teaching the kids. Small things like doing the English worksheets, nothing about the Islamic studies. Then this evolved into an opportunity to go over and teach English to the children there.

To be honest I didn't even used to pray, I didn't even observe my diet, in terms of halal requirements. My parents felt that by going to this pesantren (Muslim religious school) in Jakarta, I will learn something about my belief to make me a better person. But when I decided to leave my job and I told them that I was going to stay there for a longer period to teach, they were apprehensive. They are influenced by what they read in the news, and they think Indonesia is a place that has more affiliations to terrorist groups. They are concerned that it might impact my future at work too. My elder brother's reasoning was that when I apply for another job in the future, they are going to ask me what I did during this break, where I travelled and why, and they may conclude that I'm an extremist. Especially if I apply for civil service jobs. But I think this is a concern that is valid. So maybe I'll only continue to do short visits.

So, yeah. For now I go there for a long weekend maybe every three, four months. This pesantren is pretty well equipped, it's a boarding school. For every three paying students they will take in an orphan for free. These students are really motivated. They're like 12, but they wake up at 3 or 4 a.m. to memorise the Quran. They try really hard to do well. It humbles me and inspires me. They have a direction in life, and then I think, "Look at me. I'm 29, 30. What am I doing?" I need to remind myself that money, that expectations of others, are all secondary.

Ng Shi Wen

Ex-accountant

Well ... people make mistakes lah. It's not as if I wanted to land myself in here. My wife keeps saying that I so old already, still don't know how to think. Maybe she is right that I didn't control myself because I didn't think I'd lose so much. But this thing is not entirely my fault. I guess you can say that I am gullible and too careless to trust the wrong people.

Last time I studied accounting in uni, that's where I started. I was pretty good with numbers since I was young, plus my family was rather well-to-do then. My father came to Singapore from Xiamen in Fujian Province, China. He married my mother who was born in Singapore, and I have seven other siblings. We were quite a large family then. I had the freedom to do what I wanted to, and studying seemed like my kind of thing, so uni was where I headed to. Accounting suited my character also; I just have to work with numbers at my desk. I'm quite introverted you see; the other jobs need lots of talking and selling, so I don't like. After I graduated at 23, I had to look for a job. Just nice, there was an opening at a shipyard company, so I applied and got in. I stayed in the company all the way till I'm 59 when the incident happened. It was a good and stable job, so I didn't have the intention to change job. I always believe it's better to stick to one company, so got more chance get promotion, you know?

I met my wife in the company; she was working in the office as a clerk. After dating for a while, we got married, but I was already

43 when I had my first child. I knew that I would be old before they turn into adults, so I have the need to save for their school in the future and all. My wife stopped work after we got our first child, she is now a housewife. With my mother and father staying with us then, I had the burden of being the breadwinner. Luckily, I stuck with the company and slowly but surely along the way I got my promotions. After about 30 years, I slowly climbed to the position of chief finance officer. The overall in-charge of company finances.

Life became easier for my family as I climbed the corporate ladder. My salary increased, but that was not the entire reason why finances were more comfortable. I also invested in stocks in my free time, which earned me quite a bit. I started when my friend introduced it to me during my first few years of work, and I thought: why not give it a try? I invested a little of my savings after careful calculations and research. Income was slow then, as I did not have much capital to invest. Plus those stocks that I chose were the safer ones and they have small growths. Anyway, I shouldn't bother you with the technical terms, they are complicated. Basically I chose the safer ones lah.

Usually I head on to work early in the morning, leaving the house at 6 a.m. to drive my way to the west. It's not that my work starts so early lah, just that I want to avoid morning traffic. It has become a part of my life routine to wake up early anyway. I leave when my children wake up, and get back late, so I can't spend time with them. We only do so during the weekends, so my two girls spend the bulk of their time with their mother. I guess that's why we were never super close, but I think we all still enjoyed our time out on the weekends and holidays. Also, I spend most of my free time exploring things on my own as that's how I like it.

When I say life was good at home, I meant that I would be able to take my wife and two girls out for movies every weekend. Occasionally we'd go for cruises and overseas trips, we even go for staycations and buffets when I accumulated enough loyalty points on my credit cards. Oh yeah, I have quite a few credit cards. I needed them to loan money for investments. I also liked to collect stamps, notes and coins from all over the world. Buying and selling currency is a way to earn money too. My wife didn't know exactly how many cards I have or how much I made, actually. She just manages the finances in her own account and our joint accounts.

After I became the chief finance officer, I was able to look through all the accounts of the company. I realised that much of the money usually would be sitting somewhere earning no interest when it was pending for some transaction. A friend's friend then told me about this opportunity for a high-risk, high-returns stock investment. I thought that I would be able to earn some cash from this, but I had no capital. So I borrowed from the company without anyone knowing. I thought if I could earn and put the money back where it comes from, there won't be any issues. I didn't really know anything about that friend, nor did I deal directly with the transaction. It was a stupid decision to trust him, I'm not sure why I did. Perhaps it was greed, or perhaps I just wanted even more for my family. At first I did earn some money, but slowly the stocks began to lose some money. I was worried and asked that friend, but he assured me that it was normal and I should just keep monitoring. I wanted to pull out but I couldn't. Later I told him to cancel, as the stocks went down further, but he did not respond. I had to use more money from the company funds to cover my losses. It was a mistake to use company money, but my biggest mistake was to trust someone else with risky investments.

After my case was discovered by a company staff, I was immediately suspended. The company filed a lawsuit against me, and I lost everything. My family was shocked and devastated at the suddenness of the issue, and my wife had depression for a year because of this. We had to downgrade to a smaller house, and I had to use my kids' childhood savings to buy a flat. Thank goodness they have been saving up quite a substantial amount from all the pocket money they received. My family then was also harassed by heartless reporters who just wanted a juicy piece of news to write about. Unable to get a word out of my wife, they fabricated interviews which deeply affected us. We did not want my elderly mother-in-law to know about it or read about it in the newspapers as we fear for her health, but these reporters were just incessant and a nuisance. I myself was in an emotional turmoil and mental torture, as the case in court dragged on for another seven or eight years before the final verdict was given. While waiting for my sentence, I had nightmares and was often unable to sleep. I was deeply troubled. Often I would turn to gambling to de-stress, especially with the convenience of the MBS casino. Nevertheless, I stopped soon after, as my wife was concerned and we made the effort to put my name in the list to ban Singaporeans from entering.

I feel bad for my two children, how they have to adapt to the sudden change in their life. Prior to the fall, I actually bought a condominium for us to stay in. My family was rather excited as it was the first time they get to move to a new house. However, instead of a happy move to a new condo unit, we ended up moving away from the familiar Marine Parade area to the Bedok HDB flats. My two girls had to adapt to the new environment and lifestyle of more frugality. The lucky thing is, I still do have some funds to pay for their college which I did not touch, so I was glad for that.

To get my mind off things, I went around looking for work. Some old school mates introduced me jobs as receptionist at Hotel 81, another offered me a minor accounting position, and I signed myself up for part-time taxi driver. It does not earn me much but, I guess it is better than nothing. Once I get out of jail, I will go sign up to be a security guard. I will continue working into my old age to keep myself active. For now, I will just sit in jail and read whatever my wife and girls bring me, do some work in here and exercise a little. I'm the oldest inmate in my cell, so generally everyone is rather respectful lah. Many youngsters would take turn to wash the toilet and I do not have to do it as I am so old already. They are nice youngsters who made the wrong choices in life, just like me. I try to stay positive also, through the monthly letters I receive from my family. I will keep trying to be strong, for myself and my family. Without them, this part of my life would be really difficult and unbearable. After all, all of that was what I did out of love for them.

Wee Min Er

MANAGING

CHAPTER TEN

MANAGING

Hostess Agent

My name is Roy. I'm 26 and I'm in my final semester of NUS Law, waiting for my bar exam. Yeah, a soon-to-be lawyer. I'm currently doing some part-time work. You know the girls in Thai discos? Have you ever wondered where they come from? Well, I'm their agent. I've been doing this for more than a year already. Of course I don't normally go around telling people I do this kind of work. No one in law school knows. Only my army buddies and a few of my close friends know about it.

You thought that only ah bengs will be in this line, isn't it? Well, you are half right. There are some ah bengs in this line too. But anyway there are a lot of well-educated people like me in this line as well. I have friends who are signed on SAF (Singapore Armed Forces) pilots, university students and many more. You have to drop your stereotypes about university graduates. We are not perfect human beings, or what. We do the things that interest us whether or not it is legal. As long as it hurts no one I am okay, for now. It's like chewing gum. We just happen to really love spending time in Thai discos. You need to understand that we're already hanging in Thai discos anyway, so we're just earning a little extra income out of our usual hangout place. No one's gonna get hurt. I know it is illegal and if anything happens I will get into real trouble. Well, after all I am a law student, right? [laughs] But honestly, nothing will happen. They have nothing against us. We only have verbal contracts and all our transactions are in cash. If they ask us anything about the flights we book for the girls from Thailand to Singapore, we can just say we book it for our "Thai friends". That's the worst-case scenario. But honestly, I guarantee you nothing will happen to me.

Simply put, people look for me when they need Thai girls to work in their clubs. But it is not as simple as that. I am responsible for them because I'm also their housekeeper, manager and basically everything, when they are here in Singapore. Most girls come as tourists. So they are only here for 30 days. Usually, I don't have to look for girls. Maybe they know me through a friend who worked for me before, or maybe they're a friend of my friend. I have quite a number of Thai friends, so I am very lucky. I also have different social media platforms that help me get girls: Facebook, Line or Thai online forums. All I have to do is to put up a short job description and the salary. If anyone is interested, they can then contact me. The girls will send me their photos and I will assess their suitability. I assess them based on their looks, English-speaking ability and so on. The most important is that they're outgoing. Some agents like to hire quiet girls to create a pool of choices, but me, I don't usually hire them. Boob size? [laughs] Doesn't matter. Of course, the bigger the better right? [laughs] But I'm not picky.

Anyway, like I said, some are friends of my friends. I trust their recommendations. In this line, you need a lot of luck because you are taking a gamble. You never meet some of them before they touch down in Singapore. Based on their photos, messages, calls and sometimes your friends' or ex-girls' comments, you have to decide whether or not to bring them over. Sometimes, if you're lucky, these girls can bring in a lot of sales for the club. You will earn more. If not, it is just the basic pay. Honestly, I don't really earn a lot out of this. When I get a job, I am offered around $5,000 to get a girl for a particular club. But yet, I earn only $200 to $300 per girl on average. That's ironic, right? Because from the $5,000, I offer my girls $3,500 or more for their work. It is a very competitive line. There are so many agents around. So have to keep my rates competitive and offer the girls more. I still have to pay for their air ticket, visa, lodging, even their local SIM card. Occasionally if the clubs are nice, I can claim the air ticket from them or they provide free lodging. But usually, I have to pay all these out of the $5,000. After subtracting everything, I'm only left with $200 per girl on average. The most I ever earned out of a girl is $1,000 over. She brought in a lot of sales for the disco. The boss was very happy because she was the hot favourite. I was very happy with her too. [laughs]

I have around 30 girls under me at any one point of time. It's important to keep a pool of these girls. But it is not so simple, because these 30 do not come in for work all at once. Well, it will be great if they did. Lesser work for me and I don't have to waste petrol to fetch them from the airport in batches. It sounds a little confusing, but basically I have a constant flow of girls coming into and leaving Singapore. For example, I have 30 girls in Singapore this week. Maybe next week, five of them will leave because of their visa. But another group of four or 10 girls will come in to replace them. So at any one point I will have around 30 girls with me.

My payment system is quite simple. There's no such thing called minimum pay in this line. Agents offer what we want to the girls, but I have to take into consideration the "market rate" offered by other agents, the club's offer, and the girl's past experience. I usually offer the girls around 70 per cent of what I'm getting from the club. We have to keep our offer competitive. Anyway, to get the full 70 per cent, they will have to hit X amount of sales of tequila shots or flower garlands and what have you, for example $5,000. If they don't make their sales target, I have to subtract the shortfall from their pay and give it back to the club. This way, I'm always able to get my "basic" pay. It can't be that I work for free, right? And honestly, $200 to $300 for one month of work is not a lot.

If the girls exceed their sales target, they get a bonus. This bonus depends on the additional sales they generate. After subtracting my share and the club's cut from the additional sales, the girls get their bonus. So if my girl brings in an extra $8,000 of sales, the club will give me a bonus of $4,000 or more. The bonus also depends on the club. You can negotiate for more if the girl is really good because the boss will want to bring her back again. She's your bargaining chip. But you cannot be over the line and ask for too much. You still have to maintain some sort of connections with the bosses. After all, they're your long-term clients. So usually I don't ask for more unless the amount is really too miserable. Out of this $4,000 I will give 50 to 80 per cent to the girls and keep the rest for myself. So you see, the girl who got me $1,000 she was really good. Anyway, I keep the bonus payment system vague so there's room for negotiation later.

I got into this industry at a time when it was just starting to take off. I had an army friend who'd been working as an agent for a while already, and he roped me in. He told me agents could easily earn up to $10,000 a month. The girls? They can earn around $20,000 to $30,000 for just their one month's worth of work. They go back, kiao kah (Hokkien: put feet up) for a few months then come back here again. Easy money for everybody. But times have changed. There are so many agents now. And the customers who visit Thai discos are smarter now and less willing to spend. There is an ample supply of pretty Thai girls and there are so many clubs around. So you see, customers have a lot of choices.

Also, these girls always use the same "girlfriend" tactics. When Thai discos first started, guys fell for these tricks easily so it was easy to exceed the sales targets. The guys feel special because the girls are so good at making you feel like they were genuinely interested in you and you were the only one. Honestly, before I started working as an agent, I'd been a victim of this girlfriend thing too. [laughs] But after a while, I realised it was just their way of hooking you to get you to buy drinks and flower garlands or take care of them. These days, regulars are better at avoiding the girls' moves when the girls try to get them to buy shots or flowers. But I have to say, Singaporean guys are still suckers for the girlfriend thing. They're still willing to take care of them, bring them out, even start a serious relationship. I have friends who've married these girls. They're so gentle, meek and dependent. Different from the independent and demanding Singaporean girls. That's why Thai discos are still popular in Singapore today. If there's a demand, then people are going to supply it.

I am currently working for three Thai discos and honestly I'm more like a sub-agent. Some people do this full-time. Compared to them, I am just a part-timer. The full-timers can easily have 100 over girls under them. I usually only have 30 over. There is something like a hierarchy in this line too. But we don't really have a boss or whatever. I think of it as a form of collaboration. But anyway, the discos usually have a few full-time agents they work with. These full-time agents can choose to sub their work to sub-agents like me. I usually get job offers from these full-time agents. But I also deal with Thai discos directly at other times. Below my sub-agent level, are the sub-sub-agents. We call them kah kia (Hokkien: underlings). But I don't really engage them. They take a cut. I'm already earning a miserable $200, so why will I want to give part of that to someone else?

Connections are very important in this line. Other agents, disco bosses, Thai friends and even the girls themselves. It really helps a lot if you speak Thai in this trade. Usually agents are able to speak Thai. Conversational Thai at least. It helps us in our job. Plus, I have a lot of Thai friends who give me free contacts. They refer girls who are interested in the job or people who are intending to travel to Singapore. Earn money and travel at the same time: who wouldn't jump at that offer? The girls who previously worked for me will also introduce their friends to me for free most of the time. Sometimes, the smarter ones or those who have already worked a few times here in Singapore under other agents, will ask me for some money when they introduce people. But I maintain good relations with the girls. I treat them well, so we are like friends. So usually they won't ask me for money.

The girls I hire are all real young and pretty. I like to hire new faces because customers go for novelty. But I do bring back girls who have done a good job previously. It is easier if I were to hire all "old birds" but I can't always do that. When I bring new girls over, I will have to babysit them for the first few days. I have to be with them and show them the ropes. I have to let them know their sales target, how to go about doing it and be very stern about it. Some of these girls, they don't really care about getting sales. Usually those who come are doing okay or well-to-do back in Thailand. They just happen to want to tour in Singapore, break up with their boyfriends or simply need a break. So when they come here, some don't really care about the sales. They just drink and party all night. Have fun and all.

So usually what I do is that I will pair the new ones, the ones who just arrived, with the old ones, the ones who have been here for three weeks or more. That's the good thing about having different batches of girls under you at once. You don't always have to be there since these "old birds" can bring them around and show the new ones how to do the job. So usually when they are doing their work, I am not around in the club. It is hard for me to always be around since I have girls working at three clubs. But then again, I would rather be doing something else. I have school in the morning, I need to rest. Sometimes you go inside the club and you realised it is half full? And you think that the club's business is so good? Some of them are just agents in there. Not all are customers. Some agents like to sit in the discos throughout the night, but I don't. I just need to be there on their first few days of work to monitor and guide them and check their weekly sales record with the club. And on days when they get real drunk, I have to come down and carry them home. If they are doing badly, they will get it real hard from me. Generally, I am quite a laid-back agent. I don't really scold them or force them to do things they don't want to, but that's only if they're putting in an effort. At least some sales and not like zero sales every night. That's too much.

The smarter and more experienced girls will usually try to suck up to me. Literally. Something like politics. They will seduce me, offer me hand jobs, blow jobs or the full set. You know they are up to something when they ask you down to fetch them home and when you arrive they say that they don't want to go home. What does that mean? My house then! Since they are so lonely and they need someone, why not? I gain a "girlfriend". I will take special care of them when they are here. Win-win situation. And I will not have this "special relations" with others until she goes back to Thailand. Exclusive short-term relations. But honestly, I don't love her. It's just an "I use you, you use me" kind of thing. We know that. So if another comes along after she goes, I am open to it. I don't ask to try them out. I can. But I don't. I only do that when they offer themselves and I find them attractive. I am not that low.

How long will I continue with this? Well honestly, I have no idea. It is something like an extra income to me and since I am already immersed in the Thai disco scene as a regular customer, it makes sense for me to be in this line. And it is not easy, alright?

Nobody taught me all of this. You have to learn it yourself. Initially I have friends to guide me as they are also working as agents. They introduced me some contacts and taught me how to get girls. But I can say that I picked up most of the negotiation and people skills along the way. The people skills I've learnt will be useful for my law career in future. [laughs] You need a lot of those in any line. But then again, I know I will probably stop doing this when I pass my bar exam and get my licence. After all, I'll be an actual lawyer by then.

Olivia Sng Mun Yi

Paralegal

Today I went out with Lynn to buy lunch. And then after buying lunch, right, I went to buy Gong Cha, but she don't want to buy Gong Cha. So there's a dress shop beside, and she likes to shop. I also like to shop. Then after buying Gong Cha, I went into the shop. And then she already picked some dresses that she wants to try. And then she turned to me and said in jest, "I always spend money when I'm out with you!" So I got a bit du lan (Hokkien: pissed). So I buay song (Hokkien: irritated). Most of the time she buys more than me. Legit. She buys more than me. I was buying Gong Cha, she went into the shop herself. How can she say that every time she comes out with me she spends money? Nine times out of, like, ten times right, she will be the one buying. So it's like, how can she say that she spends money every time she comes out with me? So I was a bit angry and I think I was a bit … I take it to heart. I literally took it to heart.

Yah, so that's what happened today. I was super angry all the way, from when she bought the dress, all the way until we went back to the office. Lynn likes to walk, so after we eat lunch already right, she'll say, "Want to go and walk around?" She's always the one that jio (Hokkien: invite) me to go out and shop. And we always end

up with two hours lunch break. So it's like, "Always ask me go and shop and then you go into the shop and buy clothes." And then we went to Marina Bay Link. She bought another dress. I also never buy. Every time you're the one who initiates and then you say you always spend money when you go out for lunch with me. But my soy sauce chicken noodle was so delicious, it made me feel better. And then I think right, that if I die the next minute right, I don't want to die being angry at someone who isn't even close to me. So that made me feel better too.

There are two lawyers in the office, one is the big boss and the other one is the junior associate. So we don't care about them, we also don't control them. They usually give us a lot of freedom. They will just let us be lah. Like last week Gavin was not in Singapore, so Lynn told James, "We want to go and walk around." And then James was like, "Okay, go ahead, have fun!" Like that. So if there's nothing for us to do, then we are not needed lor. Then this week also, Lynn left first. And then I left later because James also told me, "You can leave now. Get out of here soon, you're not needed here." That was like about 3 o'clock? Actually for like the past week right, we came in on time, but we get to leave early. Like, there was one day we knocked off at 2 o'clock. And for next week right, Lynn actually asked Gavin whether we can come in late, and leave early. So clearly stretching the limit lah. But Gavin said it's okay. But he also said he prefers to have someone in the office, because it's like when people call, you don't want to give people the impression like, "Why this office is officially opened, but no one is there to pick up calls?" So Gavin said yes can come in a bit later, and can leave earlier.

Next week Gavin and James are both not around. So it's just me and Lynn in the office, so there won't be any work for us to do. And also for the next next week, it'll just be me and Lynn as well. She said that she's going to spend three hours on her lunch break. She's going to like, eat for one hour, and then two hours she'll go shopping. I'll follow her lor.

In the office both of us actually have a wide spectrum of responsibilities, because right now it's just the two of us support staff only. We do ACRA (Accounting and Corporate Regulatory Authority) filings, we make sure that whatever the company needs to register is properly registered. Or we register the lawyers, because they are foreign lawyers, so we have to register them with the Law Society of Singapore so they can certify them to practice in Singapore. I'm not sure about Lynn, maybe for her it's more of, like, admin work. But for me, I do paralegal work because I used to work in a law firm. There will definitely be admin stuff, like filings, tabbing the pages and all that. But most of the time we handle legal affairs.

This firm is focused on global transportation finance. Global transportation has two big areas: aviation and maritime. James focuses more on aviation, Gavin is more focused on maritime. We are the middleman. This is a fun fact lah: actually, Singapore Airlines, Korean Air, they don't own the airplanes. The planes are owned by the banks. So we are the middleman between the banks and the airline company. Let's say Singapore Airlines operates 3,000 planes, but they're all rented from different banks. And we make it all happen. Now I'm working on Sriwijaya, the Indonesian airline, Jeju Air, Ryan Air, Emirates, Lufthansa, United Airlines, and all that. Singapore Airlines is one of our biggest clients, but I personally haven't had hands-on experience doing Singapore Airlines files lah.

We also do private jets. So recently there's this Hong Kong-Australian businessman who bought a second-hand private jet, which costs millions of dollars. It's just for his own use, but these are the people who are rich lor. Buying the aircraft is one thing: to maintain the plane, to go for servicing and pay for fuel, it's millions after millions, so these are the really rich businessmen lor. Because they cannot contact the bank directly, they need the lawyer in order to rent the jet from the bank.

Lynn deals more with monetary stuff. Like, she's the keeper of the petty cash, she orders stationery, toners, and all that. Anything that requires like, you know, payment that kind of thing. So, we order art pieces and all that, and she deals with the invoice. But we don't have to deal with the payout, we just need to get them to fill up the form, and then we fax it to Chicago, because the accounting department is not in Singapore. We're just a law firm. We got nothing. We also don't have that kind of money to pay out for all these things. So Chicago will make payment via wire transfers.

For example, we rent plants from plant companies. Yah. Office plants. We don't buy them because when we shift office, these plants might not fit the layout of the new office anymore. So these two guys, they will come and water the plants every two weeks. They will wipe the leaves. I think one month is about $200 plus. But we realised watering once every two weeks doesn't work, maybe it's our weather or our humidity level, or maybe it's air-conditioned, so maybe the plants feel it's too dry? Or maybe I don't know, like, maybe in a stressful environment the plants can feel the stress? James has anxiety issues actually. Because he says he cannot take stress, so he'll need to listen to music or something. But sometimes the music he listens to is, like, Guns N' Roses, not the jazz, soothing kind. So I also don't know and I don't really care also. And if the music is too loud Lynn will tell him off lor, so like this colleague she will just voice whatever she wants to voice lah. So I told my boyfriend, "I don't know whether is it politically astute to just say your piece," but like I said, she worked in American firms previously, throughout her career life, so she prefers to be open lah. And Gavin also encourages us to be open.

But for me, I'm still trying to get used to it. Like just now Gavin was asking us, does it affect us if he wears a suit, does it put pressure on us if he wears suits every day, then we have to dress up every day also. But he wears suits because it's a habit already, like the Americans they wear suits everywhere, and maybe because their weather is kinder also. But he says it's a habit, and he says that he feels like he can work better in suits. Maybe it's the confidence, I also don't know. But if Gavin says can dress down, I will just dress down. If Gavin says there will be visitors – now the requirement is like, if there's Chicago visitors, he'll prefer us to dress up a bit lah, at least not in red floral dresses and all that.

But I think Lynn also don't care, because that time we had a visitor from US, she wore this bright yellow flower dress. But I was in black and white lah. I mean it's like, if I don't wear it to work, I won't wear it on Saturdays and Sundays also. Because in my previous job I go to court very often, so I'll usually be in court attire. Since I bought it already, if I don't wear it now, it'll just be sitting in my wardrobe. And then soon it will turn yellow, all these white shirts … so I might as well just wear it lor. I don't see a point to wear it on Saturdays and Sundays, because on Saturdays and Sundays we dress down what. So that's my point of view lah, I don't feel so strongly about the attire.

But Lynn was saying, "If Gavin wants us to wear corporate attire right, I'm going to resign." Then she says, "Unless the company gives me an allowance to buy." Maybe – I also don't know, maybe at her age she can speak like that? And also maybe because it's the culture of her previous firm lor, it's a US firm. And also maybe because she married a German husband? So, maybe the culture is a bit different lah. To me it's like, I would prefer to err on the side of caution, yah. If don't need to say so much, just don't say so much.

But when Gavin is not in the office, James will be in his shorts and T-shirt or singlet and straw sandals, then Lynn will be in her usual lor. She usually likes to wear floral dresses, and floral dresses give people the kind of feeling that it's not too appropriate as a corporate attire, especially not in a law firm. I try not to be so floral on Mondays to Fridays, in fact I haven't worn any floral dress before. I'm usually in more toned-down colours, like grey, black, white, navy blue … I do wear more dresses though. But if I want to add some colours maybe I'll add like an orange flower flare skirt? And er, plain top lor. Not the whole attire is floral lah.

But my colleagues, they are definitely fun people to work with, because they have a lot of funny questions to ask, like settling down and all that. I feel that it's very refreshing lor, this is the first time I'm working with Americans. In my previous company it was very local. My colleagues were mostly locals. And definitely there will be differences lah. I generally feel that the Westerners are more chill and easy-going. So Gavin says that now we can just close office at 4:30 and go for a drink, or now we can go for lunch for two hours, or he can buy us sweets every two or three days. So now we appreciate this lah, but it's to a point where I hope he will stop buying so frequently lah, because it's really not healthy also. But that's him lor, he has a very sweet tooth, he likes to eat – he buys for us also because he doesn't want to eat alone, also not very nice lah, like every day just enjoying the sweets personally. And also, as a big boss, he also wants to show that he is generous, you know, employees' welfare.

So usually, that's what I do lah, I spoil my bosses lor. Actually not spoil lah, but technically speaking, yah … spoil. So for example, they will ask for food recommendations. They probably also don't know that we don't really go to those kind of places they go to for lunch. Cos usually these kind of places are more high-end, more for business lunches. But to them it's like, normal lunches can also be done at these kind of high-end restaurants. Most of the time they do sandwiches lor. They are not fully immersed in our culture yet. They will go to like – recently they like The Daily Cut, it's like a salad bar kind of place. So you can choose your protein, and then you can choose how many proteins, and then it can add up to $17, $18? Sometimes $22. For salad. Because of the protein that you choose. Let's say wagyu beef, there's like different grade, how much fats. For those people that are, like, watching their diets lor, like those bodybuilders. My bosses are not on a diet, but they just have the spending capacity lah. So to them it's affordable! Because they also eat food that's like $400 or $500, so to spend $20 plus for a meal, it's nothing.

And also for Gavin, his relocation fees are very high. Every month the housing is paid for, I don't really know how much, but maybe $8.8K? Just for the house. He stays at Orchard. For James, recently he found a penthouse near Katong area. It's 4.1K. It's like less than half of what Gavin's place costs, but the location is further out, and you'll probably have to take a long bus ride. But he stays with his girlfriend. His girlfriend also got relocation package and, according to him, her package is better than his, so it's not hard to afford a penthouse that kind lor. It's a double-storey penthouse.

See, quite good to be an expat. But also depends on the industry lah. Like my boyfriend, who works in animation and design, let's say he gets relocated to Vancouver, you think he got money to stay in this kind of big-big houses meh? Oh, and the relocation package also includes the children's school fees, like international schools. Like, for Gavin's children, they're studying at an American school. Because, if you think about it, relocation inconveniences them. All their family members are in the US. So in order to request someone to relocate, you must have a package that's attractive enough lah.

And Gavin also gets like a $100 haircut at Orchard, near his house lah. He actually asked me to find a salon for him, but he says this current hairstylist not bad, so I guess just don't change. And it's like, he can afford mah, so just don't change lor. If you change to another hairstylist, firstly I don't know whether it's good or not – I personally don't engage such expensive hair stylists what, and then it's like, his hair a bit challenging also lah, because ... not much also mah. So if he thinks this hairstylist is good, then stick with it lor.

Travel expenses are also part of the relocation package. So let's say end of the year they are all returning to their country, one is US the other one is Ireland, it's included in the package lor. If the trip is more than 10 hours, they fly business class. So their entire family flies business class – cannot possibly be Gavin flies business class, and then his wife and three children are in economy class what, so everyone will take business class lor. Sometimes his work trips are below 10 hours, so it'll be economy class. Gavin will ask Lynn to find the business and economy fares. And if the difference is not too much, maybe $1,000 – it's considered not much – so he will top up $1,000 for business class.

As of now, there's nothing much that I don't like about working here. Really nothing much leh, because I just started working here two months ago. Maybe as the company grows it'll be different, but for now, there's nothing much that I don't like. Gavin is looking at bringing another shareholder in, and he knows the dynamics will shift. A shareholder usually doesn't come in alone, especially those high position shareholders. They will bring in their junior associate to help them. Because these shareholders, they don't have much to do, they delegate the work. So they will bring in their junior associate. And the junior associate will bring in their paralegal. So when you decide to bring one person in, you're actually bringing three people in. Gavin says he cannot afford to have someone who's not the right fit joining the office. The office is just four of us, so if you have someone who comes in and have attitude problem and all that, cannot work with this, cannot work with that – it's not like you can change seats. No matter how you change right, you still have to face the person somehow.

But so far working here has been very good. If the company grows to like 20 to 30 people, or 100 people in a few years down the road, we definitely cannot have flexibility like we have it now. It doesn't make sense if everybody takes advantage of this flexibility, the company probably cannot function lah. So Gavin always says, "Take advantage of it while it lasts."

Candy Lee

Hostel Manager

My name is Muthu. I am accounts administrator in a backpackers' hostel. Total we have three outlets in Little India. Here I manage the check-in and check-out of the guests. Check-in time, I entry everything. Take photocopy of passport. And then ask them to sign the terms and conditions. I record their name in my book also, then okay. Check-out time they need to sign only. This one is gents only can stay. For sure, 100 per cent girls cannot come and stay. I know you think hostel always got all this funny business. But some hostels still traditional like that. In India got a lot of this kind of hostels. Here that kind of problem all don't have. One hundred per cent cannot. Maybe all this European people like that.

Also if the guests got any problems or feedback or what, they will come and tell me. Most of the time their problem is got a lot of talking and then very noisy. So they will come and tell me. Because here is open-concept. Total is 28 beds. Double-decker bed.

I work every day eight hours. Got night shift also. But I never take night shift. Night shift cannot. Night shift more money but health problem. Humans need their sleep. I also work only five days. Most of the time if no guests coming, I will do the online advertisement. My company have Booking.com, Agoda and Expedia. So I checking the reviews all that. My area is internet marketing and all. See what

the customers say, then try to improve.

When don't have customers, I will sometimes go outside and talk to people. Over here mostly Indian people so okay. Little India have everything. Beside here is the haircut place. I go there and talk to the people. All friendly all good. But then I cannot practice my English because mostly here is Indian people.

I like talking to customers a lot. I think that one very important. If you talk to them, they will come back and stay. Got guests every time come back to Singapore, will stay here. Like they doing business or what. I keep talking to them about their work, they very friendly. They boring, I also sometimes boring, so sometimes we will come and talk. I tell you. The Sri Lankan people very good. Rich people they will bring me to go watch movie at night. Sometimes Sundays they will take me and my girlfriend go watch movie or have food. They are very, very nice. You talk to people you can get this kind of benefit. If you scared-scared, don't want to talk to people, then nothing.

Here got all kinds of guests. Mostly from India. European also have. Europeans talk little bit only. Sometimes have Singaporean. Singaporean cannot stay very long. Because there is a law in Singapore. Government say: I give you house then why you must stay in hostel. So they can only stay seven days. But we ask them to check-out one day, then come back and check-in. This people mostly do the gambling then lose their money. Go casino. Then they have to sell their house. Some Singaporeans I don't like. Come to the room, show their IC, say I am Singaporean I only will give you $10. I say no cannot. Here is $16. Everybody $16. Then they keep showing their IC. This one cannot. I must talk to them slowly then they can understand.

Hotel to manage very difficult; account manage is very hard. Sometimes okay, some fun also have. Sometimes fighting, some

Malaysian people coming. They do a lot of drinking. This one happen last month only. Then one guest come and tell me that they fighting. But this kind of thing, I just call police can already. I don't need to get involved. This kind of guests sometimes spoil my mood all. But okay, very few only. After a while they talking then they okay. Never go jail or what.

That time I was looking for job in India. I have one friend working in Singapore. He say have this one vacancy here in Singapore. So I talk to the boss on the internet, we doing the Skyping, all okay. Then I come to Singapore. I work here for two and a half years. Last time I work in India as a marketing manager. I have master's in Business Administration. You know Singapore have Singtel. The company I worked for is Airtel. They are doing the landline and broadband. I am a group leader in charge four or five person. Then I help them with everything. I give instructions to them. We in charge of marketing ideas and all that. This one, very good job. But salary not good. I earning over there 40,000 rupee, about $1,000. Over here I earning two or three times of that. Also there I work six days a week. Twelve hours. So come here, I can earn more. Salary in Singapore very good. But Singapore also very expensive. I staying in rental flat in Sembawang: $800. Very expensive. India rent is $200.

Singapore is good. Everything very clean and nice. I think 90 per cent of Singaporeans good. Everything I ask any help, suddenly they giving help. India no helping. But trains in Singapore I don't like. Too much talking there. When Singaporeans talk, sometimes I don't understand what they are talking. That time I first come to Singapore, everyone saying this "Tekka Mar-kate, Tekka Mar-kate". I am thinking what is this? I confused. Then they write down then I know "Tekka Mar-kert". India talk better than Singapore. They talk the proper grammar, proper sentences.

I bring my girlfriend to Singapore from India. She now working in Mustafa Centre. Doing the cashiering. She say she don't like working there. Because there working hours not very good. Over there she don't like her manager. Not very friendly. But she okay lah. We collect money here, go back India and get married. Weekend we go out. Weekend going Marina Bay, Sentosa. Last time going Botanical Gardens.

Now I am 26 years old. I want to go back India next year with my girlfriend and get married. [smiles] Get a house and start business with my brother. Doing finance. We will have a joint venture and make profit.

Samuel Devaraj

Ship Repair Manager

It is about time I retire. Age is catching up and as the days go by, I realise that I can no longer do this job. It is not physically tiring but mentally draining. I think I'm a failure. I achieved the targets I set for myself but it's hard to actually say that I have contributed to the society. I always dream about giving back, not in terms of money but in terms of energy. You all call it CIP (community involvement project), my time no such thing as CIP. It's just help or volunteer. But now at this age, the only giving back I can do is to myself. [chuckles] Senior citizens, right? I have no regrets working in this industry for almost 40 years now. But how I wish I was able to retire earlier and then I can achieve my dreams. A lot of these foreign workers under me, now very rich abroad. Always call me ask, "Abang, when you want to come visit me?" Now they become big-time towkay already. Last time, all come here, don't know anything. I teach them because I also last time like them. But wouldn't it be good if these guys were local?

Last time I lived in Queen's Close, army quarters. Near the railway track. Shiok (Singlish: fun) life. My grandfather was a politician. Very rich guy. First person in Kembangan to own a car and TV. How not to? Every meeting he attended, he gets $500. That time you know. So I always get money from him. I was his favourite grandchild. I always wipe his head because he botak and sweat a lot. Now I look at myself, same lah.

Being a politician can never be on my list. I never do well in school. How to do well? If it's not track and field season, it's softball. I come to school, no books, only my training kit. [chuckles] Even if I don't give up on school, school gave up on me already. I thought of being a sportsman once, but Singapore really cannot make it. It's not about the athletes. We have really good athletes, but those up there are a bunch of fuckers. So I gave up on that dream. Whoever tells you to follow your passion is bullshitting you. You have to be passionate about the work you're destined to do. Maybe that's just how I was brought up. Growing up, I was very disciplined in everything else but school. I think I was made for the army.

But back to my father and Queen's Close, I have always wanted to be a soldier. Given a chance to sign on, I confirm sign on one. Last time people wear uniform got pride. The boots kilat (Malay: shiny) until can see own face. Uniform, starch until can stand up. My father was a WO2. He drove the car for the Queen when she came long time ago. See if I can find the photo.... Don't know where I put his things already. The stick got termites so I throw away. His battalion was also the only one that fought real war. Konfrontasi and the communist fight. He almost went crazy when his best friend – forgot his name – got killed by the Indonesian forces. After that people say the body was chopped into pieces. Don't know true or not. But luckily, he okay, so they send him to transport battalion after the wars.

Then comes me and my siblings. One by one register for NS, all rejected. Only my elder brother got accepted. He became a cook. Lucky by then we already transferred to HDB flats. If not, don't know where to hide face. But okay lah, he became a chef at hotel after NS. So the skills quite good. At least better than me, registrant only. With a certificate from VITB (Vocational Institute Technical Branch), I tried applying for jobs. All rejected me. Last, I applied for apprenticeship to be scuba diver repairer. At this company called Selco.

Every day dive in and do same thing: underwater hull cleaning, wash propeller, all that. Tiring job. Six days work week, I think worse than army. But what can I do? I wasn't educated. Total five of us work together. The faster we finish the job, the earlier we go home. I worked for four years there until my friend – what's his name? I don't know, I forget, I just called him Ah Teck – got pulled down by the anchor. Only his feet was found at the anchor. Other body parts all gone. We call naval diving unit. But they did nothing. Say visibility low. So me and my brother Rashid dived in to search. We only managed to find his boots. He was a good guy. Speaks Malay like a Malay but babi (Malay: pork) cannot miss. That was the last time I dived.

After that I had to find another job. I wanted to do something ship-related. That was the only thing I'm an expert in. That time, shipyard was a big thing. Everybody wanted to work at shipyard. Engineers very valued, not like now. Nowadays I don't know why people take engineering. No job, take for what? But not say I was an engineer anyway. I just worker only. Youngest worker out there. Twenty years old working with the Thais. I spoke Thai just like them. Every day they laugh at me. Call me "Crab" because my body turns red working under the sun. But I told myself that I will become a supervisor in six months, which I did. After that company sent me to SP (Singapore Polytechnic) to do my part-time diploma. Pan United very good. Take care of me very well. Every year go holiday no need to pay a single cent.

Once I got my diploma, I worked even harder and gave myself

five years to upgrade until I become ship repair manager (SRM). But last time different. It's not about what certificate you have but whom you know. I was just lucky my name rose up very fast and I became a manager in four years. The only Malay SRM in Pan United. But it was hard work. No rest at all. Every day work. Last time a lot of projects and they always want me to do the job. Especially this Australian vessel captain. His name is Paul something, French guy. Very fat. Every night invite me to captain's table and eat ice cream. Australian rules very leceh (Malay: troublesome). Paint must be their standard, which means that the paint cannot be releasing certain chemicals. They protect their sea a lot.

I also worked for KT shipyard for a few months in Pasir Gudang port. It was a desperate job I had to do. If not, no makan. But Malaysia really cannot make it. You just imagine ah, I deal with the captains at kedai kopi (Malay: coffee shops). That's their work culture. Friday, people haram from working. They come late and after prayers, all go home. Whether you Muslim or not, all go home. Now you know why Friday, Johor make it a weekend already. Some more these dato' all forever asking for their 10 per cent. Call themselves dato' but small profits also makan. Jialat lah, work there.

I enjoyed working at Pan United, although at times I don't get my weekend breaks. When we work, we worked hard. When we play, we really enjoy. I will always remember the days where we had sports tournament. These Thai workers just wanted to hantam me hard. They were dead good with sepak takraw. I remembered my supervisor Pongsiput, I called him Pong. He libas (Malay: flip to kick) the takraw right straight to my face. I was angry, but what can I do? This is sports. So I return him a favour with a tapak (Malay: kick) and the ball went straight to his balls. No more Father's Day. But at the end of the day we were a family. They get married and I went to Thailand to visit them. Thais are the most hard-working bunch I've ever worked with. Very loyal too. Very different from the foreign workers we have today.

Pan United was the longest place I stayed with. It was where I started and where I thought I'd retire. But after 18 plus years working there, the effects from economic recession started to be felt. Pan United couldn't sustain so they bungkus (Malay: pack up) here. The Pan United you see today is the cement and construction side. They just use the same name but the big boss is different. For eight months, I was left with no job. I basically sustained from my savings. Alhamdulillah, I eventually got the job here at this company, ST Marine.

The nature of my job in ST Marine initially was very boring. They put me as the department head for painting. The pay is much higher than Pan United but honestly, I'd go back to Pan United any day. I manage all my anak kelings (Malay: Indian children). Every project, same process. Set up staging, then sand blasting, then paint. My aim is to work till mega yard open just to see how big this shipping industry can go. I don't know why are they planning for this mega yard because now there's really no project. That's why they get me out from operation side. Even Keppel closed one wing. But I still want to see that project happen. It's like my baby, this industry finally became an adult. But nothing to be proud of lah. Most of the workers all foreigners. My company's scholars also came from India and Myanmar, like Nagaraju and Thant Zin. They are really good, but of course lah, they come here to work and live. Survival skill, of course anyone will be the best in this situation.

The work environment here is not as fun as Pan United, but it's okay so long as I still can give my family food, okay already. But I honestly don't know how long more they will extend my service. Every year I must sign contract because I reach 60 years old already. I want to retire but it will be boring once I stop working. But I also know that I need to rest. Atuk dah tua (Malay: Grandfather is already old). But I think confirm plus chop, I won't last long here. Next step is the end.

So you better work hard. Study hard, get some work experience here, then if can, go migrate. Go to places that need you. But always remember to buy a house here in Singapore then rent out to people. So if things don't work out you can always come back and restart the process. As for me, maybe next year I apply to be softball coach. But first I have to trim my tummy.

Said Effendy

HEALING

CHAPTER ELEVEN

HEALING

Clinic Assistant

My name is Ying and I am ... 50 plus lah, this year. I have two children and both I and my husband are working. My husband works as a factory operator in Jurong Island, while I work as a clinic assistant in a GP along upper Bukit Timah.

I work as assistant for almost 35 years already. This clinic for about 19 years, and before this I work at two specialist clinics, one cardiology clinic about 10 years, and one neurology clinic about six years. Those two clinics were at Orchard Road. I quit the job because of my children lah. I want to spend more time with my children, that time they were about five or six years old, and this current job is near my house. The specialist clinic's pay was around $1,600 plus OT. Now this clinic hor, the pay is very little, started only with $1,000. After 19 years only $1,300. My husband lor, tell me not to work, he say Orchard very far, ask me to spend more time with the children. But yah lah, quit the Orchard job also good, I always go shopping during lunch time. See those OL (office ladies) dress so nice, I also must keep up, cannot lose to them, must make use of my time to go shopping. Even though high pay, I spent a lot, really a lot, save no money. Now I work here, no time to go shopping; even if got time, here also don't have shopping centres for me to shop.

I only study until O Levels. I didn't study any medical or nursing courses before work. My first training was taught by the wife of the doctor in the very first clinic I work at. The place you work will have those old nurses that will train you lah. Then, you work there for a few months, by then you should know already. At least three months basic training, then you will know one. Not very difficult lah. All the clinics, it is the old staff that will train the new people, the doctor don't do the training. Some do dressing, some do registering for the patients, then some do preparation of the medicine. Workload depends on how many staff the clinic have. I don't like blood, the doctor knows so he ask the other staff to do it, so I have never done dressing in my life before. [laughs]

Every day, Monday to Friday, I start work at 9 a.m. I open the clinic, then register some patients and wait for doctor to come at around 9:45 to 10. Then throughout the day, I will stand behind a counter, do the registration for the patients, prepare and give out medicine. Standard one hour lunch break, the clinic will close for one hour then re-open again all the way until 5:30 or 6. During work, mostly I talk to my partner but sometimes I will talk to patients, especially the regular ones. All sorts of patients come to my clinic: the old, young, men, women, very sick until like dying and the not sick but act sick also have. Those non-regulars like to ask stupid obvious questions like what time the doctor is coming or is it my turn yet. If the doctor come already, of course you will see patient moving in and out of the room what, and then if it is your turn, I will call your name what.

The regular ones like to talk to me about everything. Really everything and anything that they feel like talking about. Sometimes they will give me and my partner free gifts like pastries, bread – mainly food. Sometimes like during Chinese Lunar New Year, the older uncles and aunties, ah gong and ah mah categories, will give us angbaos. Got one time about Christmas, one patient gave me a pair of Flip-Flops (branded sandals) saying it was a gift for causing some trouble a few years ago. I think maybe they know us too well already, close enough so they will give us things out of generosity. But sometimes they will want us to help them, like helping them register through phone or call them when their turn is nearing. We usually only receive the free gifts from regular customers because of their goodwill, but we will never receive gifts from the suppliers or the drug salesman, later people accuse us of bribery or what. Such cases are so sensitive, we dare not play with the rules.

The best thing about the job is that it is so near my house that I don't have to take bus to work, I can just walk to work, save time and save money and, also, the doctor will give two month bonus at the end of the year. I think the most memorable part of my experience is during the SARS period in 2003. Every time have to wear the mask, so stuffy, so hard to talk and so uncomfortable. Then when you see some patient coughing non-stop, the whole clinic like freeze in fear, all scare die, so funny.

I think the hardest part of my work is that there is always so much work to do. Sometimes I must multitask to finish all my work, and crowd control is always problematic. Angry and noisy patients are the worst. More important thing is that I always have to be focused, especially when dispensing the medicine. If I give out the wrong medicine or give wrong person, then cham liao (Hokkien: there will be trouble), right? It happened before leh, but luckily the doctor is always there to help us cover up. But the doctor will always scold us for being rude to the patient when they ask those obvious questions. Whether we are rude or not, or whether the patients are the ones that are rude, as long as they complain to the doctor, the doctor will sure take side with the patient and scold us first. What to do? We need the job, cannot possibly resign over this kind of small matter.

I don't see any chance for promotion or what lah. The clinic so small, we only got five weekday and weekend assistants plus the doctor, and the doctor old already and is very happy with the small clinic, so don't think that he will expand the business. Plus now with the PG (Pioneer Generation) thing hor, the clinic is busier than ever. Other than more business to do, my job scope has not changed since 19 years ago, but my colleague's job scope changed a bit.

My colleagues and I still okay, our relationship is good. But sometimes need to be careful. We don't have any clock-in system, and because the doctor always comes in later than us. We have to be very careful to come to work on time or else some staff will complain to the doctor that so-and-so is late. Yah, all the staffs are females, mostly aunties in their late 40s lor. I don't know why, but doctor don't want to hire any male workers. Maybe because female workers can help the doctor when he need to check on the female patients lor. Not only my clinic, I think almost all the clinic in Singapore, all don't have male clinic assistant one lah. Aiyah, anyway, the pay is so low, I don't think any men will want the job also lor.

I think I will retire about 60 to 65 years old. By then I am too old to do this kind of job that need so much focus. I scared I will dispense wrong medicine to people. After retiring, maybe I will take a part-time job at Old Chang Kee selling fishballs and curry puffs. Work about four to five hours enough. But for sure I don't want to work at supermarket, need to carry so many heavy things, cannot handle it, too old for that. [laughs] Maybe by then my children all married, have their own children and I can be a happy grandmother, bring my grandchildren go shopping or play at the playground. I don't know lah, it is still too early to say.

Alan Ang Wee Chuan

Doctor

My name is George and I'm a doctor. I'm in my late 20s and I've been working as a doctor for six years since graduating from NUS. I started my housemanship (internship for doctors) during my first post-graduate year. In my time, it was a series of three rotations through three different departments at three different hospitals. So in one year, I did four months rotations at NUH, KK (KK Women's and Children's Hospital), and SGH (Singapore General Hospital). During the housemanship, what interns have is a "Provisional Registration"; we don't have the authority to sign and chop our name on the documents, the documents have to be counterchecked and countersigned by our seniors. Only after we pass our housemanship, then will we get the "Full Registration"; only then can we use our chop and signature everywhere. In a sense, only then will you get the actual responsibility and recognition from people. When we were interns, we started out like about $3K per month. When we became a MO (medical officer), we get graded by performance, so we get small increments year by year based on our performance. So currently, I am getting about $5K to $6K per month.

I wanted to be a doctor for many reasons. Firstly, I have an older cousin from my mum's side. He is a doctor and he graduated from medical school when I was six. When I saw that, in my little idealistic child's mind, I thought, "I want to be a doctor like him." It was sort of like a crazy childhood dream that came true. Secondly, I would say that this is a very unique job, there is no other job in the world where life and death of your client is in your very hands. So you get to learn and experience things that no other job can offer. Thirdly, I would say, for lack of a better word, shall we say, it's convenient. When you do medicine in Singapore, the moment you graduate, you are important to the government, you don't have to hunt for a job, it's there for you already. It is easy for the career to take off lah, in a sense.

Being a doctor anywhere in the world, I can tell you, is not easy because of the nature of the job. Other people may make mistakes, maybe the company will lose some money; we make a mistake, and people die. You can't measure life with money. So it's a very serious kind of job, you need to be really aware of what you are doing.

At the same time, because it's a service job, you need to know how to read people. You got to be aware of cultural issues – in Singapore, cultural issues are all over the place. You really got to know who your patient is, how to approach them, how to help them in a way that they will accept. Basically, you got to be careful of taboos. In the area of medicine, it is a very touchy thing, you deal with people's bodies, people's health, you see.

Third, it is the intensity of the work. I mean other than lawyers lah, no one else works as long hours as we do, especially in a place like Singapore. If you are rostered for a night duty, you come in to work at 7:30 in the morning on the first day, you are practically on a high gear all the way through the whole day, then through the night again until the next day, about 12 noon. You go home at 12 noon, you go and sleep and the third day, 7:30 in the morning, you are back to work again. In the bad old days – now the junior doctors have more welfare, lah – in the bad old days, you will get it about seven to eight times a month. Essentially, it's a tough life and even if you love your work, you love what you study, being on high gear that long, so many times a month, you will eventually get tired.

In the past, there were more males than females doctors because medicine was a very patriarchal thing (quotas limiting women to less than one-third of applicants accepted to medical school in Singapore were lifted in 2012). Now it's about even, but if you want to talk about the care, the concern, and the healing touch, you have

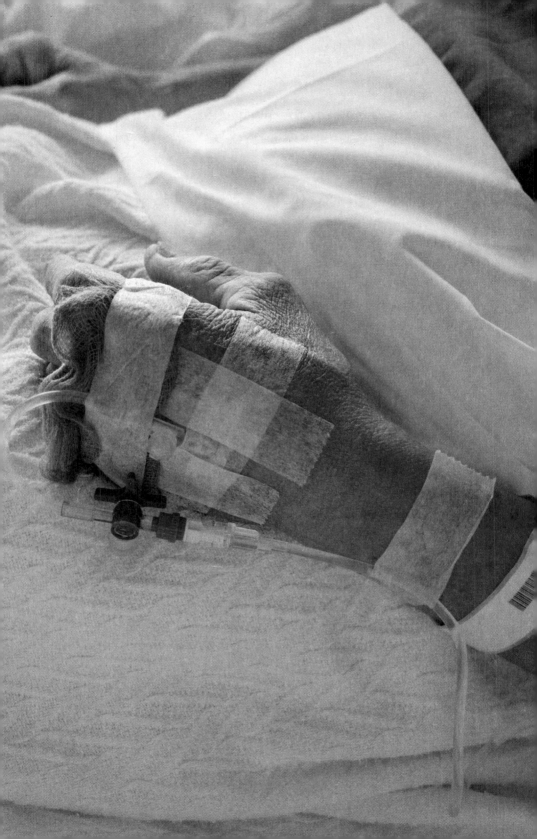

to look at sub-specialities. Most guys like to go into surgery, A&E, the very so-called macho things. Girls, they like to do paediatrics – maternal instincts. Especially in the past, the number of women in paediatrics was overwhelming. Rarely have I seen a female surgeon. They do exist, of course, but not very many.

Currently, I am working in the dermatology department. Basically we look at skin problems, but there's some overlap with other fields of course, because women and children are our patients as well. We (male doctors) have been taught from day one that we have to have a female colleague when we are doing consultations for female patients to avoid the legal repercussions. It is a must to have a female colleague, whether is she a fellow doctor, a nurse, or even a clerk, if you are desperate. However, it does not work that way for the female doctor, they don't require a male colleague if they do consultation for a male patient. I believe it's a societal thing. [laughs]

I get into work about 8 to 8:30 in the morning. Look at the morning list of patients in the clinic, go to the wards, look at referral letters, go for lunch, after lunch another round of clinic consultations in the afternoon, and then that is about it. I go home usually about 5 to 5:30 in the evening. I am very thankful that my current posting is not affected by the "36-hour shift", because we are an outpatient department. I mean in the wards, yes, there was the infamous 36-hour shift, which I had a good five years of. Again, in the bad old days, it used to be 36 hours, by the time I graduated, they limited it to 30 hours and now, my juniors are getting only 24 hours. This, I feel, makes a lot of sense. You cannot afford to have a tired doctor who makes mistakes, you need to rest. In the past we probably didn't have enough doctors and it is a "work culture". You got to be tough, you can't throw things to your colleagues and leave, it doesn't reflect well on your performance. I am glad people are using more logic and common sense to think that sleepy doctors are the most dangerous doctors. After looking at the lives of my seniors, I have given up the dream of climbing up the ladder. They handle more paperwork than they handle patients. I signed up for this to save lives and help people, not to sharpen pencils. I'd rather not deal with administrative work because I prefer the good honest work.

There are a few happy moments. When you have been with a patient long enough, you see them recover, see them well, they leave the hospital, then when you bump into them again and they recognise you even after months or years, those are very happy moments. Second category will be when they write compliments. Of course, all the talk about serving without expecting anything in return, sure, but a nice word every now and then to the doctor who is working so hard, actually makes a lot of difference. A smile from the patient is actually worth more than any amount of money you can make. Interestingly, the most painful thing is not when the patient dies because after a while, you come to accept that, such is life. The most painful is when you get patients who have been blinded by the internet, especially with all those nonsense floating around in the internet. It is tough for a layman to understand what you are reading, let alone to know whether such information are real or fake, or whether it applies to you or not in the first place. These are people who do not have medical background, they read things at face value and freak out. They usually get the completely wrong impression of what the doctor is trying to do. In the past, it used to be "Doctors vs. Traditional Superstitions/Supernatural Remedies", now it is "Doctors vs. Mr Know-It-All on the Internet". It just breaks down the relationship between the doctor and the patient.

If I have kids and they want to be doctors, I would definitely want them to follow their dreams. But first I need to find a wife, lah. I'm actually quite surprised, I used to think that medical will marry medical – same social class. But apparently not, some of my friends have married paramedical people such as therapists, pharmacists, not just purely doctors or nurses. Probably the social class issue has much to do with having a partner with the same wavelength, having a shared and common topic would be important.

Currently, I am still serving my medical bond. After my bond is finished, I'm considering joining a private group. I'm also trying to complete my masters in paediatrics, but I still need a lot of training. After six years in this field, I can provisionally sum it up as: love the job, hate the system. The amount of red tape, the work culture and the high gear-ness. Things are changing, they are getting better of course. I am looking forward to the future and I hope that this profession need not always be so high gear all the time, we need to rest as well.

Alan Ang Wee Chuan

Nurse

My name is Mun. I am turning 31 this year and I am happily married to my childhood sweetheart. We've been married for two years and we're living in a five-room HDB flat. We moved only five months ago. I used to live with my parents and my four other siblings and I always complained about how packed and noisy the house was, but now that I'm living alone with my husband, it feels a little too quiet sometimes. I am currently working as a senior staff nurse and I work five days a week. I work in three rotating shifts, meaning on some days I will do morning shift, sometimes afternoon and the other days will be night shift. It all depends on the week or the roster for the week. For morning shift, I will have to be at work at around 6:30 a.m. and I'll get to go off at 3:30 p.m. For afternoon shift, it will be from 1 p.m. to 10 p.m. and if I have to do night shift, I will start work at 8:30 p.m. and I'll end at 7:30 a.m. For morning and afternoon shifts, I'll work for eight to nine hours and for night shift I will work for 11 hours. When I reach my workplace, there will be roll call and attendance taking before we depart to our areas. I like morning shift because it's the best time for me to have dinner with my friends and catch up with them. My husband comes home late on some days, so I'm able to have dinner with either my family or my friends. Sometimes I'll go back home over my stipulated time because I'm always involved in projects, so the meetings will hold me back. And I'm also in charge of the duty roster for my colleagues, so I'll have to stay at work longer to plan the roster. Sounds tiring, right?

Thank god for me, my workplace is not that far from my home. I live in Boon Lay and I work at NUH. It only takes about an hour to get to my workplace if I take the public transport. I love taking public transport! I don't know why people are always complaining about our trains and buses. I like long bus rides. I usually travel during off-peak hours so I can be alone and enjoy the journey. It gives me the time to contemplate about life and just rest.

I'm in the A&E department, so the room is always so tense and we are always rushing to treat patients. It's a little different in the A&E. There will be three kinds of patients. Okay, actually it's four. The first one is for those who comes with illnesses and we will have to manage their symptoms, like find out what's wrong and all till they get better – either to be discharged or to be admitted to the hospital. Then there's another group of patients who come in critical conditions and we will try our best to save their lives. We'll give medicines, intubation…. There will also be patients who are not breathing anymore, or in other words technically dead, and we will try to resuscitate them using CPR or defibrillators. The last group is for the patients who shouldn't be at the A&E! Please spread the word for us ah, if you're not in a critical condition, please visit a general practitioner instead. Mild injuries or ailments like stomach aches or sprains shouldn't be at the A&E department. Sorry lah, but we nurses get so angry about this because these people who don't need immediate treatment make up more than half the cases we have to deal with!

Maybe this is why I've turned into a hot-tempered person. I used to be a very patient person, but recently I've been told by my colleagues that I've became very snappy and impatient. How do you expect me to remain calm and patient when you've got to handle stubborn and rude patients every single day? Aiyoh. I don't think many people know how difficult it is to be a nurse. I think it takes loads and loads of patience. I seriously think we are underpaid. It's not that I'm not satisfied with my pay. I get to bring home around $3 to $4K plus a month, alhamdulillah. And I think that's not too bad because I get a bi-annual bonus also. But when I say that we're underpaid, what I meant was that the things we're expected to do exceed human capabilities.

Okay, let me explain this to you. I think all of those people who are working in this line must have experienced this or can at least relate to this. It's normal for us to get punched by patients, be it intentionally or unintentionally. We nurses should probably get treated too. [rolls eyes] We will get punched usually when we are trying to treat the patients with injections or if the patient struggles when we are trying to keep them still. Some of them are really violent, especially the elderly. They like to grab whatever that is near them and throw it at us. We not only face physical abuse, we face verbal abuse too. From both the patients and their relatives who visited them or sent them over. Verbal abuse from patients is manageable for me. Usually I'll turn a deaf ear to their rants and scolding and just try to give them their treatments. What is not okay for me is when the patient's relatives or, in most cases, the patient's children ordered us around and even worse, complained about our services.

Sometimes they say things like, "Oh, this nurse is not doing her job well", "She is hurting my father", "She is not gentle enough", "She is doing things too quickly, it's so rough" etc. Some of my patients' relatives even blamed me when the patient's condition worsened. Like hello, I am not god, I am not in control of such things! And we are helping to save their lives, for goodness' sake. The least they could do is appreciate our work, right? They expect us to give our fullest attention to their sick parent but they don't know that we have to handle so many patients at a time. We can't possibly give all our attention to just one patient, right? The weird thing is that sometimes it's not the patients that overreact but their relatives. They think the patients are going to die when we don't treat them immediately, but the truth is that they are not in a critical condition so we'll only attend to those who need immediate treatment. They like to exaggerate only, so irritating.

Patients these days are so picky and demanding. Some are snobbish, rude, and even mean. For example, patients in the wards sometimes spit their food on the nurses. Can you believe it? Some of my colleagues have to go to counselling because the things we go through can be mentally and even physically abusive. I know it's part of our job to take care of our patients but not when we're abused. But not all patients are like that. I love those cute little old uncles and aunties. Some are really, really sweet, they understand and appreciate the littlest things we do, like when we help to carry them or help them walk. We actually don't need much to be happy. Just a simple thank you or a smile from the patient can make me really happy.

As a nurse, you're exposed to the life stories of your patients. It's saddening to hear stories from parents who just lost their children in traumatic accidents, or when we couldn't get to save the patients' lives. Our sadness just doesn't stop there. It's already sad that we couldn't save a patient but seeing their relatives cry over their loss is even more heartbreaking. Sometimes I bring my sadness home, I won't be able to sleep peacefully at night, I will think about what I could've done better to save that patient's life. I bring work matters to home on some days. And when I say work matters, I don't mean paperwork, I meant the problems I faced at work. Like, because I couldn't express my feelings and let it all out at work, because we're expected to remain calm and composed all the time, because we're supposed to be professional in front of our patients and not show much emotions over the loss of lives, I do it all at home. On some days I cry myself to sleep.

Even my husband has commented on my behaviour at home. I can get angry at the slightest things lately. Like if he doesn't do something properly or misplaces something, it could cause a fight. It could be because I'm pregnant too. I just got to know that I'm pregnant today. I haven't told my husband yet. I'll probably tell him when he gets home. The only person I've told is my mum. We've been waiting for this baby for two years now, and I'm not ready to tell the world about it.

I don't plan to tell my colleagues about this yet because if the head knows then I'll have to be shifted to the counter. And I don't want to do counter work because I'll have to answer calls and complains from patients. That is the last thing I want to do at work. My mother wants me to tell the people at work so they could take care of me or at least keep an eye on me, but she doesn't understand how bad it is doing counter work.

I think about quitting a lot but I always tell myself to endure a little bit more. I've worked really hard and been through so much to get to where I am now. It would be such a waste if I were to just quit and start a new job with lower pay, right? I don't even know how I ended up being a nurse. I wanted to be in the police force when I was younger. But now that I'm a nurse, I get to save lives too, so one part of my childhood dream is fulfilled. After secondary school, I went to JC. And then I felt that I wasn't happy there, everything was so rigid and all we ever did was study. So I dropped out of JC after my first year and went to poly instead. I advanced my diploma in Emergency Nursing after polytechnic, and then I got a degree in Nursing. I'm planning to pursue my masters degree in a few years' time. You need to constantly upgrade your skills and knowledge. That's what I've been told by my seniors, so that's what I'm doing.

Anyway, even if I wanted to quit I don't think I'm allowed to lah. There is just too much work, too many patients, and a lack of manpower in the hospitals in Singapore. I will be on my feet for more than eight hours, running around. If I'm lucky, I'll get my one-hour break and I get to rest and eat. If not, I'll have to gobble my food and get back to work. And when I'm really unlucky, I get no rest at all. Sometimes we even forget to go to the toilet. Once I get home, I'll be too tired to do anything and I'll just sleep for the next few hours. I do get my off days. I get 23 days of leave annually. But I have to ballot for leave among 200 staff in my department. The result is I usually don't have time for my family. I'll have to work on public holidays and when my family has an outing or go on vacations, I'll be stranded at work. I get really sad sometimes when I don't get to spend time with my family, but I've accepted the fact that I'm a grown-up now and I have a family to support.

Last time, patients would respect their doctors and nurses. Now they argue with us because they think they know it all. After all, they read it on Wikipedia. Might as well just study from internet then lah, no need for the years of education that I went through. And in Singapore, people think a nurse is just a high-class maid. They can't even feed their own parents or help take them to the toilet. They think their hands are made of gold ah? I don't know if they are just snobs or plain lazy. My god, they're your own parents, can't you just help them? Sometimes I would rather work in a Third World country where people are more appreciative of the small things.

Sure there are the good sides of this job, like how I won some nursing competitions, I get to attend events as VIP. And of course, how many people get to experience saving someone's life? But I think there are more cons than pros to this job. I wouldn't want my child to be in the same profession. Although I've learned so much and become a stronger person, at the same time this job has changed me into someone ugly. Not on the outside, but on the inside. I don't want my children to go through the same things that I did. But if they really want to be a nurse, then I'd prepare them mentally. To be a nurse, you cannot take things to heart and you must learn not only to deal with your own emotions but your patient's emotions as well. You have to have a big heart and you have to be forgiving. And life as a nurse is really unpredictable. You may just be talking to a patient happily and the next day, they might just leave you and the world. Life is like a rollercoaster ride. Sometimes there's ups and sometimes there's downs. Sometimes you save patients, sometimes you lose them. And being a nurse, you just get used to the fact that everything is temporary in this world. You'll learn to appreciate things and people better. I think that's the best take away any nurse could have.

Nur Atiqah Binte Rosli

Monk

I often tell people, this is not a profession. It's more than a profession … it is [laughs] … it is a 24/7 life, if you will. But there is work to be done as well, so in a way it's work, we call it Dharma work, but it's just a name. So in some ways it's work, but in some ways it's not work. When I was not a monk yet, I was in the tech industry in R&D,

software engineering and also in consulting later on. It was almost never work, I was just doing my hobby, and I just happened to get paid decently. [laughs] I was doing computer engineering, but that was way back.

There were many factors involved before I decided to become a monk. Erm, at some point you basically got to ask yourself, "Okay, is this what you want to do for the rest of your life?" I ask myself, "Okay, is that all I am going to do? Is that what I am going to do?" So I decided, okay yah, I want to do more than that, I want to go and explore and experience what I have been reading about in the Buddhist text, and not simply read about it, but go and experience it myself. That in the nutshell is what drove me. But there were other factors that push me in this direction, like my exposure to Buddhism, the various retreats I attended, the various masters – in particular my late ordination teacher. He gave me the confidence that yes, even in this day and age it can be done, it's a worthwhile goal. As the MOE advertisement many years back post: "Do something worthwhile in life, be a teacher." [laughs]

So when I ordained, my mum was actually quite happy, yah, being a Buddhist herself, my dad is also a Buddhist but he was quite upset. Yah, for various reasons ... but over the years, eventually they accepted it and they supported me. I think it goes the same for all parents, it's not that monkhood to them is bad or anything, but it's just this fear of uncertainty. It is not a well-trodden path, at least for most people. That's why most parents traditionally would think yah, find a girl, find a job and then settle down, have kids. Cos this seems to be what everybody has done, and human beings are still around so ... well, it seems to work. So when someone suggest to do something else, like, no, I am not going to get married, I am going to stay a spinster or a bachelor for the rest of my life, then people are like, "Huh? But what about your family? Your kids?" Oh, I am not going to get married. Then people are like, "Gasp!"

So in Buddhism, ordination is the start of our training. From what I heard from my friend in Catholicism, it takes about maybe eight to ten years before a person becomes a fully ordained priest. There's no further thing, the further things like being a bishop or archbishop and so on, those are more appointments and duties, it's not in a way additional training, they would have retreats also. But for us, ordination is the start of the training, you only complete when you are enlightened, so we don't really have a three-year enlightenment course or something, although the Buddha did highlight some teaching that say if you do this consistently, seven years, or even seven days you can get enlightened.

So yah, counselling is part of what we do. I was trained as a counsellor last time when I was in university, but not as part of my course, it was part of the Buddhist society. We collaborated with Shan Liu counselling centre, so they trained us as like, para-counsellor I guess, to serve as mentors for adolescents in secondary schools. But we also trained to handle cases involving sick patients, the terminally ill, the elderly, different categories. I consider it a privilege, out of the cohort who were trained, they pick about five or six of us to start actual counselling, so it really started off there.

Training establishes a basic set of skills that are very useful, but many times I find that it's life experience that allows me to connect with what the person is going through, that helps with the counselling. It's a lot like driving: whether you have a licence or not, if you can drive, you can drive lah.

I ever encounter one case where the person was a teenage boy, was just at a point where he and his parents were so disconnected already, it's a bit too late. So this is where I have to come to terms and say, "Well, what can we do?" You know? And it is a very humbling experience as well to face that, that no, we are not omnipotent. We can only do what we can, but there are many other factors that come before us, how they live as a family for all the years. You think a few sessions with me is going to solve it? Sometimes this is part of the message, to get them to look at it honestly and have realistic expectations. So yah, I've encountered cases where I just can't help.

Last time when I was newly ordained, or even last time as a layperson, I would get very frustrated when friends ask me questions, and I give them advice and instead they would follow some other person's advice that turned out to be wrong. I would be like, "See? See?" But these days I won't feel that way. I would say that, for the most part, I am more concerned about whether they get the help they need. So sometimes if I know that the connection is not there or that whatever I say cannot go in ah, then I might as well don't say any more, I may refer to another person or get another person to talk to him or her. So the focus has shifted away from me and more towards that person. The important thing is that the person is helped.

Many times in my lessons, I challenge my students: do you think that you can simply go to some temple, or church, or this or that, or even some high monk or lama or Rinpoche or you know, and they just "Omnomenomenom," and then, wah! I say, "If that can be done, then I pose you a question: surely in terms of compassion and wisdom and powers, the Buddha is more superior than whoever it is, and if the Buddha is omnipotent, then why didn't the Buddha just solve everything for us?" Even me – maybe I'm not very compassionate – but even me, I would just: click! Okay, enlightened already! And maybe snap three times, you know, just for good measure. [laughs]

So yes, we cannot highlight this enough, but we must be careful how we do it. Because unfortunately some members of other faiths use this to cast doubt on Buddhism. In JC, I had this friend, Magdalene, and one day she said: "Hey, do you know something? Do you know the Buddha is not a god?" I was like: "Yah, what's new?"

Then she's like: "Huh? You know?" and I was like, "Yah, of course I know!" Because many Christians, in this case she's a Christian uh … she could have been any other religion but this is an actual case. The thing is that in many churches, they take time to teach young adherents about what Buddhism is or is not, many times confusing the hell out of people, yah. And sadly sometimes even giving distorted answers. For me if I ever share anything about Christianity or other religion, I would quote literally from the text, like Matthew 19 and 25, which I often quote, and I would tell them to go to biblegateway.com, which is an official site, and read for themselves as well. I would not give them further interpretation. But that's beside the point, the thing is, then she said : "Then why do you worship the Buddha, since he's not God?" I was like, "Since when do we worship him?" That's the thing lor, many times they would get teenagers to go and question their friends, "Er, but Buddha is not God, why you worship?" And when the Buddhist says, "Oh yah, why ah?" Then they tell you, "You should worship the one true God blah blah blah…". [laughs]

So yah, when we do a blessing, at least for myself, the last thing I want is for them to think that I have some Harry Potter magic that you don't have to do anything and I just "Ding!" and you are okay, you know? That's why my blessing service takes longer than usual because I want them to have the right understanding. When I bless a building, I almost always insist that the family or the workers must be present. The point is this: as we do the service together, do the chanting together, it leaves an imprint, a memory if you will. It's my hope that having gone through the whole house doing this service, when you are about to quarrel, you're reminded, "Ah! I was here once with master and my family members, and there were teachings given, we did some chanting, and how did it feel at that point in time? Do I want to calm myself down or do I want to be hot-tempered now?"

So people have this kind of misconception that monks should

be totally disconnected from worldly affairs. To me, this is not so realistic. Some people expect that we shouldn't have handphones or be online, but then how do we serve the community? There were some Thai forest monks that were here, we actually gave them the space to do a photo exhibition. It's very inspiring lah, to see those pictures. But then people start to have the idea, "Wah, these are real monks. They all stay here got air-con. You see Thai monks, they don't have air-con, they live in atap houses, you know, zinc roofs, and they walk barefooted." And so this is the image that people have of what monks should be. And then when they see monks in Singapore, then compare, like they go "tick, tick, tick," on a list like that. To me, it's okay if people think we are not doing monkly things. If they come to my face and tell me, I will explain to them, but if they don't then so be it, you know?

Honestly, sometimes I'm very frustrated with the state of things, with how things are, with the religion, with the legacy we have to uphold. Even now, sometimes in class I ask them, "Do you think everything is rosy?" It's frustrating you know. To me, sometimes facing these challenges only makes me pull up my socks and say, "Hey, I've got to do more." But I don't say I will never quit. Who knows, maybe next week when you call the temple, they say, "Oh, the monk has gone home." Who knows, you know?

Vincent Lok Weng Seng

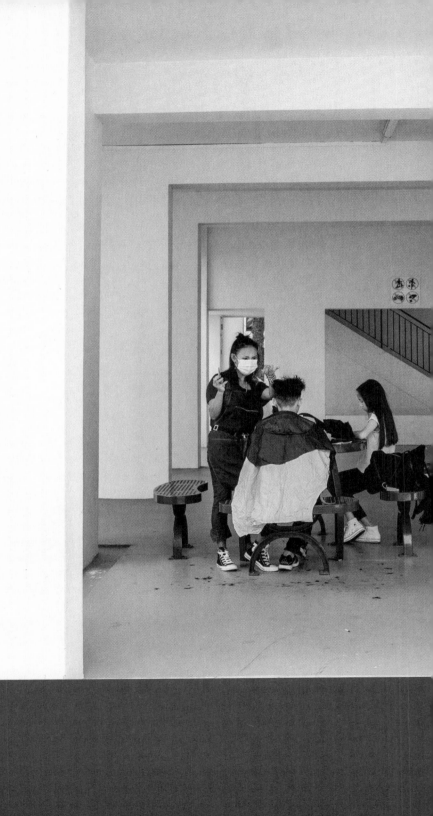

GROOMING

CHAPTER TWELVE

GROOMING

Wedding Groomer

What? You want to interview the people who make the pelamin (wedding dais)? That's them over there. You all can go smoke and chit-chat behind the pelamin. Just don't take too long. We need it to be up and ready by tonight.

What? Then who am I? I'm the pak andam (groomer) for this wedding lah. You want to interview me for your project ah? Can is can but got one condition. You must promote my company Bestman Services. Steady ah? So now you want to interview me or not? Okay, we can talk as I do my things. You're Muslim, right? I thought you were a Chinese kid just now.

You don't smoke? Weak bro! But okay, fast game (colloquial: quickly). [grabs a plastic bag filled with yellow rice and red roses] You follow me from the back then if I stop it means that it's time to say the selawat (Malay: supplications). If you don't believe in these kinds of things, just shut up and pretend like you reciting something. This one is not for us. It's for the bride and groom and the success of the event.

Can you record the conversation? Sembarang (Malay: anything). Record my conversation yesterday pun boleh (Malay: also okay).

What's important is you promote my company. [laughs] I started this company not long ago. About one year ago. Some people say I'm too young to be doing these things. I'm 24 years old. Aiyah, but people say anything they want lah. At the end of the day, what they say won't give me food on my table. What I do is more important.

Of course, when I started this business I was still working. Work for a logistics company. [pauses to throw some yellow rice and roses, then recites supplications] So as I was saying, I work for a logistics company. Do nothing one lah. I did more during my National Service days. Let's not talk about studies. I cannot study one. Not like you ah, boy, NUS! [laughs] I was so loved by ITE that I spent an additional year doing my Nitec. Then after NS, I applied for higher Nitec but never get. So boh pian (Hokkien: no choice), I do kerja bodoh (Malay: stupid work) like logistic ah. I had to.

I had to work. My parents both too old to work already. And my abang, kakak (Malay: brother; sister), both married already. So they have to jaga their families. For me I don't think I'll get married anytime soon. Just continue supporting my parents okay already. They also need me. Sial punya (Malay: jinx the) government, swallow my money. Expensive you know, my parents medicine. Charge so expensive, subsidies so little. But all these will pay off some day.

Although the government still chee bye (Hokkien vulgarity) we still have to survive. But doesn't mean we can't enjoy.

When I was working with 3G Logistics, I look forward to my weekends. Every weekend was always busy for me. If not taking photos for weddings, I'll be performing kuda kepang (traditional Javanese dance depicting a group of horsemen). No stop. But if I take photos that day, I cannot go kuda kepang. It's a one whole day work. But okay lah, last time quite fun. And besides, makan was free. Biryani every week bro, mana nak dapat? (Malay: where to get?)

I don't get a lot of money. Especially when I perform kuda

kepang. But it's just something I do since young. The Siji Loro troupe watched me grow up, and I got to see what the Malay people did to this tradition. Melayu bunuh Melayu (Malay: Malays kill Malays). This haram, that haram, everything haram. Rather just live in a cave. [pauses again to sprinkle some yellow rice and roses, along with water]

You just imagine, things like what I'm doing now also they say haram. How can that be? I am reciting verses from the Holy Quran. The only thing haram is them! Kepala pantat (Malay vulgarity). Yes, it's a Hindu tradition but it has now become Islam way. It's been like that for so long. Why now then you want to say it's haram? That's the reality of this community lah. But you just have to keep on pushing.

Okay. Back to the story of how I started. After a while, I realised that I really liked spending my weekends at people's wedding. Upholding traditions and ensuring everything runs smooth. So I save some money and went for the kursus mak andam (Malay: bridal grooming course). It was awkward. Most of them there were girls. That's why they call it mak (Malay: female term) andam, not pak (Malay: male term) andam. But quite fun lah. I learn about make-up and how to tie ikat samping (type of short sarong). Not very hard for me lah, since I've been engaging with Malay culture my whole life. But girl make-up, rabak (colloquial Malay: out of control). Most girls think make-up can change them into another person. Act like they can be Nora Danish (Malaysian actress) for a day. [laughs] But now one year already, I really think I can even make males look like females.

It's not about the make-up, though. Now, everyone can watch a YouTube tutorial then can be their own mak andam already. Confirm got more to this. So I asked around until I met this mak andam called Mak Su. She taught me all these spiritual things.

You know we can even know if the bride is still a virgin just from potong andam (hair cutting ritual)? Males don't need because most of them confirm not virgin already. Either you believe or don't believe only. But it is accurate. We do it so that we know how to naikkan seri (Malay: increase the beauty) of the brides. We can only hide the ugliness if we know what is ugly about them. No, it's not the make-up that will make them pretty. It's the prayers we say and the kind of air bunga (Malay: flower water) we give them. The more experience you have, the more beautiful you can make them.

Even the ritual we're doing now, adat merenjis, is to make the place beautiful and protect it from bad spirits that could destroy the event. You ever wonder why some events, they order enough food but on the actual day, not enough? Or you think for yourself lah, how is this void deck, the place where we all play soccer, can look so beautiful on the wedding day? It's not luck, bro. So we have to do all these rituals for the bride and groom, even they don't believe in it. Which is okay. Just don't go around telling people that what we do is haram. Spoil market.

But, even when we know all this, it was hard finding clients. And you want to know why? Because makcik and pakcik (Malay: aunties and uncles) once again say it's haram. They say it is a job for women only. Pak andam cannot touch the brides. Stupid one. Our job is to make them look pretty and neat, that's all. If the dress is too big, we pin for them. We style their hair, put make-up and sometimes put on inai (Malay: henna) for them. Not like we dress for them. Think what? They still baby? But when mak andam do these things for the groom, suddenly okay. [long sigh]

If you want to talk about this problem until dawn, also won't finish. But cut the long story short, I eventually found my way through. Me and my friends, all the ones that the big bridal companies won't hire because we're guys, we decided to work independent. That's when we founded Bestman Services. Our services are largely for males but of course, since we're trained, we can dress up the brides too. If they feel uncomfortable we have a mak andam from another company to help us at a slightly higher price.

The key was Facebook. I tell you one, Facebook changed our lives. Oh yeah, and A.B. Shaik (radio personality and event organiser), you know him? He also helped us a lot. Always promoting our services during wedding showcase or even wedding events itself. He's a nice guy ... who is rich.

Suddenly client bookings came one after another. Big companies start to know us. Then slowly they outsource their assignments to us. Now we're fully booked for the year. Malay weddings you must always remember, it's not about this year, it's about next year. Planning start one year before the big day.

I don't know what I did to receive this from God. Miracles really do happen. You really have to believe in yourself and believe in Him. Even if your own parents don't believe in you. [chokes up] Adoi ... emolah pula (Malay: so emotional).

Of course, I understand why they didn't support me. Everyone said that this job was for girls. Apart from my 9 to 5 work, photography used to be my additional source of income. It was this additional income that I used to pay my parents' medicine. For me to suddenly stop doing that and kuda kepang to focus on my grooming services job, of course it was tough.

So now it's been three months since I left my logistics job. I now do middleman jobs for small things related to weddings. Dessert table, photography, kompang (malay drums), gamelan, kuda kepang of course. And even things like arranging transport for receptions. The commission I get from arranging all these almost the same as my salary at logistics. Sometimes even more. But if business that month not doing well, I come back to 3G Logistics as part-timer. Help carry heavy things. My boss there still wants me back lah.

But for now I'm concentrating on Bestman Services. So far, by respecting all these traditions my business has been doing well, and with God's will it will get even better. So remember later when you graduate NUS already, don't think we stupid, you know. We stupid in many things, but confirm got smart in some.

Said Effendy

Tattoo Artist

What did I do before? I had so many jobs, like lots and lots of jobs. I polished cars for a week. Yeah. [laughs] I did decorations for like, say it was Christmas, I would put decorations up for different banks cos they basically had a contract with my boss, right. I was a visual merchandiser, so I worked in Levis. The company that brings Levis to Singapore, yeah, I worked in the creative department. That was like the most adult job I had lah. And then, I worked in the airport.

I left my job after two years with Levis. It was a fun job but the pay sucked lah. Then someone asked me to try this out. So I did, lah. It was, you know, I got an apprenticeship. I was lucky. So my apprenticeship was like two and a half years and the rest is basically working in a few different shops before I got my own. How long have I been doing this? Thirteen or fourteen years.

So, I started doing it from home, on myself first. [points at legs] All this, yeah I did it myself. Then my cousins and my uncles and then whoever wanted a free tattoo ah, I would do it for them. It was crap, ah! It was basically scratching, ah. Scratching is like a term for a bad artist. When I used to work on my cousins and they were like, "Yeah, I want a really big cross on my back." I was like, "Okay." "I want it to be very detailed," And I was like, "Okay." So after I did it, right? Basically, it looked like a kid with a crayon did it. [giggles] Yeah. And when I see them now, they're like, "Hey, when are you gonna fix it?" I'm like, "Uh, not so soon lah." [laughs] Because it's so big, lah. It can't be helped sometimes. But it's free, you know! So you can't complain ah.

So basically I was a scratcher for a bit. Then I progressed lah! I did it for six months at home. Then I finally met someone who wanted to teach me, and after I was better, he decided to take me under his wing. I was his apprentice for two and a half years. Basically, whatever I earned, he would take 80 per cent. Yeah, it was a bit of exploitation, but he wasn't a bad guy, it's just I didn't know what I was entitled to. Actually, you should give about 50 per cent, so I was getting 20 only. Then, after I left my apprenticeship, I went to a couple of places, maybe two or three different shops that I worked at for a year, half a year, sometimes a year and a half. Before this shop, I had another shop on the same level but another unit down this way lah. Same building. I got it with a friend, and we're not friends anymore because we just couldn't work together. Yeah, lots of ego, lots of jealousy, you know, stuff like that. It was always about money, so after those two years I managed to get this shop.

I get about 20 clients a week. I do a minimum of 70 people a month, ah. Yeah, 70 clients a month. Lots of them are repeats. Maybe about one-third are repeats. The rest are new, one-timers. I do walk-ins also. Like, if a hot girl walked in now, I would ask him [points to customer] to go home, then I would do her lah! [everyone laughs] No lah. If I have time, I'll do walk-ins, but usually it's by appointment lah. Yup. When you have appointments, you can run the business better because you know what to expect. You know how much you're gonna earn, unless they cancel lah, but walk-ins.... If someone relies solely on walk-ins, you have to have a crew. So if anyone comes in, they can do at any time. Yeah, so I go by appointments.

It's pretty common in Singapore to see someone with tattoos lah. It's very common. It's just that, I mean I don't know about America, but you see a lot of people who are pretty traditional here, this being an Asian country, right? So if you got tattoos, people think, you know, you're a bad person, or you just got out of jail, or … yeah, that's about it lah. Oh, and if you have tattoos, you can't get some jobs in Singapore. They won't allow it. Like, if you're a cop and you have a tattoo, they'll kick you out. Because I guess in the Singapore handbook, if you have tattoos, you're a criminal already. For example, in the police handbook, if two guys are walking on the street, one guy has tattoos and one guy is dressed nicely, the guy in tattoos is the criminal. That's how the handbook works lah. So, for example, a couple of years ago when I used to go to clubs, the police like to have random raids. Yeah, so they come in and the guys with tattoos have to go out. The ones without tattoos, or the tattoos are hidden, you don't have to go out, you can stay inside. But the guys who got tattoos gotta come out, then they take a statement, then you gotta listen to a talk, then you gotta take your particulars down, then you gotta like…. Yeah! This is from my experience! Many, many times. There was one time … my mum works in a pub, she's like a cashier, right? And I came to pick her up after work and there was police inside and they made me strip in front of my mum. Yeah, because they wanted to see my tattoos. Stuff like that.

I guess the worst thing on a regular work day is sitting down the whole day, lah. Sometimes you get cramps in your back, and they say it hurts your eyesight if you don't have enough light, you know, and … I mean not exercising, I used to sit down the whole day, right? It's bad for your circulation and stuff. Health stuff lah. The worst thing is when a customer doesn't come for their appointment, then you basically waste a whole day. There's nothing worse than that.

Ideal? Somebody books a full-day session, then I only work with one person, yeah. Then I don't have to reset, you know? But I work 12-hour days ah! I start my day around 11 a.m. or 1 p.m., depending on who I have in the morning. Like this whole week, including today, I've been working 11 to 11.

What's the longest someone has sat for a tattoo? One customer sat from 11 a.m. to 3 a.m. the next morning. But I mean, not all the way, lah! We had lunch, four or five breaks – smoke breaks, you know. It was just him the whole day. Yeah, this German guy, he's a model and he flies to Singapore when there's this fashion week. Every year, he's invited, and he always comes here to get a tattoo. Yeah, his whole body is filled. Maybe 70 per cent filled with tattoos, ah. How many times has he come? [he and his customer burst into laughter] By himself or…. With me, never! [laughs] No…. [recomposes himself] How many times? A lot, a lot. Um, six, seven times already.

But his story is pretty sad. He missed one year, and I just thought he quit modelling and stuff, but then he called me the next year and said he wanted to make an appointment and then I was like, okay. So anyway, he came back and he looked very gaunt and very skinny. Because he's a model he has a full-on six-pack and everything, you know? And he says he has freakin' cancer. He says he has cancer, yeah. He had cancer the last year, but he's in remission. Then, I did his tattoos, then he told me, like … he told me something pretty sad, he said, lah, "After you get cancer, you kind of know your body really well and if you see something on your body, like there's a bump, you freak out." So when he was here, his last day of the tattoo that I was doing for him, he goes, "My neck feels weird. I may not see you the next time I'm here." Yeah. So, he left after the tattoo. I haven't heard from him yet. That was the beginning of the year, January or last year, December. Usually, he'll say that the tattoo is really good and stuff, but I haven't heard from him. Yeah … so actually I don't know if he's still alive, you know.

You know Singapore doesn't have an age limit for tattoos? We don't have an age limit. Yeah, we don't have – who's the youngest

I've worked on? Fifteen. But, you gotta listen to the whole story. I'm morally correct in my head lah, okay? So, she's 15 years old, she comes in, she has lots of tattoos already, and she wants to do a full-back piece. I said, I do it for you if you bring your mum, and her mum really came. So her mum comes to the studio and she says, "I'm just here to see the place and make sure the needles are clean, because if I don't follow her, she'll go by herself." So I told her mum like, "So you understand that this is a full back. It's a very big piece right?" She said, "Yeah, I know." So the mum was here when I did it. There's no law, but I played it safe, lah.

But you guys can only drink at 21, right? So that's worse lah? Right? Okay, the difference is, you guys, your government closes one eye when it comes to drinking because that's growing up, you know. You go to a party, you drink, you know? So, that's what I think is a good thing about American government. Singapore, we say when you can do this, there's no in between, but it's pretty weird because in Singapore the laws are a bit weird. At 18, we are trained to kill people. We are trained to kill people in the army, you know? And we are drafted, it's not voluntary. They call us to go. We always shout, "Kill, kill, kill, kill!" You know, that kind of shit, but we can't watch a restricted movie. A restricted movie is 21. You can kill someone at 18, but you can't watch some titties fly, you know. That's backward, right? And if you talk to people who make these laws, they have reasons for it, which is dumb. But people are still doing it, kids are still drinking and stuff, you know. You can't really stop it, eh?

Would I want my kids to do the same job? Honestly? Of course. Yeah, there are two reasons. You know how much money Singapore's number one artist makes a month? Thirty thousand Singapore dollars, a month. That's more money than a pilot, you know. Yeah, Elvin Yong. He makes about $1,000 a day. And he's booked for a year, or two years in advance, man. When my kid is born and he shows an interest in art, I'm gonna teach him. I'm gonna send him to art school, you know. Then I'm just gonna sleep and let him do everything! [laughs] If my kid loves art, do it lah!

Let me tell you something. If you're 27 years old and you haven't had something to do, you're gonna shit your pants, lah. That's what was happening to me, ah. I had no idea what I wanted to do with my life. Until my brother-in-law said, "Eh, you can draw, you know. Why don't you try tattooing, you can earn a decent living." So I did lah! I bought the machine and, you know practiced on him, practiced on my uncles and I'm lucky to be where I am lah! I earn a decent living, ah. I don't earn $30,000, but I sure don't earn peanuts. That's for sure, y'know. I earn a pretty good living.

And you have to make money, man. Singapore is a country where you pay non-stop for everything. Tax. For medical, for so many things. Scary ah. Rent is expensive. I live with my mum. Everyone lives with their mum, in Singapore. It's not, I mean like, it's nothing to be ashamed of because everyone lives with their mum. Only when you get married in Singapore, then you get your own house. You'll be incurring costs that are ridiculous. I have my own house actually, but my house isn't in Singapore, it's in Thailand. Yeah. I go every month. It's expensive lah, but when you're in a long distance relationship, you got no choice, you know? And she comes here. Every month lah. No, most of the time I go there because Singapore doesn't like Thai people coming here. Singaporeans don't like anybody coming here, you know. Like, the government has this thing where they think everybody wants to live here, which I doubt lah. So Thai people, when they come here, right? Sometimes they'll turn them back, you know, for no reason. Yeah, just go back to Thailand.

What's the reason? They have no reason being here. Like, okay, let's say there is a lot of Vietnamese people in Singapore that work as ... basically the ladies of the night lah. They sell their bodies and shit, you know? So, like I said about the police handbook in Singapore, if you have a tattoo, you're a criminal. Now in the handbook for Customs and Immigration, if you're Thai, you're here to work. If you're Vietnamese, you're here to work. They figure no one's here for holiday. So they send the girls back. Yeah. That's how they run shit around here.

So far I've apprenticed eight people. One of them is more famous than me ah. But I really hate him lah. [everyone laughs] You know they say, I wouldn't wish it on my worst enemy? I would wish everything on him! [laughs] I wish he would get crushed by a safe or something. He's a dick lah. The polite way to describe him is a dick. But you would like him lah. I don't know why, girls seem to like assholes. [laughs]

Long story short, right. Eh, this guy, he gives me a fucking sad sob story, "My mum is a single mum, and I need to support her, blah blah blah." You know? So I try to do the right thing and take him under my wing. Within the first two weeks he stopped coming to work, and I was like, why aren't you coming to work? He was like, "I don't have money for the bus." So I give him money for the bus. And two weeks later he stops coming. He said, "Oh I don't have money to eat!" So I started buying him lunch and dinner. So, six months down the road, he's supposed to start work at 1 o'clock, he kept coming at 2:30. So I said, never mind, you start at 3. He kept coming at 5 o'clock! Okay so last straw, right, was just before he quit, or just before he disappeared, right? I brought him to another location where I was supposed to move and I told him this is where we are moving in a couple of months, so the next day, he just disappeared for two weeks. Just disappeared like that. Cannot contact him or anything. And then, his Facebook resurfaced again. And he said, I have a new shop. Guess where? Yeah, he opened the shop in the place that I showed him. And now he's more famous than me.

Advice, ah? Don't trust anyone except yourself. [laughs] I'm very, very cynical when it comes to work, ah. I could be wrong, lah. I could be 50 per cent wrong, but I think I'm 50 per cent right. You cannot rely on anyone in the world but yourself, really, ah. You need to get through a lot of shit. A lot of bullshit, man. You meet so many fake people ah. You meet so many people who want to befriend you because they want something. And the worst thing is manipulating someone by pretending to be your friend lah. That's the worst. Words of wisdom? Yeah don't just ... how, what did I say, ah? Yeah. The only person you can rely on is yourself.

Perlita Contridas

Barber

Yeah, you can talk to me while I cut his hair. People around here know me as Cik Mamat, and I've been a barber for 37 years. I was a part-time barber back then and I had another job. I quit in 1992, as they might retrench me any time under the new management. I needed a stable income to support my family of five. I got a better paying job as a delivery driver. While working as a deliveryman, I saved a lot of my money. Eventually I stopped working there to be a full-time barber. You see, I didn't really like being ordered around, although I was paid good money for someone with a Primary 6 education.

So in 1999, I opened a barbershop with my savings. I shared a space with a Chinese salon. After the rental lease for the shop ended in 2005, I decided not to continue. [sprays customer's hair with water] Despite my long years of experience, it doesn't always mean I earn a lot more. On average I get 20 customers a day, but on some days I get only one customer.

I don't charge that high. One haircut is around $6 to $8 for children or adult. Although things in Singapore are more expensive compared to 20 years ago, I have enough to feed my family. I don't need to spoil my family. I'm not here to make a lot of profit; so long as I break even. Besides, I get exempted from paying taxes, as my annual income is not that high. People are always complaining that they have to pay so many taxes – income taxes, road taxes, service and conservancy charges – but I don't own any private vehicle or property, so I don't have to pay for these. The government is smart, the more things you try to own, the more they make you pay. So I try to reduce on unnecessary spending – buying only what is necessary.

One of the most important things in this job for me is to maintain a good relationship with the customers. I live around here, and I might bump into my customers. I will say hi and ask if they're satisfied with the cut. If they are not, then I will offer them a free haircut. That is how I build a rapport with my customers, and that's why I have many lifelong customers. These customers know that I know what they want, and I know what hairstyles fit them. This sense of familiarity keeps them coming back.

These young people can cut nice hairstyles for the customers. Right now the hairstyle trend is the undercut that fades. There are times when customers ask me to cut that hairstyle too and I learnt to cut just by looking at it. I must admit though, I've been losing some customers who prefer to go for the modern barbers, but that's fine. I believe that old barbershops still have their own charms. There's something about the simplicity in our décor, and the items we use that keeps people coming back. It feels homely, not made up. There are still many old people who come back to my shop to get their regular cut. They can also bring money to me. Some of them are taxi drivers who will recommend my shop to their customers. I don't have Facebook or these new gadgets to publicise my shop. I don't need to, now it's hard to find old barbershops like mine, it's a novelty. One day, people will all come back to find old barbershops.

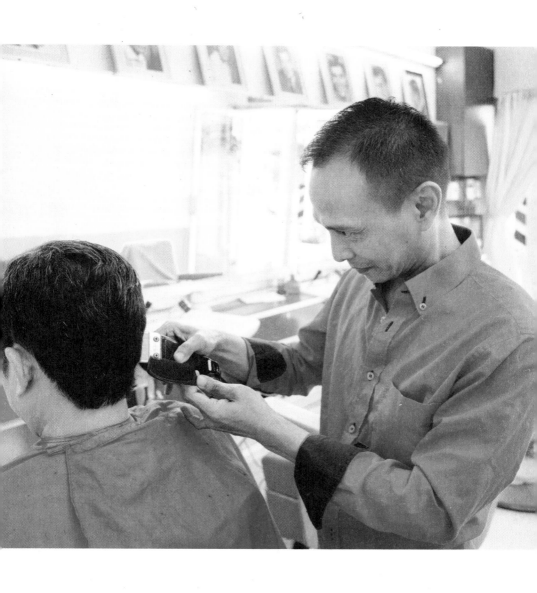

The rental here is cheap. I pay about $60 a day for the rental, and the rest I bring home. There are only two seats for haircut.

So we work together. It's a communal space here. [shopkeeper from next door comes to borrow some air freshener] You see, sometimes the shopkeeper beside me will come in and borrow things for his shop.

I think what is unique in Singapore is that although it is multiracial and most people are Chinese, you will find most barbers to be Malay. It's a Malay thing; we have it in us to have such craftsmanship. You look at just the Malay's handwriting, it's naturally nicer. Another thing also, we Malays are more patient and flexible. Sometimes we get customers who want many different styles, and we try our best to accommodate to them. I've got requests to go to the houses of old people who can't walk to my shop to get a haircut. I try to accede to their requests, but the charges are higher to cover my transport costs. There was also once when a Chinese family called me to cut the hair of their deceased. We are multiracial. Melayu tolong Cina, Cina tolong Melayu, sama-sama happy (Malay: Malay help Chinese, Chinese help Malay, everyone's happy).

Inasmuch as Malays are good barbers, there are also bad Malay barbers. Some of these bad barbers eventually are out of job because of three main reasons. First, they take drugs; secondly, they have many wives in Batam; and thirdly they bet on horses. You become obsessed with these indulgences, and you lose lots of money on this. For this, I must say Chinese people can be good barbers. They are very hard-working when it comes to work. But there are very few Chinese barbers. The Chinese usually learn how to cut from scratch and they are passionate, so they can cut hair. Tapi barber Melayu lagi bagus (Malay: but Malay barbers are still better). Some of us were born to be barbers; it's in our blood. Now old barbers will be gone after my generation, and I would be lying to say that I'm not sad.

Such traditional skills should be passed down to the young bloods, but if they have no passion and they were not born to be one, then I cannot do anything, right? Now people are obsessed with the trendy hairstyle, but one day the trend will pass, but not traditional barbers.

Whatever it is, I know for sure that so long as I am still alive and healthy, I will still be a barber. I don't have high education; I cannot work in many places that allow me flexibility of work hours. I will still want to serve my customers lah. They are like my family. Some of them come back just to talk to me here. [gestures to the area in front of the shop, equipped with coffee table, foldable chairs and a guitar] That's what keeps me going.

Seri Ariyani Binte Zulfakili

ENTERTAINING

CHAPTER THIRTEEN

ENTERTAINING

Drag Queen

Must sign form all ah? Ha, why cannot use real name? Just use lah. Okay, how about you use my drag name? Then can promote me. Dahlia Rose. [puckers lips while crossing legs]

Okay, I started drag when … wait, actually I fell in love with drag when I was young. When I was a young gay boy, I played with fabric, made costumes … and you know the Lego bricks? I made heels! So I was like okay, maybe I want to be a girl. I didn't know any gay people until I was Sec 1, then you know what, I thought to myself, I think I'm gay. Then I discovered dance and there was this group called Voguealicious – they were the strongest gay dance group back then. They were very loud – hotshots and whatnot, skimpy outfits for dance competitions. So I was like, what is this cross-dressing thing? When a few of them started dressing as a woman to perform, I was like whaaat is this? [high pitched voice] This is what I've been looking for!

So yah, I really found the world of drag when I was Sec 4. It was introduced to me and then I started seeing all these people doing shit and *RuPaul's Drag Race* came along. I watch from Season One all the way! When the first one came out, I was like, "Oh, this is what the business is about." So I went researching about this business and the drag culture. I thought, like, okay lah, drag like happy-happy and get some cash for yourself. Then I started to take it seriously and obviously wanted to be booked, but people don't know that I do drag and they don't know that I want to do drag professionally.

So two years back, when I started NS, a friend introduced me to the organiser of Herstory (a monthly lesbian club party). So she was like, "Bring her in, ask her to try out!" I was sooo nervous for my first try-out. Basically when NS started, my drag life started. And I was like, "Wah, this is two extremes". Okay never mind, then I went for the first show – it went well and subsequently the big boss was like, "Okay you know what? You're hired and we're gonna have you every month from now on." And I was like, "Oookay!" After a year of joining the show, I learned the tricks of the trade ah.

I'm actually freelance lah, so as and when I'm booked for a show then that's when I work. Let's say for a club, I'll be at the club say around 6 in the evening. Get ready and event starts at about 10. Then you mingle around and performance time is about midnight. And then after that, mingle all the way till the end. Usually after performance you get the pay – cash or usually by cheque. We also have to do rehearsals. But then it's based on events. Let's say it's a one-day event, like a random event they do and decided to invite a drag queen, then there's no rehearsal. Just come and on the day itself, you see the stage, adjust music, lighting, all. But if you're booked for a clubbing show, there will be two rehearsals before the show day. I usually work with a lot of people and there will be group numbers and stuff. If you solo, usually there's only one rehearsal. So the recent one where I perform at Taboo's Handbag Nite, we only met for one rehearsal and that's it.

How much we get paid is again, based on events. We always set a price for ourselves. We have this thing called drag mother, so, like, mothers who teach us how to do drag and polish us. Usually drag queens ask what is the pricing, but for my case, I'm more of an independent drag queen. So I won't … how to say … listen much to the mothers lah. [laughs] I just set myself cos I like to be more independent like that. Usually, how drag queens charge is based on number of performances. So on that night, let's say you have to do two songs, then get more lah. Also consider how big is the event. But roughly so far in Singapore, we won't accept lesser than $200. We get drinks on the house, free entry to the club – it's a good deal! Right? It's a good deal! One night … wait, wait, wait, not even one night, girl! Thirty minutes show already get $200. Two hundred dollars will drop on you. [pretends it is raining money] But in Singapore, there's a no-tipping rule, right, so you can't tip a drag queen. If get $200, then $200 you get. In US, people tip the drag queens so you get your basic pay and when you perform, the more amazing your performance is, the more elaborate your costume is, the more people will be like, "Yaaas!" And give you tips, then you be grabbing that money! So, they earn more. I think I got my first tip at Handbag Nite. The other drag queens were like, "Yas, take sepuluh dollar" (Yes, take the $10). "Take! Take! Take!" So I was like, "Yes, gimme!" So on top of the $200, I think I got like $40.

I am actually proud to say that I'm the youngest working drag queen. Youngest. I'm 22. No other person my age has a home club. Every weekend without fail, I'm here. The boss likes what I do – they're proud to have me and I'm proud to have them too. But yah, I mean, it's a growing process. It's a challenging job. It's not easy to put yourself in a character and sell that character. And for someone who wants to do drag…. Drag is like an investment. I invest on the clothes, the heels, the make-up. I invest time and effort in performances. After I invest money and time, obviously this is the product I'll be selling – Dahlia Rose. So I get recognition and pay lah, of course.

It's a business. I am a package and they pay me accordingly. But of course if you give me $80 pay, I give you $80 show. Don't expect me to give you full. For example, home club minimum $200 which is normal rate. Then for a private event, [whispers] I did one for a celebrity I can't say … uh, it was $400. If I'm a brand-new queen, I will ask them how much they want to pay me because I don't dare put the price on myself since I'm not known yet. I don't want word to go around like, y'know, like they say, "Eh, Dahlia asking for high price but she new queen." But you don't want to down-sell yourself! Cannot be like, okay lah, I take $100 only … if they hire other drag queens next time, they will be paying the same price and say, "I got Dahlia for $100, how come you so expensive?" Spoil market lah, like that! So, the drag community works together. Like a business, right, got market all? If you want to be a working drag queen, that's how it works.

But then again, it's all about status. We have the more senior drag queens and you have the younger and newer ones like me. Senior drag queens are obviously more expensive since they are experienced. Anyway, if you want us to host the whole night, of course it's expensive. Thinking about costume change, thinking about what to say, the theme … it's not easy. We have to talk and talk and talk a lot. Not easy. So the organiser of Herstory, for example, she's the host and the queen of the area, of course she gets more lah. The senior drag queens are usually the ones whom people go to, to get to the newer ones. For my case of Handbag Nite, I was introduced by the biggest drag queen – you could say that she's the RuPaul of Singapore. She was the one who invited me to Handbag Nite to showcase new talent – she loves new talent. There's also Vanda Miss Joaquim from Tantric who is ah-maaazing. She is the one who got me into drag and who was my idol when I was young. We became friends and got closer after a few drag shows, then she invited me to

Tantric anniversary night. It was a big event like, girl, please. From then on, I got booked for Altitude because of Vanda Miss Joaquim again. So basically it's more of a community of drag. Like whoever can't do a show or think that this doesn't suit me and might suit some other queens, we like to, y'know, share. It's a small community but it's definitely growing, especially because of the new upcoming drag competition for new queens. If you wanna go, next Friday okay, I'll be there. Anyway, I was thinking lah … I already have a home club and bookings, so I think I have enough to start with. Let these new queens who have never done drag before or haven't got any bookings … let them have it.

Actually right, drag's still an issue in the gay community lah. Because you see, gay is man on man what, so you would want to still fit in the masculine male stereotype. Not all gays are soft-soft one, okay? Gay men want masculine men. So the gay community think that, ew, he dresses like a girl and make-up and what. They don't like it. We are totally taboo. It's different lah. People don't understand what's different … they think we want to be a girl, but not necessarily. Yes, we enjoy this. Because why? Drag to me is like an armour. It makes me powerful and for a night, I can be someone else. The opposite sex some more. And you know you look good. [laughs] I feel more confident. Drag is not just dressing like a woman. Of course, drag queen means female impersonation but in a drag queen world, there are many types of drag queens and multiple identities. People need to know! Okay, so we got "fish queens" like me – they like to look as feminine as possible. Don't ask me why "fish", I also have no idea! I myself have to go Google, okay? Anyway, when people praise you they usually say "Girl, you look so fishy!" We also have the comedy queens and trans queens and clown queens who are super artsy-fartsy. And then you have the pageant queens! Alamak, girl! Cannot mess with them eh, they really take drag very,

very seriously. I have never been in a pageant before but I'm going to one in December hopefully. It's called Miss Two-Faced – like Miss Universe. But the thing is, there are many categories such as evening gown, drag performance or talent and drag as a man! So you're gonna show yourself as a girl, then show that you still look good as a guy. It's called Two-Faced for that reason. I already signed up and I'm so nervous but I'm going! Argh, just thinking about it makes me so nervous!

You got watch *RuPaul's Drag Race* or not? It's a good show but, wah, now every gay guy also want to be drag queen. Wah lau, I don't get it! Last time used to be like, ew, drag. But now everyone is living for drag! But okay lah, I'm the kind of person who doesn't chase for fame or what. I just like what I do. C'mon, I looove drag since young. I clearly remember not knowing what wigs were. I cut out paper and staple long strips and make it a wig. I know drag has been with me since young. I was in dance crews and stuff, so I just love performing lah. My home club now is my home. Whatever other shows I have, my home club shows come first. I'm actually blessed lah, because I started out differently from other drag queens. Usually you have to try different clubs, impress them, show them what you look like, what you have to offer, what queen you are and mix around with other drag queens, then you get booked for a show. If a club sees a potential in you, then they take you. But for my case, I'm blessed that my first show was in my home club.

Anyway, you know I work in a lesbian club, right? Usually other drags work in gay clubs. That's a challenge for me in the drag community because I grew up in a lesbian setting. Usually you start in gay clubs then go to lesbian clubs, but mine is the other way round. I'm not hating on gays, but I love working for lesbians. You feel appreciated! It's nice and there's no drama. Everyone's there for fun and they enjoy the show, but if you go to a gay club, their ego

ah … they will say things like, "Girl, I can do better." So when you perform in a gay club, your standard must be high up there. You must break the stage so that these gays can't say a single shit about you. This is why I was sooo nervous for my Handbag Nite show. But then again, I don't want to be someone I'm not. I want to be Dahlia, and if you don't like it, fine. But so far, so good, people recognise my drag character more than me myself. I went Tantric last Saturday as a guy then the boss was like, "Who is this?"

Speaking of these experiences, you also have bad days lah. People think that drag queens are very bubbly, fun and don't care about anything. So for example, the reason why I like lesbian clubs is because you girls have a bit more respect for drag queens. But in gay clubs, people will be like, "Oh my god, your hair!" Then they touch here, touch there, touch your face, pull your hair. They don't know boundaries! Men will be men. Actually some butch also like that. They think we are here to just make them laugh and be an entertainment, so all they think is "be my entertainment". They don't care. There was a case at Handbag Nite … you go to gay shows before? No? Okay, there is a big cultural difference. When I perform, I feel different. Some straight girls go to gay clubs and think they're the queen, I don't know why. They pull our costumes and one time things heated up and they were told to get lost lah. We are not a toy for you guys. We put in so much effort in our costumes and if you are in love with us, just tell us. Don't you dare start pulling our hair and what. We are human beings too. We dress up like dolls but we are human. Don't think of us like a joke, y'know? These experiences are quite bad. Then you have straight guys who wait for you after your show…. Wah, that time a few black guys waited outside the club after the show and, okay, don't get me wrong, I like black guys but no bitch, no.

Apart from these things, being a drag really gets into your head.

You look so feminine and when you look in the mirror, you think to yourself, "Aw, you're such a pretty girl." But when you take off everything, you become a guy. It might get into your head. It did get into my head. I was like … why do I enjoy drag so much? Why? Do I want to be a trans? Am I happy to be a girl? I would say we are the in-betweens. Like we can be a guy, and we can be a girl. Then I mentioned that I attract straight guys, right? I was really thinking, "Wah, should I turn trans?" But no. There's no need to change sex when you can be both, right? Anyway, do you know we also have straight girls who do drag? We call them "bio queen" because they are biologically women. They do over-the-top make-up and costumes to the point that people can't tell whether you're a girl. But okay lah, stare at the boobs a bit, look real … you know she's bio queen already. But Singapore don't have lah. We have drag kings – women who dress up like men.

Your module about jobs, right? Okay lah, can see it this way. A job to me is like selling yourself. If you work at Starbucks, you're selling your skills in making coffee and interacting with customers. If you work at Sephora, you're selling your make-up skills and knowledge. For drag, you're selling a character. I guess it's just more expressive lah, compared to an office job. But y'know, drag queens only do drag part-time. They usually have two jobs. In Singapore, sadly to say, it's not a stable job. So you have to get a regular job then this drag job is a side thing. So after NS, I have to find a job. But in the US, drag can be a full-time job! I wish I can do that but cannot lah. Even if you're an actor at Mediacorp or what, you still have to have a proper job.

With regards to family right, my family also religious. They pray five times a day! But this is my face when I leave home. [points to face] They know I'm feminine, and I think they know I'm doing drag? I don't know lah. I'm always ordering heels and dresses but the reason I told my mum is that I'm selling these things macam business. As for the make-up, she just thinks I do make-up for other people. Like a package thing lah, have clothes and make-up. So I can cover lah! But I still think she knows it's for drag. Mum always knows. They just don't want to confirm it. She got ask, "Why you always with guys?" Or, "Got put make-up ah?" But never really address it. I have a lot of boyfriends and I date a lot, so they always see like I kejap (Malay: sometimes) with this guy, kejap with that guy. Most drag queens won't tell their mothers. It's a double life. Sometimes I sit down and think of my life and Dahlia's life…. Girl, it's two extremes! But sometimes what we struggle with is balance. I like Dahlia so much to the point that I have more girl clothes than guy clothes. My make-up pile is getting bigger! I invested a lot and I don't even want to know how much I spent.

Mostly, that's what drag is. It's not a known job in Singapore. But people need to know it is a job. It's taboo. And, wah, if you bring in religion, even worse … y'know like Islam … don't even go there! We drag queens attract people to come to club and boost alcohol sales. So, I'm actually a satan. [laughs loudly] Like, come buy drinks and watch me! Sometimes that's the aim. Drag queens are in clubs to attract people to come, and when they come they obviously buy drinks and boost alcohol sales. It's part of the business too. How to say ah? You imagine McDonald's have Ronald McDonald, confirm more kids come and buy happy meal what! People use mascots to attract people – we are the mascots of the club, sort of. People know more about drag now … but mostly in the LGBTQ community. I enjoy what I do and y'know people say it's a nice job to have but it gets tiring. A job always starts out fun but eventually it can become a hassle. That's why I try to change here and there and up my costumes.

In drag, to keep your business going, you have to explore. I think drag has evolved and when you watch *RuPaul's Drag Race* from Season One to Season Nine, you will see how much it has changed.

Last time you can go to Zara, get your dress and heels – drag already! But now, no. Drag is about crazy costumes and eccentric stuff. Now people like comedy, so you have to be funny. Have to keep yourself current and grow. Last time people like Whitney Houston, now people like Beyoncé or Rihanna, so must adapt. You gotta keep up with the trends, if not people will get bored. I like to keep it fresh and current, but it's not easy to entertain everyone. So my motto in drag is "I will sell what I'm selling". Whether you like it or not, I will sell it to you until you like it. I won't morph myself too much to make you like me.

Siti Nurfatin Binte Raja Ali

Tennis Coach

Hey, my name is Hamid and I'm 27 years old. I've been a tennis coach for almost 10 years already. I picked up tennis when I was 16. I just love the sport. It was never part of my plan to be a tennis coach actually. When I was in my poly days, I was just coaching my younger brother who was only nine back then. He began to love tennis as he saw me playing. So I just taught him. He became one of the top five pro players in Singapore today. He has won a lot of competition and titles. Then I figured, maybe I can do something along this line. But I have to do NS first after I graduated from poly. So, while between waiting for NUS and my ORD, I started coaching people. I was 22 during that time.

So basically as a tennis coach, I train almost anyone who wants to play tennis – be it locals or expats. But mostly my students are expats, and their wives and children. Well, it's the rich peoples' sport. So yeah. My youngest student is four years old. My oldest is 50 years old. Different groups of people have different motives for training. From what I observed, locals pick up tennis because they want to play the sports seriously. Their goal is usually to represent school, get rankings in Singapore and overseas. They usually train with me twice a week minimum. Some hardcore ones can be seven times a week! Crazy. [laughs] As for the expats, most of them train just to keep themselves occupied and healthy. Some of them already have the skills when they come to Singapore, but they just need people to play with. So, that's why they hire me. Some of their wives are housewives, like tai tai, that kind. They play tennis to kill time only. They always play once a week, but those that play twice a week usually have group session.

Usually I'll teach them at their place. Most of them stay in condominiums, so they have tennis courts. For those who are staying in bungalows or terrace houses, they will sometimes use their friend's condominium or public court. The time of training depends on the students. For housewives, usually around 8 a.m. and 10 a.m. Seven is too early for them cos some need to prepare their kids for school, and breakfast for their husband and children. They wouldn't wanna play at 11 a.m. cos of the sun and heat, and they wouldn't wanna get tanned also. As for the kids, normally is after school time around 4 p.m. and 7 p.m. The working expats tend to play in the evenings, around 9 p.m., cause they knock off from work pretty late. Each training usually lasts an hour. Except for the hardcore ones lah, they want two hours. I anything. So, I usually confirm with all my students the timing for training one week before so I can plan my schedule well.

For the kids, it's easier to plan cos their days and timing are quite fixed. Teaching them is also easier, cos they will listen to me. So they cooperate with me well during training. As for the expats – the men only okay! They are pro usually, so they're like my playing buddies. I'm just paid to play! Isn't that fun? [laughs] But the housewives a bit hard. [shakes head] They all don't really know how to play sometimes.

But they play with me as well cos their husbands also play with me, but their husbands play with me at night. During the day, they can have many plans and then very hard to confirm timing with me. Sometimes, they wanna play in group, with the other housewives. Then need to coordinate timing all. Then one have this on this day, one have that on another day. So hard to even confirm on a timing. So leceh. Wah, tai tai lives … everyday also got something. I thought they should be so free, just sit at home shake legs. [laughs] During training, it can be even harder. They want to play, but then later so fast they complain that they are tired already and all. But then that is when my creativity comes in handy. I will make sure if I'm training the housewives, I try not to make them tired easily, instead make it an enjoyable one for them. They are different from kids. Kids need games but tai tais like them, you need that "wow" factor, like show off to them a bit of skills, then let them practice. Oh, they love facts also! For example, I'll tell them, "Do you know that Nadal hit differently from Federer?" And then they'll be like, "Serious? Tell me more about it!" And I'll start my grandmother story with them. And they'll be very, very excited to know about it. So I just entertain them. But then, sometimes, it's good to make them feel tired a bit also cos they'll feel healthy and that their money is not gone to waste. In managing them, I always make sure there is minimal physical contact as far as possible, if can, zero. This is to protect myself as well as to give the image that I'm professional and I do not take advantage of them.

Well, this job can be quite hard, but can be easy also, depends…. But okay lah, it's good money, man! So, it's a good job, although travelling is a bit of a chore. Like you have one hour of training here, and then travelling to another by public transport. A bit tiring, but it's okay. My rates are pretty good. If I'm feeling lazy, sometimes can take taxi. The rates tennis coaches charge is different, but on average it's about the same. Some charge different rates for children and adults, some same rates. Me, I charge the kids at $60 per hour, for the adults at $70 per hour. But those who stays in the east usually $80 per hour, like that, cos I live in the north what. Pay more for my transport. But you know, for pro coaches, right, like those who used to be players and teaching good schools like ACS (Anglo-Chinese School), RI, etc., theirs can reach like $120 per hour. Imagine that! But I don't think I have to raise my rates as of now. I'm fine with it now. Plus, I'm getting more and more students already as my reputation grows. My students recommended me to their other friends to be coached by me. It reached a point that I have so many students that I started employing coaches. Cos more students come in when I was already in NUS. So, I wouldn't want to reject students, but at the same time I need to focus on school too. Then I figured, why not I get coaches and take commissions from them. So, currently I have nearly 100 students and six coaches under my wings. It grew pretty huge, now I have my own club that I set up myself.

Previously I'm doing this job on a full-time basis. So, I started my coaching in the day around 8 a.m. till 11 a.m. So, during the 11 a.m. to 2 p.m. window, I can relax, though sometimes there are students who don't mind playing under the hot sun. Then after lunchtime till night will be coaching again. But this is not every day. There will be times I end work pretty late, and there are times I end work early also. When I was still studying in NUS, it was on a part-time basis, plus I got coaches also. But now, I let my coaches run the show fully, so I can work full-time in the engineering sector. This cause I don't want my certs to go to waste. I previously studied Civil Engineering in NUS, so now I'm a civil engineer.

Actually, more than just my certs, it's also for my housing application. I just settled down with my wife. We got married about a year ago. So we're in the process of getting a new house. Currently, I'm staying with my parents. I applied for BTO flat at Punggol. And to apply for BTO right, you need a CPF contribution continuously for one year so that you're entitled to the $40,000 grant from the government. If I just do my own tennis business, I won't have CPF. But now, I'm working as an engineer, so I will have CPF and I can get that $40,000 off for my house. Better, right? Must be a bit kiasu lah. House is so expensive in Singapore! Also right, since I'll be working as engineer until I finish my reservist which is around 50 years old, I think I'll be able to clear most of my house loans, and so I have less things to worry. That is the way to survive. In Singapore, you can't depend on the government. You can't depend on just CPF. You need to find other ways of growing money. And I chose tennis to grow them. Engineering is just a temporary one until I finish my reservist.

I'm not saying I'm so money-minded or what. But then again, that's life in Singapore. You need money for everything. And you need to think and plan ahead. Like buying house, finishing up the loans and all. Life's not easy. And now I'm married, I have more responsibilities on my shoulder. I have a wife to support. Life is more difficult now than last time. [laughs hard] Joking! That is the magic about married life – you see the wife and you feel happy, no matter when things get harder or what. And frankly, having my wife, that's enough for me. But at least now I'm in a more stable job, with standard office hours, so it's pretty relaxing, just supervise and get updates.

I still do coaching though actually, cos if I don't play at all, there goes all my skills. I need to constantly train also, but only once a day, which is sufficient. And plus, it can be a good form of side income too! For example, one day I get $60, seven days I can already get $420. And if I were to multiply this by 4, I get $1,680 a month. I can save more of my engineer salary and spend on necessity using these coaching fees. I wouldn't wanna take up too much coaching also, since I have a job. And I must make sure I make time for my wife too. Sometimes when I'm coaching now, my wife will follow me to my students' condominiums. She uses their gym while I coach my student at their tennis court. It feels like both of us go exercise together. Then after that we go home together or go dinner.

Another reason why I want to do this business – my students. Actually, I've always dreamed that 70 per cent of my students are Malays. I've not got a single Malay student now. But, at least that's the aim I want to achieve in five or ten years time. Deep inside, I know it's gonna be tough. But I really want to bring Malays to another level. I want them to be different. I am determined to bring them out of that shell cos I'm proud to be a Malay, and being in this sport for more than eight years, it makes me feel good.

I want to let our Malays learn to be different, and learn to get out of their comfort zone. Like me, I play tennis. I'm being different. Not many Malays play tennis, right? Wherever you go, you hear Malays play soccer and etc. But as for me, nope, I'm different. By doing that, I'm also getting myself out of my comfort zone. You can see the pattern. From what I observed, right, most of my Malay friends that I know, when they graduated from NUS, their next route will be NIE, which I think is an easy route to success. And I was so determined not to go down that route. I want to learn the hard way. If we strive enough, they cannot look down on us. Don't get me wrong, I'm not saying going NIE is wrong or what. But, it's just my 5 cents opinion. You know, people out there really look down on Malays, and I want to show them otherwise. They say tennis is not like the Malay's kinda game. It's the rich peoples' sport and it doesn't suit Malays. Ugh! So yeah, I've always heard that kinda stuff. [sighs] But it's okay, it's normal. Used to it. They bite hard, but I'm gonna bite harder! They'll see more Malays playing tennis.

Shabirah Binte Mohammed Sidek

Bet Collector

My name is Lai Wei. This year, I 28 already. I am married to my Thai wife, Looknam. How we met, ah? I met her in Planet Paradise lor, the Thai disco that I always go. She was singer there. The first time I see her, I already fall in love with her. She was different from the other girls there. My whole life ah, marrying her is the best decision I ever make. Three months ago we just had our baby girl. She is really very cute. Every time I look at my small family, I feel really blissful. But I have to admit leh, have children in Singapore really very expensive. We accident lah. [laughs] We not prepared. Before our girl come, we don't have a lot of saving on our own. Milk powder lah, diapers lah, doctor, vaccination and what, they all need a lot of money.

My wife cannot work in Singapore lah, because her English is really jialat. She's been here for two years but my friends still got problem understanding her English. I need to be their translator if they want to communicate. It is really bad. I don't want her to go back to Planet anymore, so the responsibility to bring money home lies on me. Now we staying with my younger sister in my mother's four-room flat. Five years ago she pass on already lah. But she left us with this flat, fully paid for. Heng, she got buy insurance also. So after she passed on, we use the insurance money to pay fully for the flat. If not ah, wah, it will be really hard for us to buy a flat in Singapore. How to buy? Kan ni na (Hokkien expletive), so expensive! She also left some money for us lah, and together with some insurance money, now our life is okay. I don't really have to work until siao to put food on the table because I have that sum of money to tide us through. But I know lah, sooner or later it will finish also.

I do many kind of work before, but my whole life still never work full-time before. Factory, KBox, waiter all do before. Aiyah, I don't like to be bound to a schedule. It's just not me lah. Anyway, now very hard for me to keep a full-time job. My wife and I always going to Bangkok to see her family mah. We spend around three, four months here then we go back to Thailand and stay with her family for maybe one, two months, like that. Depends on whether I can get my visa extended or not lor. If not approved, then I will have to travel to Cambodia. In any case, I love Thailand leh. I would actually migrate there when I am old and retired. But for now, I want my daughter to study in Singapore. Better future here. So I will stay for her sake. I want her to be different from me lah. I want her to succeed in life and not be looked down upon by people. The society looks down on people like me. But I don't care.

I don't know if you count this as a "job", but these days I'm a horse racing bet collector. I do this a few years already. I work with my partner. One will be stationed in the club room, while the other will be using a computer at home and directing the one in the club room when to collect and when to stop collecting bets. I am the one stationed in the club room. Usually, the people who place their bets with me are uncles and aunties in their late 30s to early 70s. I know them well lah, I do this how long already? They will just come to me before a race starts to place a bet. After the race finish, they come to me to collect money straightaway if they win. I usually have to carry at least $3,000 to $5,000 with me when I'm working. People get angry if you don't have the money when they win. This one is long-term business, so it is important that we pay them on the spot if they win. Like that, then they will come back to us the next time mah.

Thinking back, the starting really not easy hor. I remember the first time I do this ah, I had to walk around and ask people if they want to place their bets with me. You have to be really thick skin leh. Walao, eh, lucky I am hor. But really lor, very hard. There are a lot of collectors around in the club. Some of them do this for how many decades already! You newbie walk in, try to steal their business,

then you realise everyone already have the one collector he is used to betting with. It is not easy. Luckily, the aunties and uncles gave me chance. They see that I was young and trying really hard. So they just placed some small bets with me initially.

Aiyah, also because I know some people there lah. My ah gong (Hokkien: paternal grandfather) did this after he retire to earn extra money and to kill time. I came to know about this through him as well. My ah gong's customers know me, so they just placed their bets with me to support a bit lah. My ah gong die long ago already lah. But he was friends with many of the aunties and uncles. So I had this advantage when I first started. Also hor, the other collectors knew my ah gong also. So they got give face lah, never treat me like competitor or threat. It is actually a very nice environment. But then again, you don't really want to mess around with the people inside. You don't know their background.

This one ah, technically illegal lah. The government does regular checks in the turf club. But if they catch you collecting bets in the venue – touch wood hor – they will only ban you from going in for one year. Like that niah lah. No criminal records or what. My ah gong got kena this before. So I know what are the consequences. If I am ever caught in this, I will just switch roles with my partner lor. But for now, nothing happened yet. Whenever they conduct checks, we will know. The collectors and betters all look out for one another. So I will just call it a day and pack up. I can go home early and spend time with my family. Buay pai (Hokkien: not bad) lah.

But, if it's my partner get caught then it's not so simple already. I also don't know why so different, but from what I know, if the police raids the house and finds out that you are doing all this in your flat, you will be caught and charged. You house will also chongkong (Hokkien: confiscate). So my partner has to be very careful when he works. He always on the TV when he's working at home. You have to understand leh. It is very chaos one. When I collect bets, he must look at the numbers on the screen and tell me to continue or stop collecting any more bets. Sometimes he will shout and then sometimes his neighbours will be du lan. If they call police report him, he cham (Hokkien: to get into trouble) already. Everyone involved in this will also kena. It is not as simple as me, the one collecting bets, get caught. When there's records and computers, it is more complicated. I can just say that I am doing this alone since there's nothing against me when I am working. It is different for him. He has all our record. Everything is against him.

But I really like this job. I only work on days when got horse racing. Wednesdays, Saturdays and Sundays. Unless got public holidays or special races, if not I just work three days a week, seven to nine plus at night. Three, four hours maximum. It is a really easy job. But you have to be smart lah, and must be heng also. On good days, easily can earn up to a $2,000 to $5,000 one shot. I got earn $5,000 before leh! Only one time lah. Usually we are happy with $1,000 plus per day. And that means around $500 to $800 per person. But there are days when we just break even or we lose money. But it's okay. You cannot always be winning, right? This one gambling leh. You lose some, you win more. When people win a little, they place higher bets with you the next time. The money comes back to us eventually. It's just like blackjack. In the end, the banker always win.

Usually we offer 1:2 for the popular horses and we have quota for the number of bets we collect for these "red" horses. For the "black" horse, it can be as high as 1:10, and got quota also. Although I work with my partner, we are both part of a gambling syndicate. There are other pairs working like us as well. My company also collects 4D (lottery). But it is too much work and too little money already. I tried for a while and realised, aiyah, cannot lah, so I quit doing that and focused on horseracing.

The group has a website that allows us to know the odds so that we can tell the aunties and uncles and key in the bets. Last time when I was collecting 4D bets, I would also key in the numbers and the bet amount into this website. Now all very high-tech already. Last time ah, my grandfather used to keep all these record books to take note of the bets. But now, we can just do it anywhere on a computer and internet. My wife also got help me key in the numbers if I too busy. But it's not as simple as collecting money on the spot when people place their bets for horse racing. You have to go down to collect the 4D money from them. Sometimes, you are too lazy to collect before placing a bet for them, and you decide to pay for them first. And then, something happens, they MIA. Gone. Your money is gone. Although I do earn a cut if anyone strikes 4D, but it is not worth my time. Horse racing is so much easier and more straightforward. My partner and I are just the kah kia. But that's good enough for us lah. At least this means that we will always be either breaking even or earning money. We don't have to be worried about incurring a loss, as the company takes care of it. We only take a cut when we have winnings.

Got one time ah, there was a miscommunication with my partner. You know sometimes the bluetooth device suddenly cuts off the connection by itself? Because of that, I was cut offline from my partner and I took in more bets than I should. My partner was really angry with me when we were finally on the line again because the group has already collected the maximum amount of bets for that horse and if it does come up as the winning horse, we have to pay from our own pockets. I mean, I can just run away with their bets or refund them. But I will kena scold from the aunties and uncles and no one will place any more bets with me. So it is a must that we pay up if the horse really does win the match. But luckily for us, the horse did not win the race. And because the bets were extra and my partner could no longer key into the system, we got an extra $1K plus apart from our cut that night. Sibeh song (Hokkien: extremely satisfying). But days like this are really rare. We don't do this on purpose because we know what will happen if the winning horse was the one that we collected extra from. We have to pay them out of our own pockets. Too much risk lah. Although I don't think our big boss would mind us collecting extra, but we don't do it because it's too dangerous. Got people do this! But you will never know lah, if just suay, how? So we just stick to the rules to be safe.

But nowadays, I really have to start thinking about the future. Now I got daughter and my family to look after. I'm not the same man. I have to be less selfish and think for them. I love them and I want my daughter to grow up in a nice environment with a father to love her and pamper her with all the things I don't have when I was small. That bastard left my mother and me when I was young. I didn't have the chance to spend time with him, much less be loved by him. I doubt he loved me anyway … I don't want to be like him. I want to be a responsible father to my baby and a loving husband to my wife. You can say that I am trying to make things up. Maybe I am, to make up for the hole in my life when I was growing up. It doesn't matter lah! All I know is that I will do all it takes to give my family the best. Honestly, this horseracing thing isn't working out too well. It can't give them the life I want them to have. So I'll just have to find something else lah. But no matter what I do, I do it for them.

Olivia Sng Mun Yi

Animal Show Presenter

I started working with animals when I had some time before my masters degree. So that was when I started working full-time in the zoo. It started as a random interview – I've always wanted to do it since I was a kid – so I applied for it and got through. I have been there five years now, currently as a part-timer.

I'm educated as an engineer and I was doing a PhD but I quit because I didn't like it. Now I'm doing an operations job in a healthcare company. So you can say I have experiences in a few different fields. I also recently had the opportunity to do some modelling. I do ramp shows and runway walks for local designers both in Singapore and India, and I do photoshoots sometimes. It's all been fun to try, but I think the zoo job is one that really goes to my heart.

I've always had a heart for animals. When I was maybe seven, back in India, I picked up a puppy from the street and brought it home with me. I was living with my grandparents then because my parents were here in Singapore. So I told them that I had to have this dog, that I had to keep him. They said okay, but when I went to school, they took him and put him back in the slum somewhere. I was so mad! I ran to the slum and tried to look for him until it got late. In India, it's not safe for a young child to stay out late, so my grandfather came to look for me. He was so angry. We never found the dog.

Anyway, my job in the zoo is to host shows, which means to present the animals to the public. Besides that, I clean and help the seniors train the animals. I've spent two years working at the zoo during daytime and, as of now, three years doing the Night Safari. Working in the zoo is more interactive because there are more sessions with the public; talking with them, giving them more information and so on. The Night Safari is more like a show, where I don't get to interact that much with the public.

I actually like the glamour that I get from the Night Safari because you are the only presenter in the show and you get to work with the animals – yeah, really show off a bit to the crowd and show them how good you are at this. During the show, the animals do exactly what they are told, because that is what they are trained to do. They are so smart. But there is a cool factor and everybody is looking at you. You got like the attention of a thousand people and you can crack some jokes because all eyes are on you. But I also like working at the zoo during the day, where you get to interact more with the visitors. It is fun because people have very interesting questions. So it's entertaining to listen to all of their perceptions of the animals. And giving them more information helps me feel a bit more knowledgeable as well. I feel like I'm also eroding some of their fears. For example, I used to handle a lot of snakes and bring out snakes while talking to people. Most likely, a lot of people don't like snakes, right? So it is good to ease their fear for snakes and basically tell them that they're not as bad as they seem.

Sometimes people can be so ignorant about animals, even basic facts. They look at a lemur and call it a dog. It amuses me. Obviously, I'm not going to laugh in their face. It's interesting to see how people are so different. I've seen a lot of Westerners bringing their kids to me and the snake, and they think that it is okay to let their children touch the snake. Even though they might be afraid themselves, they don't pass the fear along to their children. It's different with Asian parents. They're afraid and don't let their children go to the snake, even though they want to. Then I try to get their confidence by telling them that this snake has been with us for a long time and has never bitten anybody. I'll hold the snake's head away so that can feel a little bit more confident in just touching the body.

I once saw a dad telling his kids to look at a lemur, while he said: "See there is a tree-dog." [laughs] I've never heard of a tree-dog. Sometimes you cannot really interfere, but other times I feel the need to correct them, especially if they are teachers. It's a bit touchy because you don't want to tell them they're wrong in front of their children. But at the same time, you don't want the children to learn the wrong thing. It really affects me a lot when I hear these mistakes. For example, most snakes are not venomous, but people always think they are. These kinds of things really irritate me.

I've got some nice colleagues at the Night Safari. I think a lot of the people working there are taking the job because it looks glamorous from the outside. But once they start, they realise that it's not that glamorous – most of the time we are actually cleaning, sweeping shit and feeding the animals. The only time you have your own glory is when you're on stage. Behind that surface there is a lot of hard work and a lot of people don't last long. Initially, I was told to clean the area where the otters are. They only eat fish and their shit smells really bad! Seriously, I thought I was going to faint the first few times. A lot of people want to help animals and stuff, but they don't know what they are going into. So this place has a lot of turnover – people going in and out all the time.

I call the animals by either "he" or "she". They have souls and once you get to know them, you can see they have different personalities. I worked with a lot of orangutans and it's so evident with them, so I get a bit offended when people call them "it". I won't be angry about it but I just continue calling them "he" or "she" so they get the hint.

It was after a few months of working at the zoo that I understood animals had their own personalities. For example, there are two baby orangutans. One of them is maybe a year older than the other one. So during the show, both of them have to come down the lines and they basically just swing down the line. You can so easily tell the difference between the two of them … one of them is my favourite, he is such a show-off! Like he knows that he is the star of the show, so when he is doing his line thing, he stands and poses for pictures. He knows that it's his time in the spotlight. But the other just knows that in the end, he gets his favourite food. So all he wants to do is get down the line as quickly as possible! He's really very innocent, a very sweet guy. But I like the other guy because he is so full of himself and he is a bit naughty – and I always had a bit of a thing for naughty boys. [laughs]

It's the same with the adult orangutans. One of the mothers is very possessive of her keepers – she doesn't like any other female to interact with her keepers. And this is men, human men, that we are talking about! One of the keepers played a prank on me. So in front of her, he was holding me and saying, you know, "Oh, you are my best friend," and so on. After that she started spitting at me every time she saw me. Even if she was in the tree she would spit on me from the top of the tree! [laughs] I'm not kidding. I got spat on by an orangutan because I was too close to her keeper.

Now I've adopted two birds, a guy and a girl. The guy talks and he likes to say hello and whistle a lot. So every morning, I wake up to his hello. He is such a happy boy. I took them off people who didn't want them anymore. I don't plan on having any more animals here in Singapore; I personally don't think that dogs belong in flats. If I ever had a landed property I would, but I'd never put him in a flat where I don't have space for him. Birds are good for me. I didn't plan on having them but they ended up with me. Whenever I am home they are flying around the house. I didn't clip their wings. So I close all the windows and let them fly around the apartment. Once, my sister forgot to close one of the windows and the boy actually flew away. I thought we'd lost him. That was really crazy. Literally, the apartment was like a funeral house with crying, and I missed him so much. But somehow by a huge miracle, we managed to find him. So now I am very careful with the windows ha! After that a lot of my friends told me that I should clip his feathers and don't let him fly, but no, it is his basic right to fly. He is a bird so he has to fly. He is so used to flying around the house and being a bully. I can't imagine

if he couldn't do that anymore.

I live with my family. But my dad works overseas so he comes once every six weeks. And my sister moved to Rotterdam recently. And my mother is travelling between my dad and my sister, so it is just me and my two birds for now. When they Skype with me, they always talk to the birds more than they talk to me! [laughs] It is kind of ridiculous. But they talk to him and he recognises them on Skype, so he will whistle, go near the camera and start talking to them. It is pretty cute! I didn't think that birds could have so much personality. I didn't think that I was much of a bird person but after having these two....

My sister is so into humans, saving them and all that. That doesn't matter to me – I don't really care! [laughs] Of course human rights are an important thing. But if you would give me the choice between saving an animal or a human, I'd save the animal. I mean, animals are so unconditional with their love. They don't have bad motives when they are interacting with you. They are just pure. And they have no voice to save themselves with. When you have been given the capacity to talk and rationalise, I think that you should put that into good use and help a species that cannot help themselves.

I volunteer a lot outside the country as well in different animal places. I have been to Thailand to volunteer in the elephant rescue centre with this lady called Lek. She rescues elephants from street begging and logging. She keeps them in her centre and they can do whatever they want there. I was there for one week and it was a life-changing experience. I didn't know how much torture elephants go through to be tamed. I also volunteered in this crocodile zoo in India, which is one of the largest reptile zoos in Asia. I worked with them for two months and it was pretty damn cool. They have over a thousand crocodiles and I helped them with feeding, cleaning, research and some marketing. I was actually doing a PhD at the time, but I quit it because my research required me to kill a lot of rats. And I felt very hypocritical about doing that. So I took eight months off, spent two months in the crocodile zoo, two weeks in a rainforest research station and after that I travelled quite a bit before I came back to my current job. Going abroad really inspired me to a career in conservation. I feel like we are all running after money, wearing fancy clothes – which I currently do. [laughs] But I was much happier over there because there is no pay, not many facilities. We didn't even have a TV, we just had some Wi-Fi. That two months I was really happy because I felt like I was making a difference for these animals and that was fantastic! That experience definitely changed me. I'm a lot more humble and I appreciate much more what I have here in Singapore. But at the same time I realised that people who do not have much can also be quite happy.

I met Jane Goodall last year, who works in chimpanzee conservation. She's my idol. Meeting her was a life-changing experience. She's from Britain and, when she was 23, she moved to Africa to actually live with and study chimpanzees. She's a true legend. Meeting her was really the defining moment for me. That's when I decided – you know what? School, trying to fit into society ... let's just do what the heart wants us to do. That was the biggest reason for my decision to quit my PhD.

It's hard to maintain that philosophy here, though. Because you are surrounded by people who are so obsessed with money. I don't really know if they're really enjoying doing that. I've decided that I'm not going to fall into this trap of branding and being all fashionable. I'm just going to try to live my life as simply as possible. I hope to be able to go back to India and work with the elephants full-time. That would be a big change ... but I think it's important to give it a shot because opportunities like this don't come knocking often.

Mathias Nielsen

Busker

Is that so? Has another uncle taken over my busking spot at Tampines? It's a good spot isn't it? So who's the better singer? [laughs] Yes, it has been slightly more than a year since I stopped busking at Tampines, and I miss my spot very much. The space was a little crowded, with people coming out of the MRT station and those heading to and leaving Tampines Mall, but it was mine. I had been busking at that spot for five years but after my diabetes got worse, my family pestered me to stop, especially my son Hakim, so I stopped. Late 2012, I started having difficulty walking and would frequently get lost when I make my way to Tampines MRT from home. The last thing I wanted was to add to their burden of caring for an old blind man, so I finally decided to stop after eight years as a professional busker.

How did I get started? It all started when I was 44 years old and my vision started blurring. I thought it could be due to fatigue from work and dismissed it, but a few months later, my vision worsened and the doctor said I was slowly but surely becoming blind. True enough, I celebrated my 45th birthday as a blind man. I had to resign from work as a security guard and the bills kept piling up. My only son Hakim here, was still in primary school then. It was hard, but it's all really just fate. One day, I was on my way home with Hakim after applying for a job at a government call centre, and heard someone singing Elton John's "Sorry Seems to be the Hardest Word". I asked him who was singing and it turned out it was a blind man.

That night, Hakim told me I should be like that man too, since I've always loved singing in my spare time and at family events. I brushed off his comments as so much nonsense from a child who couldn't understand that singers can't earn much, and what's more, a blind singer! But with each passing day that I went to work as a call operator, I would pass this same man singing passionately. Compared to my stable job, he seemed happier, so I started entertaining the idea. So one day after work I spoke to him and asked how I could do the same, and he explained about the procedures of obtaining a licence from National Arts Council. It took me a few years to make the move but with the support of my wife, I decided to give it a try.

Yes girl, it was the riskiest thing I had ever done. I still had to support my family and I was determined to make sure Hakim could still go to school. But Hakim was very excited for his dad to be celebrity. [Hakim laughs and looks at his father fondly]

Busking isn't like other forms of work. Being self-employed, my hours were flexible. On weekdays, I would be at Tampines from 3 p.m. to 8 p.m. Weekends, I started earlier at 11 a.m. to 8 p.m. On days when I was unwell, I would stay at home and it made me feel even worse, knowing that I wasn't earning anything. As the interchange is walking distance from my house, I would take the bus or walk. Then I would set up my xylophone. I made friends with one of the staff working at one of the interchange shops and he would sometimes let me leave my instrument in the shop. On days when Hakim didn't have school or he ended early, he would accompany me.

The people living or working in Tampines know me well, especially the Malay aunties and Malay library staff, so they would sometimes buy me food or sit and chat with me. I can't see who the people who usually give me money are, but Hakim said it's usually parents with young children or students.

My favourite song to play? The Carpenter's "Top of the World" and Sudirman's "Pelangi Petang". I played a mix of English and Malay classics, although Hakim would try to teach me what he calls modern songs. [smiles gently in Hakim's direction] Sometimes the makciks would request songs and if I know them I would sing them. Generally, Singaporeans are nice people, I have never been insulted. Though I do occasionally wonder what their expressions are like as they watch me. Are they giving me money because I am talented or is it out of sympathy? I tried to be positive since I will never know. I guess it's a blessing being a blind busker, right?

A person should do whatever they can to support their family. As long as my work is halal and I am not cheating anyone or breaking any rules, I am content. I have never begged in my life. Every day as a busker I've worked hard. I leave it to God to reward me how He deems fit.

Nasuha Binte Nizam Thaha

Musician

From day one when I was born, I was given away to an adoptive family. From day one, more or less, I don't have a real father or mother, so right through my teenaging years, y'know, it was kind of … I would say … kind of rough lah. Rough and tough life lah, because you don't have a real father and mother with you, so mostly I survived … the hard way. I used to live at the Whampoa Drive area, after that I moved out to many different places. Primary school I was at Norfolk Primary School, then later Monk's Hill Secondary School at the Newton area. And once I got employable, I dropped out, because adoptive father told me, "That's it. No more education for you. You have to survive on your own now." So I was 17 years old. I was on my own, looking for jobs to survive.

Actually my natural parents, they were Indonesians. They were from Indonesia, and then my adoptive parents, they are all a mixture y'know. So er … that's life for you lah. Besides English I also speak Malay, because basically Malay is part of the education, you gotta speak Malay, and then also Bahasa Indonesia, I guess. Once a year I would go back to Indonesia. I found out about my natural parents when I was about 41 years old. But it was short-lived. They passed away suddenly, sort of, y'know? So I've got no more natural parents.

All the time before I was Sec 2, I was listening to all kinds of music, I was everything yah. Actually when I was Sec 2, I went for my first school talent time, first time singing in public, y'know. School talent time. And those days were known for the Bee Gees, the Beatles and all that, y'know. So I sang the Bee Gees song called "Words". And my god, I got second prize. [laughs] And one classmate I met a long time ago, told me y'know, which I almost forgotten, she said to me, "I knew that time when you won that second prize on the school talent time you said you wanna be a musician!" My god, did I say that? Yah, you see? But at that time when I said I wanna be a musician, it was not a blues rock musician yet, it was all kinds of music. But then somebody, my classmate in Sec 2 passed me one blues rocking album by John Mayall & The Bluesbreakers. That one really turned me on, y'know. I found out that that music, that album, is the real stuff that I wanna do. Cos it's so realistic, so meaningful, so simple but so difficult to play, y'know, that kinda stuff. There's nothing superficial about it. I can do country, folk, pop, standards, all that, I've had to do that too. But I enjoy the blues rocking more than all that stuff.

This classmate yah, sort of my … best friend, he was also the one playing the guitar. I watched him, and all that, then somehow he got me interested in it. And he taught me guitaring on his guitar. And then, how I got my first guitar, was that we worked together, our first job, as construction workers, after dropping out of school, while waiting for NS, and whatever, y'know. So I saved up that money and got my first guitar, and this best friend of mine taught me all the way. I had a band with this friend. We somehow managed to get another guy who can play the drums, so it's more or less like a three-piece band. A blues rocking band. It was … it was … awesome, during those times. Really enjoyed the real stuff.

When I was in my 20s to 30s, those days were struggling. You were experimenting with … things. Y'know, you couldn't get to a point where you were satisfied, y'know. Now I'm contented. What I wanna do, I can do, y'know. Those days I was just experimenting, whether I'm okay, not okay, not sure. It was later then the blues thing got to me.

Right now I'm a school officer at NJC (National Junior College), I help out in the school with operations, like a handyman. When it's time to work, I work, according to the rules and regulations. I was invited by the OM (operations manager) to do this job, I guess because he trusted and respected me, that's it. I work normal school working hours. Do my normal school work – closing, opening the classrooms, taking care of students, etc, yeah. So I do Monday till Friday. I'm doing the second shift which is from 1 p.m. till 10 p.m. at night. But I get to go home earlier if nothing happens. So that's my life as a school handyman. I don't get to perform on weekdays, only when we get a public holiday, yeah, or my extra off days, then I can. Normally when I do my blues rockin' it's on my off days lah, yah.

On weekends, if I'm not going out with the family, well, my kids are all grown up already, they have their own projects, so basically I'm alone with my wife, and my wife is a very home-loving person, so she doesn't like to go out, so I go out on my own. [laughs]

Except for cleaning jobs, I've done many types of jobs before. So actually I'm a jack of all trades. Some low-standing, some medium-standing, some high-standing jobs. But the thing is, most of the time I drop out cos of my music-making. Previously I was a security guard for about six years at NJC and er … no regrets cos I get to meet all those students, the good ones especially, y'know. Really enjoyed that. Some of the most jialat jobs were menial jobs like construction work, grasscutter, gardener, yeah, waitering, hotel reception, store clerk … yeah. All these jobs – besides music – are all just a survival means. Just means to find money, that's all.

I'm living a double life: outside my jobs, deep inside me, actually I'm a blues rock man. So whatever jobs I pick and do is only temporary. I did all these jobs because of survival. The money to survive, that's all. That means my first priority is to earn a living as a blues rock man. Hoping I get a couple of nights every week to play some shows, that would be my dream, yeah. Sometimes I'm paid to play, and sometimes … er, y'know, just for passion, that means to jam around, y'know, you don't get paid, you get free drinks.

So during the weekend, especially around with my blues buddies y'know, having fun. [laughs] Here is one of the night spots, Tanglin CC. There are many others I go to, like the Jazzistic, the Crazy Elephant, the Barber Shop, Blu Jazz, and many more. Most of the time when I go to these places I get invited, "Eh, Moody! Sing some blues rock songs!" So no matter what I've gotta give three to four songs, with a band, house bands, y'know.

Like I said money is only for survival, y'know. But the blues music thing is a passion, a love, it goes on till I'm old, maybe when I'm dead and gone. But I'm gonna do the blues rocking thing as long as I'm still capable. Now I'm 64, maybe in my 70s y'know, I'll still be doing it. Blues legends, in the UK or USA, they're all elderly people. Why are they doing it? It's a culture, it's a part of their life. They will be doing it forever. And don't be surprised that the young ones, many of them get turned on y'know, by these people. So it's a regeneration of the blues. So we have new people, new blood. We need new blood for the blues.

My legends depend on the instruments. I love the guitar sound, I love the harmonica sound. These two instruments are my most favourite instruments. On the guitar, number one is, whether I like it or not, Jimi Hendrix. He can play the real blues, that is really blues, and he can play wild rock, heavy rock, which is away from the blues, but the touch is there. So I really like his style and I appreciate his skill. Johnny Winter also same category. These are the people who influenced me. Harmonica I have this Julian Wells, er … James Cotton. These are the people that really know what they are doing. There is no bullshitting! They are really best at their instruments. So I look at them like mentors. When I look at Jimi or Johnny Winter, it's how I wish my guitaring is like them. And when I watch Julian Wells or James Cotton, wow, how I wish my blues harping was really like them. That's something I look forward to. To get that kind of thing. The feel, y'know. Must have somebody y'know, who you look up to y'know, to learn from y'know, somehow. We don't learn from nothing. It must be from something that we learn: somebody.

Moody Cash is basically number one a blues singer and harmonica player. Guitaring is number two. On my own time, yes. I'm more known for singing and harmonica. Guitar is in the backseat. Cos if I play the guitar, I cannot play the harp. Y'know, the blues style harp, I cannot play. Last Sunday I just had a jam with a guy from KL, he came down, we had a good time y'know. This guy on the guitar and the harp. When they told him about me, he put aside his harp, wanting me to play the harp, and he was on the guitar, and it was a really awesome jam. Good stuff, y'know. So I'm enjoying lah, y'know. I can communicate with the blues with these people.

Well, right now, my dream … my dream … my dream is … is … to hopefully one day, who knows, if there is one angel, a backer, a sponsor, who's got a joint, where he can have a platform for me to perform as main act. So far, I've come to a level of the so-called famous, established blues rocking people, the big names yah, I'm at that level. I'm on that level with them. Every time I perform, I'm on that level with them. It's just that I don't have a blues home base, that's all. A regular joint, a residency they call it, y'know.

A couple of my buddies they already chope (colloquial: reserve) some of these places, you see. Don't say rivals. [laughs] my blues buddies y'know, like Calvin Ng and the Skive band are doing it at the Crazy Elephant, and we have the Louis Lam and the Chicken Shack, at the Barber Shop. These are the ones that are very famous here in Singapore, in the blues rocking scene. Me, I just go in and they know, "Hey, Moody!" So my dream is yah, to become a major act. Right now I'm something like, in football terms, on the bench. [laughs] Yah, you're on the bench watching the action, y'know. So I can only perform there just to support them, y'know, to help out. But to have a regular gig at their place, it won't be nice y'know. It's like a diplomacy thing, y'know. Imagine if you're better than the main act. [laughs] Then the first choice starts thinking, "Hey, this my rice bowl man." So it's ... not very nice, y'know.

You see, the thing is that in Singapore there are not many blues joints at the moment, less than five, which is ... not good enough. Y'know, unless one day we have a hundred blues rocking joints on the street. Oh yeah, that's my dream man. Monday to Sunday, you can just jump from one club to another club, then these people also won't get bored of one particular band, y'know. So I also don't get bored with the audience and I can keep jumping and jumping. That kinda situation, y'know.

So unless you get an angel ... operating a new joint, then, "Hey, I only want you, Moody Cash!" That's it! I'll be satisfied. But then on my part, I hope I can make some changes. Like, "Hey, not only me ah! You guys can come in on these days." And all that y'know? Make it different from the rest.

When I'm on stage, I feel at home. I feel at home with the blues, yah. When I'm performin', I have to interact with the audience. And when I see the audience ... dancing, moving their bodies and all that, and, er, some of them laughing, crying, some, [laughs] whatever it is, emotions, yah? That is the reward. I feel good. That means we have this communication between the audience and the performer, then that's the way it is, y'know. No point if you're just on stage, on your own, and you're not interacting with the audience, it's not gonna work that way. You have gotta get a two-way street. The bottom line of the blues rockin' is performing live. Whether you make false notes or whatever, round notes, whatever, it's live music. That's why for me recording an EP is not important. Recording and all that, hey man, it's secondary. The blues, you must feel good performing live, that's it.

I wanna spread blues music to people, y'know, and get people to understand more about the blues. It's very real. It is a lifestyle that can tell people how to live life positively, bravely, not to foul up your life, okay? I did many of my own compositions, y'know, where I injected all this positiveness. I wrote a couple of these songs which I have yet to record. [pauses] Cos here in Singapore we have a different environment, y'know. So waiting for who knows, y'know, one day I can do my own blues rocking songs, my own compositions. Here, most of the time we're doing covers, but when I do covers, I also don't do 100 per cent covers, I repaint them … ah, y'know! So people say "Hey! That's not like the original!" Cos I retouch, redo, repaint, resong, more to my feel.

One of the quotations I got from one of my ang moh buddies, y'know, it really struck me leh, saying that, "Hey, Moody, you singing that song, you're bringing light to that song." Oh, I was amazed, he can describe it perfectly. I mean, it's subtle in the meaning. You don't just hantam (Malay colloquial: do carelessly, lit. hit) the song. So when you do your stuff, you must be sincere to yourself, do it properly, and get it done. You don't bullshit when you perform.

The blues is in me. The rest of the people are outside there, it's up to them. You can't go ask people, "Eh, how good ah? Nice or not? Very nice ah?" You cannot force them. If you just sing it sincerely, honestly, people will understand, y'know, "Hey, this fella is doing the blues." Right now, I can just do the blues music, and that's it,

I'm very happy already. Money, like I said, is secondary already. Fame is all secondary, y'know. I can have one audience, I can have 100, I can have 1,000, it's immaterial. Yah, if my gravestone, you see written there "Moody Cash: Blues Singer", that's it. That would be an achievement. Not any Tom, Dick and Harry can just do the blues, y'know. Because you know, to … live, and to be able to sing the blues, it's a gift from the God Almighty. So I'm grateful.

Yeo Tze Yang